The Digitalization of Financial Markets

The book provides deep insight into theoretical and empirical evidence on information and communication technologies (ICT) as an important factor affecting financial markets. It is focused on the impact of ICT on stock markets, bond markets, and other categories of financial markets, with the additional focus on the linked FinTech services and financial institutions. Financial markets shaped by the adoption of the new technologies are labeled 'digital financial markets'.

With a wide-ranging perspective at both the local and global levels from countries at varying degrees of economic development, this book addresses an important gap in the extant literature concerning the role of ICT in the financial markets. The consequences of these processes had until now rarely been considered in a broader economic and social context, particularly when the impact of FinTech services on financial markets is taken into account. The book's theoretical discussions, empirical evidence and compilation of different views and perspectives make it a valuable and complex reference work.

The principal audience of the book will be scholars in the fields of finance and economics. The book also targets professionals in the financial industry who are directly or indirectly linked to the new technologies on the financial markets, in particular various types of FinTech services.

Adam Marszk is Assistant Professor at the Faculty of Management and Economics at Gdańsk University of Technology, Poland.

Ewa Lechman is Professor of Economics at the Faculty of Management and Economics at Gdańsk University of Technology, Poland.

Banking, Money and International Finance

1. **Innovation in Financial Services**
   Balancing Public and Private Interests
   Edited by Jan Monkiewicz and Lech Gąsiorkiewicz

2. **Carbon Risk and Green Finance**
   Aaron Ezroj

3. **Inflation Targeting and Central Banks**
   Institutional Set-ups and Monetary Policy Effectiveness
   Joanna Niedźwiedzińska

4. **Global Stock Market Development**
   Quantitative and Behavioural Analysis
   Marcin Kalinowski

5. **The Digitalization of Financial Markets**
   The Socioeconomic Impact of Financial Technologies
   Edited by Adam Marszk and Ewa Lechman

6. **The Digital Disruption of Financial Services**
   International Perspectives
   Edited by Ewa Lechman and Adam Marszk

7. **The Economics and Finance of Commodity Price Shocks**
   Mikidadu Mohammed

8. **Mergers, Acquisitions, and International Financial Regulation**
   Analysing Special Purpose Acquisition Companies
   Daniele D'Alvia

For more information about this series, please visit: www.routledge.com/series/BMIF

The Digitalization of Financial Markets

The Socioeconomic Impact of Financial Technologies

Edited by
Adam Marszk and
Ewa Lechman

LONDON AND NEW YORK

First published 2021
by Routledge
2 Park Square, Milton Park, Abingdon, Oxon OX14 4RN

and by Routledge
605 Third Avenue, New York, NY 10158

Routledge is an imprint of the Taylor & Francis Group, an informa business

© 2021 selection and editorial matter, Adam Marszk and Ewa Lechman; individual chapters, the contributors

The right of Adam Marszk and Ewa Lechman to be identified as the authors of the editorial material, and of the authors for their individual chapters, has been asserted in accordance with sections 77 and 78 of the Copyright, Designs and Patents Act 1988.

With the exception of Chapters 2, 5 and 10, no part of this book may be reprinted or reproduced or utilised in any form or by any electronic, mechanical, or other means, now known or hereafter invented, including photocopying and recording, or in any information storage or retrieval system, without permission in writing from the publishers.

Chapters 2, 5 and 10 of this book is available for free in PDF format as Open Access from the individual product page at www.routledge.com. It has been made available under a Creative Commons Attribution-Non Commercial-No Derivatives 4.0 license.

Trademark notice: Product or corporate names may be trademarks or registered trademarks, and are used only for identification and explanation without intent to infringe.

British Library Cataloguing-in-Publication Data
A catalogue record for this book is available from the British Library

Library of Congress Cataloging-in-Publication Data
A catalog record has been requested for this book

ISBN: 978-0-367-55834-5 (hbk)
ISBN: 978-0-367-55840-6 (pbk)
ISBN: 978-1-003-09535-4 (ebk)

DOI: 10.4324/9781003095354

Typeset in Times NR MT Pro
by KnowledgeWorks Global Ltd.

Contents

List of figures vii
List of tables viii
Acknowledgements x
List of contributors xi
Introduction xvi

PART 1:
Digitalization of capital markets

1 **The impact of information and communication technologies on the equity market** 3
   AGATA ADAMSKA

2 **European financial institution physical geolocation and the high-frequency trading potential** 19
   PIOTR STASZKIEWICZ, EWA ŁOSIEWICZ-DNIESTRZAŃSKA AND ANNA GRYGIEL-TOMASZEWSKA

3 **Necessity of digitalization in the capital market of developing countries in current pandemic situation: The case of Bangladesh** 38
   S. M. SOHRAB UDDIN, ANM MOINUL ISLAM AND MOHAMMAD ROBAITUR RAHAT

4 **Information and communication technologies versus diffusion and substitution of financial innovations. The case of exchange-traded funds in Japan and South Korea** 57
   ADAM MARSZK AND EWA LECHMAN

PART 2:
FinTech: Selected issues

5 **FinTechs, BigTechs and structural changes in capital markets**   81
JANINA HARASIM

6 **Critical success factors for FinTech**   101
ANNA KARMAŃSKA

7 **Systemizing the impact of fintechs on the efficiency and inclusive growth of banks' services: A literature review**   123
PIOTR ŁASAK AND MARTA GANCARCZYK

PART 3:
Digitalization of financial institutions

8 **The prospect of cryptocurrencies becoming money**   145
ANDRZEJ SŁAWIŃSKI

9 **Employing artificial intelligence in investment management**   161
TOMASZ MIZIOŁEK

10 **Challenger bank as a new digital form of providing financial services to retail customers in the EU Internal Market: The case of Revolut**   175
MICHAŁ POLASIK, PAWEŁ WIDAWSKI AND ANDRZEJ LIS

Index   194

List of figures

3.1	Turnover of DSE and CSE (1991–2019).	46
3.2	The Trend of DSEX and CSEX (1991–2019).	47
4.1	Total index financial instruments, exchange-traded funds, stock index options, and stock index futures diffusion patterns in Japan (million USD). Monthly data for 2003–2015.	67
4.2	Total index financial instruments, exchange-traded funds, stock index options, and stock index futures diffusion patterns in South Korea (million USD). Monthly data for 2003–2015.	68
4.3	Financial substitution patterns. ETFs versus stock index options in Japan. Monthly data for 2003–2015.	71
4.4	Financial substitution patterns. ETFs versus stock index options in South Korea. Monthly data for 2003–2015.	71
5.1	Opportunities and threats connected with the entry of FinTechs and BigTechs into finance.	86
5.2	Digital platforms in asset management.	93
6.1	Scree plot.	116
8.1	The bank-based monetary system with PSPs as its new component.	147

List of tables

2.1	Summary of definitions of variables and expected direction	25
2.2	Usable sample identification	27
2.3	The geographical distribution of the population and sample with the number of supervised entities in the sample	27
2.4	Descriptive statistics	28
2.5	The system estimator results	29
2.6	Stock exchange's individual effects	30
3.1	Evolution of capital market of Bangladesh (1954–2020)	45
3.2	Capital market indicators (1991–2019)	46
3.3	Mean returns and standard deviation before and after the demutualization	47
3.4	Mean returns and standard deviation before and after the starting of NGTS	48
3.5	Mean returns and standard deviation before and after the initiation of DSE info	48
3.6	Mean returns and standard deviation before and after starting of the DSE mobile	49
3.7	Mean returns and standard deviation before and after the declaration of the Shanghai-Shenzhen stock exchange consortium	49
3.8	Summary of output of event studies	50
3.9	Impact of the demutualization	50
3.10	Impact of the initiation of NGTS	51
3.11	Impact of DSE info and DSE mobile	51
3.12	Impact of the Shanghai-Shenzhen consortium's inclusion	52
3.13	Sector-wise distribution of companies not maintaining websites	52
4.1	ETF shares versus Internet users: Country-specific models, 2004–2019 (annual series)	66
4.2	Changes of market shares in the total turnover of index financial instruments in Japan and South Korea. 2003–2015	69

4.3	Changing market shares of ETFs versus options considered as total market. Japan and South Korea. 2003–2015	69
4.4	Financial substitution model estimates. Japan and South Korea. 2003–2015	72
5.1	Technology impact on the market structure in the financial services industry	83
5.2	Digitalization in the stock market	89
6.1	CSFs for FinTech	110
6.2	Distribution of the sample members	111
6.3	FinTech products used by the sample members	112
6.4	Frequency of answers and descriptive statistics	113
6.5	KMO and Bartlett's Test	114
6.6	Pattern matrix	115
6.7	Correlations	117
7.1	Preservation effects on the banking activity and socioeconomic inclusion	129
7.2	Modification effects on the banking activity and socioeconomic inclusion	131
7.3	Creation effects on the banking activity and socioeconomic inclusion	133
10.1	Comparison of the Revolut's offer to other challenger banks and traditional financial institutions	184

Acknowledgements

This edited volume is a result of scientific project no. 2015/19/D/HS4/00399 financed by the National Science Centre, Poland.

List of contributors

Chapter 1:

Agata Adamska, Warsaw School of Economics. Agata Adamska is an Associate Professor at the Institute of Corporate Finance and Investments, Collegium of Business Administration, Warsaw School of Economics. She holds a PhD and master's degree from the Collegium of Socio-Economics, Warsaw School of Economics, and also a master's degree from the Faculty of Law and Administration, University of Warsaw. She conducts research on ownership and governance in publicly traded companies, capital markets and strategic finance, and has authored and co-authored over 70 papers, chapters and books.

Chapter 2:

Piotr Staszkiewicz, SGH Warsaw School of Economics. Piotr Staszkiewicz is an Associate Professor at Warsaw School of Economics, Poland, where he works since 2012. His doctoral-granting institution was Wroclaw Economic University, from which he obtained his PhD. Piotr research areas are auditing and institutional economy. He is co-author of books, textbooks, and research papers in these fields. Piotr published papers in Poland, Singapore, Australia, Slovakia and works as an active reviewer for several peer-reviewed journals.

Ewa Łosiewicz-Dniestrzańska, Wroclaw University of Economics and Business. Ewa Łosiewicz-Dniestrzańska is an Assistant Professor at the Wroclaw University of Economics and Business, Poland, where she has worked since 1995 and obtaining her PhD in Economics. Her research interests include banking, central banking, and financial markets. She is the author and co-author of academic publications in this area.

Anna Grygiel-Tomaszewska, SGH Warsaw School of Economics. Anna Grygiel-Tomaszewska works at Warsaw School of Economics, Poland, since 2016. She holds a PhD in Economics from the Warsaw School of Economics. Anna is the author or co-author of several books and academic publications. Her research interests include financial markets, institutional economics, and behavioral economics.

Chapter 3:

S. M. Sohrab Uddin, University of Chittagong. S. M. Sohrab Uddin is a Professor at the Department of Finance, Faculty of Business Administration, University of Chittagong, Bangladesh. He obtained BBA and MBA from University of Chittagong, and an MBA and PhD from Ritsumeikan Asia Pacific University, Oita, Japan. His research area focuses on financial market, institutions, and instruments with particular emphasis on banking sector development including Islamic finance in developing countries.

ANM Moinul Islam, Asian University for Women. ANM Moinul Islam is an Associate Professor of Economics at Asian University for Women (AUW). He teaches Econometrics, Microeconomics, Macroeconomics and Development Economics. He did his undergraduate work at University of Chittagong, Bangladesh. He received his Masters in Economics from Illinois State University and his PhD, also in Economics, from Southern Illinois University Carbondale, USA. His research interests include both theoretical and empirical analysis in the areas such as Economic Development and Sustainability, Foreign Direct Investment, Capital Market, Rule of Law, Human Rights and Economic Growth.

Mohammad Robaitur Rahat, Bangladesh University of Professionals. Mohammad Robaitur Rahat is a lecturer at the Department of Business Administration in Finance and Banking, Faculty of Business Studies, Bangladesh University of Professionals, Bangladesh. He completed his MBA and BBA in Finance from the Department of Finance, University of Chittagong, Bangladesh. His research interests include the capital market, banking sector, financial inclusion, digitalization in the financial sector, and Islamic finance.

Chapter 4:

Adam Marszk, Gdansk University of Technology. Adam Marszk, PhD, is Assistant Professor, employed since 2013 in the Faculty of Management and Economics, Gdansk University of Technology (Poland). He graduated from the Warsaw School of Economics (M.A. in Finance and Accounting). He is a CFA charter holder and a member of the CFA Institute. He has authored and reviewed many publications in local and international journals focusing on financial innovations, linkages between financial markets and the economy, financial systems in underdeveloped economies, economic integration, and portfolio management. He has served as coordinator and investigator in research projects financed by national and international institutions.

Ewa Lechman, Gdansk University of Technology. Ewa Lechman, PhD Habil, is Associate Professor of Economics in the Faculty of Management and Economics, Gdansk University of Technology. Her extensive research interests concentrate on economic development, ICT, and its role in reshaping social and economic systems and various aspects of poverty and economics in developing countries. She coordinates and participates in international research and educational projects, and also works as an independent expert assisting with innovation assignments, including the evaluation of small and medium enterprise proposals, EU-financed programs, and policy design regarding innovativeness, digitalization, education, and social exclusion.

Chapter 5:

Janina Harasim, University of Economics in Katowice. Janina Harasim is professor at the University of Economics in Katowice and the head of the Department of Banking and Financial Markets. She published 9 monographs and over 150 research papers on retail banking, competition in banking, retail payments market, payment innovations as well as alternative financial services. Recently her research focuses on digitalization in the financial industry, including the expansion of FinTechs and BigTechs. She has been a member of the Committee on Financial Sciences of the Polish Academy of Sciences for ten years. She is also a member of many committees of national and international scientific conferences and journals. In addition, she is involved in business practice. In 2019-2021, she was among the 20 most influential women in the Polish payments industry. She is also a member of the Supervisory Board and the Audit Committee of one of the banks in Poland.

Chapter 6:

Anna Karmańska, University of Economics in Katowice. PhD Anna Karmańska – Department of Business Informatics and International Accounting at the University of Economics in Katowice. Computer science graduate of the Silesian University of Technology. Statutory Auditor and Chartered Accountant with over 20 years of experience in managing Finance and Tax departments of Polish and international companies. Her research focuses on information systems and technologies for business, auditing and accounting. She published nine peer-reviewed papers and chapters.

Chapter 7:

Piotr Łasak, Jagiellonian University. Piotr Łasak – (PhD, Hab.), Associate Professor at the Institute of Economics, Finance and Management, Jagiellonian University in Krakow, Poland. His research, publication and teaching activities focus on banking and international finance. Among the main research topics are financial market development, regulation and supervision, mechanisms of financial and currency crises and shadow banking system development.

Marta Gancarczyk, Jagiellonian University. Marta Gancarczyk – (PhD, Hab.), Associate Professor at the Institute of Economics, Finance and Management, Jagiellonian University in Krakow, Poland. Her research, publication and consulting activities focus on entrepreneurship, firm growth, technology management and commercialization, industrial clusters, and public policy for small and medium-sized enterprises. She is an Associate Editor of the international scientific journal entitled Journal of Entrepreneurship, Management and Innovation (JEMI), and a Member of the Editorial Advisory Board of the Journal of Organizational Change Management.

Chapter 8:

Andrzej Sławiński, Warsaw School of Economics. Andrzej Sławiński is professor at the Warsaw School of Economics, Chair of Quantitative Economics. His research interests include monetary policy, macroprudential policy, and international finance. Until recently, he worked both at the Warsaw School of Economics and the National Bank of Poland, where he was member of the Monetary Policy Council (2004–2010) and Director General of the Research Department (2011–2017). In 2011, he was advisor to the Chairman of the Polish Financial Supervision Authority. At the National Bank of Poland, he was directly involved in the process of stabilizing and opening up Poland's economy. He published a number of books on financial crises, central banking, and financial markets. Four of them were awarded prizes by the Ministry of Higher Education. His latest publications focus on the effectiveness of central banks' quantitative easing programs, the transition of Eastern European economies, and the impact of FinTech innovations on monetary systems.

Chapter 9:

Tomasz Miziołek, University of Lodz. Tomasz Miziołek is Associate Professor in the Department of International Finance and Investments at the University of Lodz, Poland. He has over 20 years of experience in the analysis of mutual fund markets. Co-author of the book International Equity Exchange-Traded Funds. Navigating Global ETF Market Opportunities and Risks (Palgrave Macmillan, 2020). Author or co-author of many research papers, including 'Nothing Lasts Forever (and Everywhere): Fundamental Indexation at the Global Level' (Journal of Index Investing, 2017). Founder and Editor in Chief of etf.com.pl, an independent, professional website focusing on exchange-traded funds, financial indices, and passive investing.

Chapter 10:

Michał Polasik, Nicolaus Copernicus University in Toruń. Michał Polasik, PhD – an Associate Professor at the Faculty of Economic Sciences and Management, Nicolaus Copernicus University (NCU) in Toruń, Poland and the director of the Centre for Digital Economy and Finance at NCU. The author of over seventy academic publications. In 2016, he was awarded the Prof. Remigiusz Kaszubski Award founded by the Polish Bank Association Board in the category of research activity for his study of the Polish payment system. The principal investigator of several considerable research and research & development projects, e.g., the pan-European study 'PayTech Impact.EU' (http://paytech.umk.pl), the studies in digital payments, payment innovations, payment system, FinTech, e-commerce, and cryptocurrencies.

Paweł Widawski, University of Warsaw. Paweł Widawski, PhD – an Assistant Professor at the Faculty of Law and Administration, the University of Warsaw, Poland and the head of the Center for Financial Services and Technology Regulation. An author of publications in the field of financial services law. The President of the FinTech Poland Foundation, an independent think tank that promotes financial innovation in Poland and conducts research projects and strategic analysis on financial regulation, new generation financial centers, governance and future of finance. He also serves as the Vice-President of the Cashless Poland Foundation, an entity focused on developing payment infrastructure in Poland and promoting financial inclusion. The former Director of the Payment Systems, Electronic Banking and Bank Security Department in the Polish Bank Association, a member of the board of the European Payments Council, a decision and coordination body of the European banking sector for payments, a member of the Payments Committee of the European Federation Banking. In the European Commission, he was a member of the Payment System Expert Market Group.

Andrzej Lis, Nicolaus Copernicus University in Toruń. Andrzej Lis, PhD – an Assistant Professor at the Faculty of Economic Sciences and Management, Nicolaus Copernicus University in Toruń. Since 2014, he has served as the executive editor of Journal of Corporate Responsibility and Leadership. He is an author of numerous publications within the area of management studies, with the focus on knowledge management, positive organizational scholarship, corporate social responsibility, public management and logistics, sport management.

Introduction

Background

In the last decades global financial markets have experienced a deep transformation in various aspects. The profound changes could be noticed with regard to, among others, the market participants, the structure and infrastructure of the markets and their environment. There are various factors that have affected the processes that were, to some extent, revolutionary and led to the development of the contemporary financial markets and, in the broader perspective, the modern financial system. One of the fundamental determinants is the substantial diffusion of the information and communication technologies (ICTs) that has led to the rapidly growing access to various Internet connections with the increasing speed and quality of these services, confirmed in almost all countries worldwide.

Over the last several years, there has been growing interest in recognizing the role of ICTs among broad array of factors conditioning functioning of financial systems. It is also argued that financial markets are to some point 'information markets'. Therefore, ICTs may reshape their functioning, as they enable information and data dissemination, decreasing market failures, *inter alia*, time delays or information asymmetries. ICTs also facilitate rapid and unbounded flows of information which may lead to decentralization of financial markets and potentially make them work more efficiently, mainly due to the fact that physically separated actors can gain new opportunities, for instance, purchase assets not available in their original location. Access to high-speed Internet (broadband network) requires particular examination, as communications systems based on wide bandwidth are notable for significant information-carrying capacity, allowing for increases in financial market activities (e.g., trading).

The impact of ICTs on the financial markets is multidimensional. Advancements in terms of ICTs have transformed the infrastructure of the financial markets, above all in their most dynamic segment, i.e. capital markets. Crucial role is played by the introduction and development of fullyelectronic trading platforms, facilitating algorithmic and high-frequency trading with the limited impact of human traders. High level of automation of the trading process on the financial markets causes a reduction in trading costs, and, consequently, facilitates more efficient risk-sharing together with improvement of the liquidity and efficiency of pricing mechanisms.

Evidently, financial markets have become reliant on ICT-enabled services and financial innovations which are boosted by new technologies, such as various types of FinTech solutions. Some of the main business-to-consumer services offered by FinTech firms are alternative payment methods, digital lending, crowdfunding, crowdinvesting, crowdlending, robo-advising, and social trading. FinTech companies also operate in the business-to-business sector, providing services connected with banking infrastructure, transaction security, payment infrastructure, investment management, and insurance infrastructure. Yet another field of activity involves services for financial regulators, dubbed 'RegTech'. In many respects, FinTech differs substantially from earlier types of digitally-backed financial services. It is more customer-centric, more highly focused on online services, less centralized; the industry operates at lower profit margins owing to more intense competition, and it consists to a large extent of start-ups rather than established financial institutions. FinTech may constitute leap-frogging opportunity for the developing or emerging economies, enabling them, for instance, to overcome the handicap of insufficient traditional banking networks by adopting payment and other services provided by FinTech companies. What is important, the development of the FinTech industry has been substantially influenced by the diffusion of ICT.

Insofar, the evidence on ICT's impact on the financial markets remains rather poor and scattered. Broad, real-world-based evidence is necessary for better understanding of the precise nature of new technologies, the ways they influence the financial markets and the socio-economic consequences of these changes. Hence, the need to assess the ICT's impact on financial markets is urgent, in particular taking into account the rapid growth of various FinTech companies that challenge the conventional incumbents such as investment companies. Are they inflicting effects positive for the economy and society, e.g., increased financial inclusion, or do they rather inflict negative effects such as new risk exposures, problems for proper regulation or privacy and security issues?

The effects of the increasing adoption of ICT on the financial markets in various regions of the world presented above, mean that these markets undoubtedly can be characterized as digitalized and the related process may be labeled as their 'digitalization'. One of the most prominent examples is the complete alteration of the trading on the stock exchanges – traditional transactions conducted physically on the floors of the exchanges have almost completely been replaced by the operations made using the highly sophisticated trading systems.

Over the last several years the growing digitalization of the financial markets has affected the socio-economic systems not only in the advanced but also in the emerging or developing countries. Consequently, the effects of the digitalization of financial markets should be analyzed in the broadest perspective possible, by no means limited exclusively to the financial sector. Trends such as increasing financial inclusion stemming from the digitalization (with regard to, e.g., transformation of the key financial institutions such as banks or facilitating easier access to the capital markets) can be associated with changes in the societies and economies. Some of these effects are still difficult to assess – digitalization of the financial markets provides new opportunities but may also lead to emergence of new threats, some of which may be exhibited only in the longer perspective. For instance, the digitalization of the financial markets can lead to higher financial openness, with the possible ambiguous effects; similar stipulations apply to the increased volatility of the financial markets and related effects on the financial stability. All these pose new challenges for all market participants and related entities such as governments or financial regulatory authorities.

What this edited volume offers

This highly valuable volume offers the reader insight into the ICTs' role in the financial markets; it includes many clearly focused papers, which are usually fragmented and published separately. It covers cutting-edge research and analysis, in the areas of crucial and growing importance. The topics of ICTs and financial markets can be classified as such, as they tackle some of the most prominent issues of the changes in the financial system stemming from the spread of the new technologies.

The volume aims to provide deep insight into theoretical and empirical evidence on ICT as an important factor affecting financial markets. It is focused on the impact of ICTs on stock markets, bond markets, and other categories of financial markets, with the additional focus on the linked FinTech services and financial institutions. For readers interested in these issues, such theoretical discussions and empirical evidence constitute a great point of reference, a complex work, and compilation of different views and perspectives.

Financial markets shaped by the adoption of the new technologies can be labeled 'digital financial markets'. Despite the economy-broad profound changes inflicted by the diffusion of ICT, existence of dynamic links between technological progress and various aspects of financial markets cannot be neglected. However, we still lack broad evidence on how and why ICT is becoming an integral element of the financial markets – this applies even more substantially to the socio-economic consequences of the emergence and development of the digital financial markets. The gap in valuable and conclusive evidence in these fields is significant, thus, it yields for elaboration a body of literature that ideally would concern the role of ICT on the financial markets, both in local and global viewpoint, from the perspective of countries at varying levels of economic development. Moreover, vast majority of the previous books focused on the applications of new technologies

Introduction xix

in the banking or related sectors of the financial system while the number of publications concerning the changes in the financial markets is much more limited. Finally, the consequences of these processes were usually not considered in the broader economic and social context, in particular when FinTech services on financial markets are taken into account.

This edited volume comprises three parts.

Part 1. Digitalization of capital markets: This part is devoted to the core topic of the book, i.e. changes inflicted by the adoption of ICTs on the financial markets, and it consists of four chapters. They all focus on the capital markets as the part of the financial markets most affected by the diffusion of the new technologies. The first chapter, *The impact of information and communication technologies on the equity market* (Agata Adamska), discusses the main changes in the architecture of the capital markets caused by the new technologies, focusing on the institutional perspective. The second chapter, *European Financial Institution Physical Geolocation and the High-Frequency Trading Potential* (Piotr Staszkiewicz, Ewa Łosiewicz-Dniestrzańska, Anna Grygiel-Tomaszewska), investigates the profitability of the financial markets' participants conditioned upon the physical distance to the main stock exchange; the discussion covers also the issue of high-frequency trading (HFT). In the third chapter, *Necessity of Digitalization in the Capital Market of Developing Countries in Current Pandemic Situation: The Case of Bangladesh* (S. M. Sohrab Uddin, ANM Moinul Islam, Mohammad Robaitur Rahat), digitalization of the capital market in the developing country is examined, using the example of Bangladesh in the context of the COVID-19 pandemic. The last, fourth chapter, *Information and communication technologies versus diffusion and substitution of financial innovations. The case of exchange-traded funds in Japan and South Korea.* (Adam Marszk, Ewa Lechman), presents the impact of ICT on the capital markets in two Asia-Pacific economies (Japan and South Korea) by studying the markets for certain categories of financial innovations.

Part 2. FinTech: Selected issues: In the second part the focus of the three chapters is placed on the FinTech sector, i.e. one of the key parts of the financial system which emerged as a result of the ICTs spread. The three chapters present different dimensions of FinTech, not only linked exclusively to the capital markets. In the fifth chapter, *FinTechs, BigTechs and structural changes in capital markets* (Janina Harasim), the impact of technology companies on the market structure in the financial industry is considered, including the attempt to identify structural changes resulting from FinTech. The sixth chapter, *Critical success factors for FinTech* (Anna Karmańska), is devoted to the identification of the critical success factors for FinTechs, adopting the perspective of their users. The last chapter in this part (i.e. the seventh in the full book), *Systemizing the impact of fintechs on the efficiency and inclusive growth of banks' services: A literature review* (Piotr Łasak, Marta Gancarczyk), aims to identify and systemize how the financial technologies influence the efficiency and inclusive growth of banking services.

Part 3. Digitalization of financial institutions: The third part concentrates on the digitalization of the financial institutions in the context related to similar processes taking place in the financial markets. It comprises three rather different chapters. Chapter eight, *The prospect of cryptocurrencies becoming money* (Andrzej Sławiński), presents selected features of cryptocurrencies such as the position of Bitcoin as a digital successor of the gold standard, regulatory stipulations to Facebook's Libra as well as Central Bank Digital Currencies. The ninth chapter, *Employing artificial intelligence in investment management* (Tomasz Miziołek), discusses not only theoretical aspects of artificial intelligence (AI) employment in the field of investment management but also its practical applications, using the example of exchange-traded fund (ETF) market. The final tenth chapter, *Challenger bank as a new digital form of providing financial services to retail customers in the EU Internal Market: The case of Revolut* (Michał Polasik, Paweł Widawski, Andrzej Lis), explores the operations of 'challenger banks' (based on digital technologies, challenging big, traditional banks) and presents the case of Revolut.

We hope that the book will be interesting for the scholars in the fields such as finance and economics. Its intended audience are those who are addressing issues of new technologies and financial markets, FinTech, financial innovations, stock markets, and the role of technological progress in broadly defined socio-economic systems. It can also be a valuable source of knowledge for students in a variety of areas such as financial markets, information and technology, global studies or comparative economics. Moreover, we expect that is also a useful material for the professionals in the financial industry who are directly or indirectly linked to the new technologies on the financial markets, in particular various types of FinTech services.

Finally, we would like to emphasize and acknowledge the role of the National Science Centre (Poland) in the preparation of this book – it was partially funded by project no. 2015/19/D/HS4/00399.

Adam Marszk
Ewa Lechman
(editors of the book)
Gdańsk, Poland – March 2021

Part 1:
Digitalization of capital markets

1 The impact of information and communication technologies on the equity market

Agata Adamska

Introduction

Ever since the world's first stock exchange was set up in Amsterdam in 1602 (Petram, 2014), the securities trading system has been in a state of constant flux. However, for hundreds of years trading took place in brick-and-mortar establishments where the buyers and sellers, or their proxies, met to negotiate the terms and conditions of share ownership transfer. The picture remained essentially the same until the advent of information and communication technologies (ICTs), which completely altered the landscape replacing human communication with computers executing transactions virtually. This transformation was not gradual or ordered; indeed the changes were abrupt, fragmentary, and affected not only the transaction process itself, but also the behaviors of the trading venues (infrastructure) and market participants. The developments in question took place in different areas concurrently, mutually reinforcing one another. However, for the sake of clarity, the presentation will follow several major lines of analysis, i.e., market processes, the incumbents and entrants, their behaviors, as well as the market structure.

The digitization of market processes

While computers were first used in the stock market as early as the 1960s, electronic trade did not emerge until almost a decade later, and it gained popularity only gradually. As ever-faster data processing and exchange methods were enabled by hardware and software innovations, the number of market participants using advanced ICTs increased over time. Nasdaq became the first fully electronic exchange with the introduction of a computerized system of quotes and volumes traded in 1971. The first (and largest) European venue that deployed computers for trading was the London Stock Exchange (LSE) in 1986 within a broader program of deregulation and restructuring that came to be known as the "Big Bang" (Poser, 2001). Floor trading did not disappear immediately; it was actually defended for quite a long time by the world's biggest bourse, the New York Stock Exchange (NYSE), with

DOI: 10.4324/9781003095354-1

approx. 10% of transactions still executed traditionally in face-to-face interactions as late as 2001 (Karmel, 2002). However, in 2006 the tide of change brought about by ICTs finally forced the NYSE to implement an all-electronic trading system (Lucas et al., 2009). The adoption of IT in the stock market has led to the digitization of the entire investment process, from collecting information and decision making to placing, executing, clearing, and settling orders.

Given that information is universally considered a pillar of effective capital markets (Fama, 1965), the application of cutting-edge technologies for data collection and processing seems to expand the overall pool of that resource. However, despite the greater amount of available information, technological progress has not eliminated disparities in terms of access to it between market participants; just on the contrary, the problem has become more acute than ever. For instance, the speed of access to basic trade and quote data depends on physical proximity to the exchange and the technology used by both the exchange and the investor (Ding et al., 2014).

ICT-driven acceleration involves not only information acquisition and processing but also the transmission of the resulting trade orders to the market. The increasingly complex algorithms not only facilitate trade by automatically executing human choices but often replace people with algorithmic decision-making strategies (Lenczewski Martins, 2019). In the United States, algorithmic trading boomed in the 2010s and has become popular ever since, stabilizing at a rather high level in the second decade of the 21st century, with the share of algorithmic transactions estimated by various authors to range from 70% to over 80% of the overall trade volume (the latter figure seems to be more accurate as it reflects not only transactions executed directly by investors' algorithms, but also those in which algorithms are deployed by brokers executing investors' orders (Glantz & Kissell, 2013)).

The development of digital technologies has enabled, and indeed necessitated, a number of changes in the equity markets at the operational level. The order queue was automated while real-time communication accelerated order execution to an average of less than 300 microseconds (Ding et al., 2014). Dematerialization put an end to the era of paper shares, which was a crucial precondition for the digitization of market processes, such as order placement, execution, and settlement. Further operational adjustments included the splitting of traditional blocks of stock into individual shares and modifying the quoting system to accommodate digital requirements. In the United States of America this involved decimalization: in 2001 a penny tick size in share prices replaced dollar fractions (Ikenberry & Weston, 2007) (previously 1/16th at NASDAQ and 1/8th at the NYSE and other US exchanges (Karmel, 2002)). Some other countries around the world have introduced quoting systems with even greater resolutions, up to four decimal places, to smooth out price movements between transactions and ensure a more accurate valuation of the traded securities.

Proposition 1: ICT development has led to the digitization of stock market processes, raising the expectations of market participants; this has resulted in a feedback loop generating demand for further ICT innovation, but the dynamic of change is now waning.

ICT-induced changes in investor behaviors

The past several decades have seen tremendous progress in the ways investors apply ICTs to achieve operating effectiveness and a competitive edge in electronic trading markets (ETMs). The automation of order processing allows investors not only to increase the frequency of transactions at lower costs but also fuels expectations as to attaining informational advantages due to faster computers and networks being connected to more efficient IT systems at trading venues. Many market participants have been drawn into a technological and informational "arms race" trying to outcompete their rivals in terms of data acquisition and processing speed (Samuel et al., 2017). This has given rise to high-frequency trading (HFT), where computer algorithms analyze market data and execute transactions at extremely high speeds. The race to zero latency has become the dominant trend in the equity market.

HFT practices emerged in the United States and have quickly spread to Europe and Asia. While there are no comprehensive data on the share of HFT in overall stock trade volume, estimates for individual markets reveal its growing significance. In the United States, where it is most popular, HFT is responsible for more than 60% of overall volume (Glantz & Kissell, 2013), while the figures for Europe are much lower: 15.41% for the LSE and 21.34% for Euronext Paris (data for 2006–2011 (Frino & Lepone, 2012)). Finally, HFT is used in all major Asia-Pacific markets but its share greatly varies across the region due to substantial differences between them. In 2011, HFT accounted for approx. 45% of total trading by value in Japan and 27% in Australia, compared to as little as 12% in the other regional markets (Kauffman et al., 2015).

While investors are often categorized by portfolio size, business strategy, and professionalism, the advent of ICTs in the capital market has brought an additional distinction between fast and slow traders differing in terms of information processing speed, alternation between buy and sell transactions, the number of orders placed and cancelled, individual trading volume, and inventory size (Roşu, 2019). The division into fast and slow traders can also be seen in intermarket operations. For instance, it has been found that the execution of a transaction in one venue is followed within 1 s by substantial cancellations of the same type of orders and then by an increase in limit orders on the opposite side of the order book in other venues (Van Kervel, 2015). However, in the absence of a clear-cut definition, the categorization into fast and slow traders is largely arbitrary. Thus, the results of most studies exploring the effects of HFT on market operations and participants largely depend on the assumptions adopted in a given paper as there are no publicly available data that would enable the identification of HFT orders, transactions, and quotes. As a result, it is difficult to conclusively evaluate HFT effects on stock market efficiency or assess their net overall externalities.

The situation is complicated by the low transparency of individual HFT firms; all that can be said with certainty is that they engage in electronic market making, cross-trading venue price arbitrage, short-term statistical arbitrage, and various other opportunistic strategies (Boehmer et al., 2018). Their veil of secrecy adds to concerns about the fairness and stability of the capital market as a whole, further polarizing opinions about HFT. The positive effects highlighted by its advocates include improved liquidity, decreased bid-ask spreads, reduced adverse selection, and faster trade-related price discovery (Hendershott et al., 2011; Hendershott & Riordan, 2013). Some also argue that the strategies of HFT firms are nothing new in the capital market; they only appear so due to their deployment in an automated environment (Jones, 2013). In turn, the opponents of HFT firms object that they increase volatility (Lewis, 2014), cause and exploit mispricing (Jarrow & Protter, 2012), and in extreme cases trigger dramatic price changes in individual stocks as well as stock indices, such as flash crashes (Patterson, 2012). Importantly, their critics emphasize the fact that fast traders may take unfair time advantage over slow traders by spoofing, pocket sniffing, quote stuffing, as well as flash and front-run orders (Lewis, 2014; Manahov, 2016; McGowan, 2010; Patterson, 2013; Serbera & Paumard, 2016).

The enormous differences in the speed of data processing, order placement, and transaction execution make fair competition between fast and slow traders practically unfeasible. This is one of the reasons why many institutional investors have departed from active portfolio management in favor of a passive approach whereby they occasionally rebalance their assets following the reconstitutions of their benchmark indices. The scale of this phenomenon is so large that some authors have written about the emergence of an index fund industry (Fichtner et al., 2017). This shift in investor behavior may be interpreted as a side effect of the tidal wave of change driven by technological progress, with the effect being that now almost 50% of mutual fund assets in the United States are managed passively (in other markets that percentage is somewhat lower at approx. 35%) (The Economist, 2019).

The fact that slow traders often avoid direct confrontation does not automatically imply that fast traders have discovered for themselves a competition-free blue ocean. In the early days of HFT, it may have seemed that the high operating speeds available to a small group of investors would allow them to indefinitely reap huge profits. One of the largest HFT firms, Tradebot, boasted that they never lost money in the course of a single trading day for four straight years (Patterson, 2013). However, over time, the number of HFT firms has grown, inevitably stirring up competition and bringing profits down (Boehmer et al., 2018). The modus operandi of HFT firms has shifted the focus from simply driving up speed to gaining a competitive advantage in the initial phase of the investment process, that is, data collection and analysis.

However, the influence of HFT firms on the equity market goes well beyond their immediate activity and strategies. Process automation and the astonishing speed of posting orders have led not only to several spectacular failures of some HFT firms, but may have serious ramifications for the broader market. For instance, on August 1, 2012, an erroneous algorithm deployed by the Knight Capital Group, acting on 212 orders from its retail customers, executed more than 4 million trades in 154 stocks totaling 397 million shares over a period of 45 minutes, resulting in a loss of $440 million (Perez, 2013). Similar accidents have also occurred in other markets. In 2013, the Chinese state-owned brokerage Everbright Securities Co. sent more than 26,000 mistaken buy orders to the Shanghai Stock Exchange amounting to RMB 23.4 billion ($3.82 billion), which resulted in a loss of an equivalent of $31.7 million (Kauffman et al., 2015). While the externalities of those events are difficult to assess, they affected large groups of market participants by triggering dramatic changes in the prices of specific stocks as well as the values of whole indices.

The latest trend arising from the digitization of the financial market is an influx of a new wave of non-professional traders. The dynamic increase in the number of individual investment accounts in early 2020 is associated with the social distancing and lockdown regulations imposed due to the COVID-19 pandemic. As a result, many people with Internet access (most of them millennials and Gen-Z members), deprived of other activities, got interested in securities trading. In the first quarter of 2020, a surge of new traders around the world was reported by online brokers to range from 58% (Charles Schwab) to over 150% (TD Ameritrade, Etrade, Robinhood) (Fitzgerald, 2020), and even 269% (Lloyds Banking Group) (Kaveh, 2020). However, since the involvement of individual investors in the stock market had been following a downward trajectory for many years, it is unclear whether this dramatic growth enabled by widespread technology-driven access to the markets is going to persist in the long run.

Proposition 2: Changes in processes and continuing ICT development have affected and differentiated the behavior of investors, increasing the heterogeneity of market participants.

The emergence of new players in the equity market

In the secondary equity market, new technologies have enabled electronic transaction platforms to challenge traditional exchanges. One of the first computer-based facilities for trade in American stocks was established by Instinet as early as in 1969 (MacKenzie, 2017). Over time, the significance of alternative trading venues gradually increased; in addition to private firms a plethora of licensed and regulated alternative trading systems (ATSs) emerged all over the world, and especially in Europe and the United States (Christiansen & Koldertsova, 2009) (in Europe they came to be known as multilateral trading facilities – MTFs, and in the United States as electronic communication networks – ECNs (Karmel, 2002)). The number of European MTFs increased from 150 in 2015 (Di Febo & Angelini, 2015) to 233 in 2020 (ESMA, 2020). Altogether, they have taken over a substantial proportion of trade volume from the incumbents: in 2018 as much as 40% of equity trade took place outside the regulated market (Oxera, 2019).

Some ATSs were designed as so-called "dark pools", with an early example being Liquidnet launched in 2000 (Patterson, 2013). Initially, they provided services to major institutional investors, enabling them to anonymously swap large blocks of stock outside the regulated market without the need to split them into smaller chunks and circumvent pre-trade transparency. Over time, this formula has become attractive for traders posting smaller orders (including individual investors). It is estimated that in Europe the market share of dark pools in overall stock trading reached a high point of up to 10% (Petrescu & Wedow, 2017), although it has slightly declined since the adoption of the Markets in Financial Instruments Directive (MiFID II; Oxera, 2019). Importantly, dark pools prevent HFT from front-running by withholding information about orders (the subscribers' buy and sell orders are matched at reference prices from other markets). Some dark pools have employed additional order placement and processing precautions to curb other predatory strategies of algorithmic traders (Petrescu & Wedow, 2017).

On the other hand, detractors claim that the information asymmetry inherent in dark pools gives the operators a major advantage over the subscribers, raising concerns as to their impartiality and equal treatment of all investors. There have been cases where dark pools granted access to fast traders without informing other participants, or protected only selected customers from HFT. Furthermore, some dark pools have engaged in proprietary trading, creating a conflict of interest due to the aforementioned informational advantage (Aguilar, 2015).

The progress in automation that enabled ATSs made them more profitable over time as market data could be sent at ever greater speeds, lower costs, and larger scales. The new entrants successfully filled the niches left by the incumbents (e.g., by launching dark pools) and engaged in direct price competition with the latter. That rivalry was taken to an international level as ATSs began to offer trade in stocks listed around the world. Although most ATSs have small trade volumes as compared to the major stock exchanges, there are exceptions. Already in 2017 the aggregate stock trading volume of the largest ATS, BATS Global Markets, exceeded by 18% the entire EMEA volume, including the LSE Group (WFE, 2018).

ICT advances have affected not only secondary, but also primary, equity markets as the rise of innovative peer-to-peer networks has led to the development of alternative financing schemes known as equity crowdfunding platforms. Although the share of those specialized middlemen that help companies raise capital remains relatively low in the overall equity market (in Europe it was estimated at less than 0.5% of the region's GDP as compared to 60% for public equity in 2014 (PwC, 2015)), the supportive approach of the regulators opens up new opportunities for these platforms. The emergence of crowdfunding as a potential substitute for traditional financing methods shows the degree to which ICTs affect the structure of the capital market.

> *Proposition 3: ICT-induced changes have enabled the emergence of new types of operators in the equity market, increasing the heterogeneity of trading venues.*

Transformations affecting incumbent stock exchanges

In the past, stock exchanges were natural venues for trade in securities which monopolized the market due to regulatory reasons, economies of scale (large venues had lower unit costs and offered cheaper services to issuers), and supply side factors (dealers tended to center around exchanges where others were already trading) (Stoll, 2006). The advent of ICTs diminished the importance of both of these factors. Process automation considerably drove down transaction costs making them less dependent on scale, while computer networks eliminated communication barriers between market participants and trading venues. As a result, many emergent ATSs attracted a portion of trade volume from incumbents by cherry picking stocks with the highest liquidity. As the most profitable trades were diverted to the new entrants, traditional exchanges remained encumbered with their role as regulatory organizations bearing the costs of overseeing the listed companies. In addition, ICT development spelled increasing capital investment for exchanges both to fend off competition and to satisfy the growing expectations of traders in terms of the speed, efficiency, and reliability of transaction systems (Hart & Moore, 1996).

Under the circumstances, stock exchanges, which originally operated as monopolistic "brokers' clubs", started to seek more flexible forms of organization to remain relevant (Karmel, 2002). Those that have transformed into for-profit companies, capable of raising external capital and implementing the necessary investments, have improved their ability to compete both with other incumbents and new entrants. In a process known as demutualization, many traditional exchanges have turned into self-listed public companies. The first to demutualize in 1993 was the Stockholm Stock Exchange, and more than 50 exchanges across the world followed suit over a next 10-year period (Padilla Angulo et al., 2014). Research results indicate that demutualized exchanges have been able to achieve superior short-term (Otchere, 2006) and long-term results (Ben Slimane & Padilla-Angulo, 2018) as compared to their traditional counterparts, leading to an increase in their value.

Once an exchange turns into a public company, it becomes accountable not only to its own members but, crucially, to its shareholders. As a result, exchanges are obliged to maximize their profits, e.g., by growing their business and limiting competition, which has led to a wave of mergers and acquisitions (M&As) as well as strategic alliances. This consolidation of exchanges in conjunction with the growing extent of their activity has ushered them into an era of global competition. Many M&As within the stock exchange industry have had not only local but also international and intercontinental implications. Although in most cases incumbents have merged with other incumbents, some have joined forces with ATSs. M&As between exchanges functioning within one country have taken place in, e.g., Spain, France, Italy (Di Noia, 2001), the United States (Arnold et al., 1999), and Japan (Kauffman et al., 2015). There have been also numerous trans-border M&As; some of them successful (e.g., the integration of Baltic and Nordic exchanges into OMX (Ben Slimane, 2012)), but others did not stand the test of time so well (e.g., the CEE Stock Exchange Group (CEESEG), which originally comprised of four Central European exchanges (Vychytilová, 2018)). Also, some intercontinental mergers did not last (NYSE Euronext survived only 12 years), while the planned mergers between Deutsche Börse and NYSE Euronext and between the LSE and TMX Group never came to fruition (Ben Slimane, 2012). Nevertheless, research has shown that most M&As among bourses have had a beneficial effect on their shareholder value, which is greater for horizontal and international concentrations as compared to vertical and national ones (Hasan et al., 2010).

The above considerations notwithstanding, the portfolio of services provided by stock exchanges has also evolved as reflected in a new revenue structure with a decreased share of trade-related services (now often less than 50% of overall revenues) and an increase in other services, both traditionally associated with exchanges (e.g., listing, dissemination of information, sometimes post-trade processing), as well as completely new ones, closely linked to ICT development (e.g., Euronext is reported to deliver software for other trading venues (Lucas et al., 2009)). Some exchanges have launched paid services for HFT firms, such as flash orders (disclosure of a market participant's order for 30 ms), direct access to market data, and colocation (placing the trader's computer at the same site as the exchange's servers). Some venues, such as the LSE and the Chicago Stock Exchange have implemented batch auctions in addition to continuous-time trading to facilitate swapping large blocks of stock between institutional clients. Similar to dark pools, batch trades only reveal some basic information, i.e., the stock symbol, time, and price (Budish et al., 2015).

Proposition 4: ICT-induced changes in the structure of trading venues have triggered a response on the part of incumbent stock exchanges, modifying their behaviors and increasing their use of ICTs.

ICT development and the situation of issuers

ICT advances have transformed the landscape not only for investors and trading venues, but also for issuers, who have had to adjust their behavior, especially in terms of communication, taking into account the ways in which information generated by them and about them is processed, disseminated, and traded on (Miller & Skinner, 2015). New forms of contact with investors encompass Internet websites and the social media; also mandatory current and periodic disclosures are now made in electronic format.

The rise of new communication channels has made it easier for issuers to reach a broad base of existing and potential investors with more comprehensive and accurate information, including voluntary disclosures. At the same time, the technological revolution has increased the diversity of information sources for investors, with more or less formal content being published by analysts, journalists, politicians, celebrities, employees, suppliers, customers, and regulators. Unfortunately, this new horizontal communication model causes information noise depriving the issuers of control over what they want to communicate, undermining confidentiality, secrecy, and classified business information. It should be noted that both reliable reports and fake news are immediately captured by machine-driven algorithms and processed in real-time, affecting stock prices, sometimes with disastrous results. For instance, in September 2008 a glitch in the search engine used by Google News highlighted an archival story about a bankruptcy filing by United Airlines, which was then run in other news outlets, including Bloomberg. As a result, the company's stock price immediately plummeted from $12.5 to $3.72, shrinking its capitalization by more than a billion dollars. However, after the information was exposed as false, the shares almost completely recovered by the end of the day (Zetter, 2008).

The development of ICTs has also influenced the disclosure obligations of issuers: not only the scope of information to be provided but also the technical requirements as to the form of disclosure, data format, transmission channels, etc. Regulations in this area are periodically amended so as to unify the diverse streams of information that are being processed by stock exchanges and oversight bodies and stored in a variety of databases. A major burden on issuers is the increasingly widespread requirement to publish periodic financial and non-financial statements in eXtensible Business Reporting Language (XBRL), which is designed to increase information transparency for the users.

On the other hand, the remote trading opportunities offered by ICTs make it possible to list stocks in any international market without cutting off the local investors (Claessens et al., 2002). By international listings, companies incorporated in countries with unsatisfactory protections for minority shareholders may send a message to investors that they are willing to meet higher corporate governance standards (Reese & Weisbach, 2002).

Conscquently, just as in the case of traders, ICTs have enabled issuers to gain global access to capital markets.

However, over time issuers have come to realize that ICT-related opportunities entail new threats. Increasing algorithm-based speculation (e.g., HFT) and software failures may instantaneously distort the market value of companies in ways unrelated to their fundamentals. There have been both dramatic drops in company capitalization (e.g., on December 12, 2003, Corinthian Colleges stock price plunged from $57.50 to $39.50 within several minutes, and then recovered to its previous levels (Stoll, 2006)), as well as surges (e.g., on August 01, 2012, the malfunctioning software of Knight Capital quadrupled the price of Wizzard Software Corporation (Kauffman et al., 2015).

Traditionally, in the process of initial public offering (IPO) companies were able to select the market where their shares were to be listed, with some large corporations choosing dual listing (with the use of American depositary receipts (ADRs) or global depositary receipt (GDRs)). Thus, the issuers were in control of the number of markets where their stocks were traded, while information about company value was usually derived from one source. The situation has become radically different. Given the activity of ATSs, the exchange selected by the issuer is now but one of many markets where its shares will be traded. For instance, in 2009 the LSE executed only 61% of the overall trade volume in FTSE100 stocks, with the remaining volume being traded on Chi-X (24%), Bats (7.6%), Turquoise (5.5%), and NASDAQ OMX (1.8%) (Van Kervel, 2015). This fragmentation of trade, outside the issuers' control, amplifies information noise with reference to stock value and increases susceptibility to inter-market speculation.

Another problem associated with technological progress and the related surge in market activity is the loosening of ties between companies and investors. The accelerating frequency of trades at declining mean volumes and the decreasing average stock holding period are manifestations of short-termism which puts a question mark over the role of shareholders in sustainable corporate governance.

Indeed, in the face of increasingly burdensome disclosure obligations, value volatility, and corporate governance uncertainty, many companies are deciding to go private. At the same time, the growing popularity of crowdfunding has provided an alternative to traditional IPOs, especially for the smaller businesses. Due to the combined effects of the rising number of delistings and fewer IPOs, the population of publicly traded companies around the world has been on a decline, contracting by 28% between 2014 and 2019 (World Bank, 2020).

Proposition 5: ICT advances and changes in the behavior of investors and trading venues have affected the issuers.

Regulatory response

Technology-driven changes in the behavior of investors, trading venues, and issues have triggered substantial regulatory response, although its degree and scope vary considerably across countries and regions due to major differences between markets in terms of the institutional environment, legislation, law enforcement, company law, capital market oversight, as well as the nature, significance, and form of informal institutions. Regulatory response encompasses the adjustment of legislation and best practices codes to the new realities with a view to containing harmful phenomena by banning certain types of conduct. In addition to such reactive measures, some regulators have undertaken initiatives aimed at stimulating desirable changes in selected areas. This process of sanctioning, prohibiting, and incentivizing has been reflected both in general regulations as well as individual decisions concerning specific market participants or types of operations.

Regulatory measures differ in terms of their territorial (local, national, international) and substantive scope; depending on the regulators' competence they may concern the legal form of regulated markets and other trading venues, reporting standards, and the taxation of transactions. Furthermore, demutualization has led to a situation where stock exchanges fulfill the dual role of both market regulators and listed companies, which undermines self-regulation (Aggarwal et al., 2007; Fleckner, 2006). As a result, in most countries regulators have assumed some of the former competencies of exchanges in terms of setting trading rules and disclosure obligations for issuers and investors.

A major problem facing regulators in their handling of new technologies is confusion as to their exact effects on the market and market participants. While some regulations are a natural response to tangible phenomena, such as the rise of ATSs, online annual shareholder meetings, and blockchain-based voting systems, in other areas the regulators lack clarity as to the consequences of technological development. In particular, the intransparency of HFT has baffled researchers and regulators alike around the world, and the jury is still out on the effects of fast traders on market efficiency.

In addition to legislative measures and the soft self-regulation rules, an efficient market also requires effective law enforcement. This is all the more important as technological development has enabled new ways of manipulating equity markets to drive stock prices up or down for the benefit of the manipulator, with the two most popular manipulation techniques being spoofing and quote stuffing (Lee et al., 2013). On the other hand, big data analysis has enabled the regulators to detect such manipulation and penalize the culprits (Zhai et al., 2018). Thus, technology has become a powerful tool for both sides.

Proposition 6: ICT-induced changes in the behavior of investors, trading venues, and issuers have led to regulatory response.

Changes in market design and competition model

The effects of ICTs on the equity market may be observed not only with respect to individual categories of market participants (investors, trade venues, issuers, regulators) but also with reference to the market as a whole. As recently as the 1990s, the main organizations that integrated the activity of market participants were stock exchanges functioning as local monopolies controlled by their founders (brokers). The role of exchanges was to bring together entities in need of capital (issuers) and those having surplus capital at their disposal (investors) and to enable the transfer of ownership of shares between the latter. The development of ICTs has disrupted this simple pattern as today's market is much more complex both in terms of types of participants and the directions and intensity of interactions between them.

The heterogeneity of trading venues, including incumbent exchanges which have turned into for-profit companies, ATSs, and large financial institutions bilaterally dealing with their customers (Gomber et al., 2017), has intensified competition. The equity market has become fragmented with both volume and liquidity being dispersed amongst numerous and diverse trading venues. This phenomenon is particularly pronounced in the United States, where stocks are traded on 13 exchanges and 40 ATSs forming a single National Market System (NMS) (Yadav, 2019). Although in Europe the number of regulated markets and MTFs is much higher (137 and 223, respectively (ESMA, 2020)), not all of them offer stock trading and few of those do carry the same stocks. This situation has given rise to intensive rivalry between trading venues under different competition models in the US and European markets.

Furthermore, it should be noted that due to ICT-induced transformations, many of the functions of incumbent exchanges have been taken over by specialized companies, for instance those disseminating information. As a result, competition in the equity market is not only horizontal, between trading venues, but also vertical, between trading venues and the providers of ancillary services (Hart & Moore, 1996). This rivalry has become additionally complicated by the demutualization of incumbent exchanges, due to which self-listed trading venues are competing for investors (and their capital) with other publicly listed companies. These complex competition mechanisms concur with a drive towards concentration as reflected in numerous mergers, acquisitions, and strategic alliances between trading venues, introducing an element of co-opetition to the exchange industry (Schmiedel, 2001).

Proposition 7: ICT progress has altered the market structure and competition model in the exchange industry.

Conclusions

The development of ICTs exerts significant and multifaceted effects on the equity market, affecting the main groups of participants (investors, trading venues, issuers), provoking regulatory response, and thus transforming both the market structure and the model of competition. As a result, ICTs have catalyzed the process of undermining some of the traditional roles of the equity market, such as financing businesses in the real economy or providing reliable information about company value. Some authors have indicated that the secondary market sector has turned into an exchange industry solely engaged in a continuous string of speculation. This phenomenon is considered yet another symptom of financialization understood as the decoupling of the financial sphere from the real sphere of the economy.

ICT adoption by the capital market proceeds in a non-linear manner, just as is the case with other cutting-edge technologies. Indeed, innovations tend to come in waves; once they are adopted, they may generate an aggregation of new solutions. In the past, such waves were caused by the use of computers and the Internet, as well as the development of specialized software. Every time, the pioneers deploying a novel technology gained an advantage that gradually dwindled over time as the technology became more widely disseminated. There are good reasons to believe that the equity market has become saturated with ICTs, but it continues to seek new solutions in the hope of unleashing yet another wave of change. Candidate breakthrough technologies include artificial intelligence and blockchain, but it is difficult to predict the final outcomes due to the early stages of their implementation. Nevertheless, ICTs have become a permanent fixture in the equity market as it would be inconceivable to forfeit the opportunities they offer, whether now or in the future. Thus, in pursuit of those opportunities, the market is certain to undergo further transformations meriting subsequent comprehensive inquiry.

References

Aggarwal, R., Ferrell, A., & Katz, J. G. (2007). *U.S. Securities Regulation in a World of Global Exchanges.* Exchanges: Challenges and Implications, Euromoney, Harvard Law and Economics Discussion Paper No. 569, ECGI - Finance Working Paper No. 146/2007, Available at SSRN: https://ssrn.com/abstract=950530

Aguilar, L. (2015). *Shedding light on dark pools.* Securities and Exchange Commission Public Statement. sec.gov/news/statement.

Arnold, T., Hersch, P., Mulherin, J. H., & Netter, J. (1999). Merging markets. *Journal of Finance, 54*(3), 1083–1107.

Ben Slimane, F. (2012). The structural evolution of stock exchanges. *Recherches en Sciences de Gestion, 6*(93), 47–71.

Ben Slimane, F., & Padilla-Angulo, L. (2018). Board restructuring and successful demutualization: The stock exchanges. *Journal of Organizational Change Management, 31*(3), 598–618.

Boehmer, E., Li, D., & Saar, G. (2018). The competitive landscape of high-frequency trading firms. *The Review of Financial Studies, 31*(6), 2227–2276.

Budish, E., Cramton, P., & Shim, J. (2015). The high-frequency trading arms race: Frequent batch auctions as a market design response. *Quarterly Journal of Economics, 130*(4), 1547–621.

Christiansen, H., & Koldertsova, A. (2009). The role of stock exchanges in corporate governance. *OECD Journal: Financial Market Trends*, *1*, 191–220.

Claessens, S., Klingebiel, D., & Schmukler, S. L. (2002). *The Future of Stock Exchanges in Emerging Economies: Evolution and Prospects*. Brookings-Wharton Papers on Financial Services, Brookings Institution Press, 167–212.

Di Febo, E., & Angelini, E. (2015). The launch of alternative trading venues and their evolution in the European union: Spanish Exchanges. *Current Politics & Economics of Europe*, *26*(3), 267–297.

Di Noia, C. (2001). Competition and integration among stock exchanges in Europe: Network effects, implicit mergers and remote access. *European Financial Management*, *7*(1), 39–72.

Ding, S., Hanna, J., & Hendershott, T. (2014). How slow is the NBBO? A comparison with direct exchange feeds. *The Financial Review*, *49*(2), 313–332.

Fama, E. F. (1965). The behavior of stock-market prices. *Journal of Business*, *38*(1), 34–105.

Fichtner, J., Heemskerk, E. M., & Garcia-Bernardo, J. (2017). Hidden power of the big three? Passive index funds, re-concentration of corporate ownership, and new financial risk. *Business and Politics*, *19*(2), 298–326.

Fitzgerald, M. (2020). Young investors pile into stocks, seeing 'generational-buying moment' instead of risk, *CNBC*, May 12 2020.

Fleckner, A. M. (2006). Stock exchanges at the crossroads. *Fordham Law Review*, *74*(5), 2541–2620.

Frino, A., & Lepone, A. (2012). *The impact of high frequency trading on market integrity: An empirical examination. Commissioned by the UK Government's Foresight Project*. https://pdfs.semanticscholar.org/4644/0e5fc9339f52c5f1f857b1ffd7e8073e2bf8.pdf.

Glantz, M., & Kissell, R. (2013). *Multi-asset risk modeling: Techniques for a global economy in an electronic and algorithmic trading era*. Academic Press.

Gomber, P., Sagade, S., Theissen, E., Weber, M., & Westheide, C. (2017). Competition between equity markets: A review of the consolidation versus fragmentation debate. *Journal of Economic Surveys*, *31*(3), 792–814.

Hart, O., & Moore, J. (1996). The governance of exchanges: members' cooperatives versus outside ownership. *Oxford Review of Economic Policy*, *12*(4), 53–69.

Hasan, I., Schmiedel, H., & Song, L. (2010). Growth strategies and value creation: What works best for stock exchanges? *Research Discussion Papers 2/2010*, Bank of Finland.

Hendershott, T., & Riordan, R. (2013). Algorithmic trading and the market for liquidity. *Journal of Financial and Quantitative Analysis*, *48*(4), 1001–1024.

Hendershott, T., Jones, C. M., & Menkveld, A. J. (2011). Does algorithmic trading improve liquidity? *Journal of Finance*, *66*(1), 1–33.

Ikenberry, D. L., & Weston, J. P. (2007). Clustering in US stock prices after decimalisation. *European Financial Management*, *14*(1), 30–54.

Jarrow, R. A., & Protter, P. (2012). A dysfunctional role of high frequency trading in electronic markets. *International Journal of Theoretical and Applied Finance*, *15*(3), 1–15.

Jones, C. M. (2013). *What Do We Know About High-Frequency Trading?* Columbia Business School Research Paper No. 13–11. http://ssrn.com/abstract=2236201.

Karmel, R. S. (2002). Turning seats into shares: Causes and implications of demutualization of stock and futures exchanges. *Hastings Law Journal*, *53*(2), 367–430.

Kauffman, R. J., Hu, Y., & Ma, D. (2015). Will high-frequency trading practices transform the financial markets in the Asia pacific region? *Financial Innovation*, *1*(1), 1–27.

Kaveh, K. (2020). Investment platform account openings surge despite coronavirus uncertainty: Is now a good time to invest? *Which? April 29th, 2020*.

Lee, E. J., Eom, K. S., & Park, K. S. (2013). Microstructure-based manipulation: Strategic behavior and performance of spoofing traders. *Journal of Financial Markets*, *16*(2), 227–252.

Lenczewski Martins, C. J. (2019). The role of automation in financial trading companies. *Journal of Management and Financial Sciences*, *39*(12), 29–42.

Lewis, M. (2014). *Flash boys: A wall Street revolt*. W.W. Norton & Company.

Lucas, H., Oh, W., & Weber, B. W. (2009). The defensive use of IT in a newly vulnerable market: The New York stock exchange, 1980–2007. *The Journal of Strategic Information Systems*, *18*(1), 3–15.

MacKenzie, D. (2017). A material political economy: Automated trading desk and price pre-diction in high-frequency trading. *Social Studies of Science*, *47*(2), 172–94.

Manahov, V. (2016). Front-running scalping strategies and market manipulation: Why does high-frequency trading need stricter regulation? *Financial Review*, *51*(3), 363–402.

McGowan, M. J. (2010). The rise of computerized high frequency trading: Use and controversy. *Duke Law & Technology Review*, *16*, 1–24.

Miller, G. S., & Skinner, D. J. (2015). The evolving disclosure landscape: How changes in technology, the media, and capital markets are affecting disclosure. *Journal of Accounting Research*, *53*(2), 221–239.

Otchere, I. (2006). Stock exchange self-listing and value effects. *Journal of Corporate Finance*, *12*(5), 926–953.

Oxera (2019). *The design of equity trading markets in Europe. An economic analysis of price formation and market data services*. Prepared for Federation of European Securities Exchanges. Available at https://www.oxera.com/wp-content/uploads/2019/03/design-of-equity-trading-markets-

Padilla Angulo, L., Ben Slimane, F., & Alidou, D. (2014). The London stock exchange: Strategic corporate governance restructuring after demutualization. *Journal of Applied Business Research*, *30*(2), 211–225.

Patterson, S. (2012). *Dark pools: High-speed traders, AI bandits, and the threat to the global financial system*. Crown Business.

Patterson, S. (2013). *Dark pools: The rise of AI trading machines and the looming threat to Wall Street*. Random House.

Perez, E. (2013). *Knightmare on wall Street: The rise and fall of Knight Capital*. Edgar Perez Inc.

Petram, L. O. (2014). *The World's first stock exchange*. Columbia University Press.

Petrescu, M., & Wedow, M. (2017). Dark pools in European equity markets: Emergence, competition and implications. *European Central Bank: Occasional Paper Series*, *193*, 1–39.

Poser, N. S. (2001). The stock exchanges of the United States and Europe: Automation, globalization, and consolidation. *University of Pennsylvania Journal of International Economic Law*, *22*(3), 497–540.

PwC (2015). *Capital Markets Union: Integration of Capital Markets in the European Union*. www.pwc.com/financialservices.

Reese, W., & Weisbach, M. (2002). Protection of minority shareholder interests, cross-listings in the United States, and subsequent equity offerings. *Journal of Financial Economics*, *66*(1), 65–104.

Roşu, I. (2019). Fast and slow informed trading. *Journal of Financial Markets*, *43*, 1–30.

Samuel, J., Holowczak, R., & Pelaez, A. (2017). The effects of technology driven information categories on performance in electronic trading markets. *Journal of Information Technology Management*, *28*(1–2), 1–14.

Schmiedel, H. (2001). Technological Development and Concentration of Stock Exchanges in Europe. *Bank of Finland Discussion Paper Series*, *21/2001*. Retrieved from https://helda.helsinki.fi/bof/bitstream/handle/123456789/7882/101105.pdf?sequence=1

Serbera, J. P., & Paumard, P. (2016). The fall of high-frequency trading: A survey of competition and profits. *Research in International Business and Finance*, *36*(C), 271–287.

Stoll, H. R. (2006). Electronic trading in stock markets. *Journal of Economic Perspectives*, *20*(1), 153–174.

The Economist (2019). The stockmarket is now run by computers, algorithms and passive managers, *October 5th, 2019*.

The European Securities and Markets Authority (ESMA) (2020). *MiFID Entities Register*. https://registers.esma.europa.eu/publication/searchRegister?core=esma_registers_upreg.

Van Kervel, V. (2015). Competition for order flow with fast and slow traders. *The Review of Financial Studies*, *28*(7), 2094–2127.

Vychytilová, J. (2018). Stock market development beyond the GFC: The case of V4 countries. *Journal of Competitiveness*, *10*(2), 149–163.

World Bank (2020). *World Bank Open Data*. https://data.worldbank.org/indicator/CM.MKT.LDOM.NO.

World Federation of Exchanges (WFE) (2018). *World Federation of Exchanges Report*. https://focus.world-exchanges.org/statistics/reports-analysis.

Yadav, Y. (2019). Oversight failure in securities markets. *Cornell Law Review*, *104*, 1799–1866.

Zetter, K. (2008). Six-year-old news story causes United Airlines stock to plummet – Updated Google placed wrong date on story. *Wired. August 9th, 2008*.

Zhai, J., Cao, Y., & Ding, X. (2018). Data analytic approach for manipulation detection in stock market. *Review of Quantitative Finance and Accounting*, *50*(3), 897–932.

2 European financial institution physical geolocation and the high-frequency trading potential

Piotr Staszkiewicz, Ewa Łosiewicz-Dniestrzańska and Anna Grygiel-Tomaszewska

Introduction

The concept of algorithmic trading is associated with the use of procedures and algorithms to make trading transactions, usually without the active participation of humans. High-frequency trading (HFT) is a sub-area of algorithmic trading. Contrary to latent trading, HFT applies the technological solution of speeding the transaction both in terms of placing and execution. The ability of the financial institution to gain a competitive advantage with the use of HFT is conditioned upon the relevant technology, distance to the stock exchange server, stock exchange regulation, and technological fit, thus it is viewed as part of the fintech financial ecosystem (Marszk et al., 2019). The investments institutions might place their servers close to the stock exchange servers thus reducing the distance of the connection (Frino et al., 2020). Because of the placement of the hardware, the time necessary to place and execute the order is shortened. Therefore, the trader gains a competitive advantage over other market participants.

To equalize the participants, the condition applies regarding the colocation of the trading servers around the stock exchange servers. This prevents only a part of the problem as the traders are legally bound to replicate the physical servers at their main seat of operation. Thus, the alternative safety procedures (e.g., to prevent flash crises) are still driven by the physical distance, which impacts the trader's profitability. Also, because the HFT on a specific stock exchange is conditioned on individual technological requirements, we lack the methodology to compare piecemeal activities on exchanges for the traders who utilize passports. A combination of those two factors contributes to the purpose of the presented research.

This research aims to provide robust evidence about the profitability of the market's direct and indirect participants conditioned upon the physical distance to the main stock exchange. The proposal builds up and extends the prior research of Staszkiewicz (2015a) and Aitken et al. (2017), among others, by widening the scope and dynamics. It advances prior analyses with the dynamic of the phenomenon and contributes to the current literature on the HFT with several aspects. Firstly, it provides robust evidence on

DOI: 10.4324/9781003095354-2

the investment institution return development across Europe. Secondly, it discusses the potential combination of merging the geolocation and regression analysis for the different stock comparisons. Thirdly, it generalizes piecemeal observations from different European economies into a more comprehensive framework.

Literature review and hypotheses development

General remarks

Following the general development of means of communication, the methods and techniques of asset trading also changed. Adopting intelligent algorithms to place and execute transactions with the use of high-speed internet enables some market participants to reach for new sources of performance advantages that are developed based on quotation volatility within milliseconds. Such algorithms provide investors with a certain upside compared to others. They also impact entire markets and their structure as we know it, beginning with questioning the paradigm of equal access to price information for all investors, to the change of perception of quotations – from traditional: discrete, to modern: close to continuous. Which in turn might jeopardize the efficiency of market allocation of scarce resources (Diaz-Rainey & Ibikunle, 2012; Upson & Van Ness, 2017; Weller, 2018; Wurgler, 2000).

HFT, being a variation of algorithmic trading, is recognized as one of the tools aimed at facilitating transactions on various asset classes, e.g., bonds, shares, futures, listed options, Interest Rate Swaps (IRS), currencies (MacKenzie et al., 2020), as well as cryptocurrencies, thus allowing to generate profit, based on short term volatility of quotations. The latest available data from the European Securities and Markets Authority (ESMA) prove that in Europe in 2014 HFT transactions amounted to as much as between 30% and 49% of equity trades and 58% to 76% of equity orders (Roqueiro et al., 2016). Robust HFT development raises questions regarding many areas of the influence of this type of transaction on markets and their participants. Abrupt and significant popularity of HFT and the specifics of HFT-based strategies (proven e.g., by the discrepancy in the percentage of orders and trades) result in the urge to regulate and supervise them (Meyer & Guernsey, 2017) also from the perspective of the protection of the ordinary (latent) market participants. However, since the impact of HFT on markets is complex, there are differences in regulatory and market approaches towards this type of transaction placement and execution (Korajczyk & Murphy, 2019; Meyer & Guernsey, 2017; Van Kervel & Menkveld, 2019).

Among others, the robust development of HFT raises also inevitable questions regarding the actual factors that contribute to the profitability of these transactions and their origin. One of which might be an operational advantage derived from the physical distance between the investor or broker server and the stock exchange server. Since in HFT, apart from the quality of algorithms, it is the actual speed of the information transfer that constitutes the potential trading upside, the shorter the distance it travels, the higher the return it generates. Thus, it is the physical distance of the servers that possibly affects the trade performance due to possible delays in trade-related information transfer.

High-frequency trading

HFT generates trading impulses to make and execute investment decisions (Labadie & Lehalle, 2010). Therefore, such decisions are free from the judgmental bias of human decisions and benefit from prompt trading sequencing. However, HFT is not homogeneous. There are two subsegments of HFT – flash trading and ultra HFT. Apart from minor differences, both are based on the ability to acquire certain information sooner than other market participants. In extreme cases, it may refer to information about orders placed by other investors, which could be recognized as a powerful upside (Chlistalla, 2011).

HFT is aimed at gaining performance advantage, especially over the classic latent trading, based on the reduction of time necessary for trading operations, combined with the exposure to millisecond differences in quotations of given assets. The expected outperformance is derived from the small profit of a single price variance multiplied by the significant volume of trade, along with the short time of holding position (on average it is less than five seconds, often less than one second) and time for order placement shorter than one millisecond (Lenczewski-Martins, 2017). HFT demands that certain technical requirements be met, which include infrastructure that is intended to minimize latency and IT software systems that decide to initiate, generate, route, or execute an order without human intervention (Francioni et al., 2017). Considering the specific features of HFT, their application is not limited solely to speculation, but also includes market-making, arbitrage, or inter-market spreading (Staszkiewicz & Staszkiewicz, 2015).

As a consequence of HFT, robust development can be analyzed both from the perspective of the market itself, as well as from the perspective of a unique (single) market participant. From the market perspective, it was proven that HFT supports growth in trading liquidity while at the same time reducing transaction costs and market risk (Meyer & Guernsey, 2017; Watkins, 2014). Raddant and Wagner (2017) also confirmed the positive impact of HFT on market efficiency, supported by lower price fluctuations and thus resulting in increased surplus and lower returns. Essendorfer et al. (2015) noticed that the increase in the speed of transactions as well as of market turnover is also credited to HFT.

However, apart from its positive impact, the abrupt and robust development of HFT as well as its expected constant refinement can be recognized as a source of additional risk to markets. Some research confirms that the robust development of HFT is related to certain negative outcome. Essendorfer et al. (2015) point to the fact that along with the growth of HFT, the average size of a single trade is reducing. Markets suffer from liquidity fragmentation and periods of excess volatility that result in flash crashes. Apart from this, the obvious consequence of HFT's robust development is that the role of a human trader becomes less and less significant in the market (Essendorfer et al., 2015).

Taking the above into consideration, both market participants and market regulators take specific controlling activities. Gong et al. (2018) noticed that in periods of bid-ask spreads being widened, CSI 300 index HFT investors need to take steps to diminish potential liquidity risk. To prevent HFT domination and the negative results of it, certain general legal restrictions, like MiFID II, were launched. HFT and other forms of algorithmic trading are not themselves directly covered by the supervisory regime of MiFID II. However, if investment firms wish to provide direct electronic access (DEA) to their clients to carry out HFT or other algorithmic transactions, they are also subject to a specific form of supervision (Busch, 2016). Also, trading companies themselves report that they use specific cap mechanisms to prevent too excessive, too abnormal returns (MacKenzie et al., 2020).

From the perspective of the HFT market single participant, the expected value-added by the use of this type of transaction may be reflected in the abnormal rate of return, exceeding the market return, also when trading in the direction of asset price jumps (Fičura, 2019). Certainly, the performance of an investor can be credited to several elements. Part of the performance can be explained with the market characteristics, including quotation volatility, asset type, and asset liquidity. However, HFT is also an invisible arena of a specific armaments race, where the quality of the trading system and of the algorithm itself may generate expected performance upsides. Thirdly, since HFT is applied mainly on markets with dematerialized quotations and with the use of electronic transaction systems, the physical distance of the trader's server and the market server may influence the result of a transaction.

Colocation

HFT strategies barely rely on fundamentals, deriving their success mostly from the ability of the trading system to place and execute the transaction with a minimum time lag. All transactions on dematerialized markets are placed and executed with the use of certain electronic systems. Therefore, this time lag depends on the speed of communication between the server of the broker or the investor and the market server (e.g., stock exchange server). If so, the physical distance between them influences the latency of quotation information and the time lag between the placing and execution of the order, which in turn impacts the trade performance.

The relationship between colocation and general performance was proven for various types of businesses (Ivarsson et al., 2017; Kudic et al., 2016; Zubcsek et al., 2017), as well as from the sociological standpoint (Tabuchi, 2019). However, there is still little coverage of the problem of the relationship between the performance of HFT market participant companies and the colocation of servers.

As early as the beginning of the 21st century, Hau (2001) confirmed that the performance of market participants is influenced by the location of the trader. Since this research was biased with internal stock exchange data sourcing, Staszkiewicz and Staszkiewicz (2015) proposed to analyze this potential impact of colocation on the performance of brokers with the independent variable geolocation of the market participant as a proxy of its potential HFT abilities.

Conrad et al. (2015) investigated the relationship between the launch of HFT to the Tokyo Stock Exchange and the quotation patterns. Their research resulted in the conclusion that HFT allowed to reduce both latency and trading costs significantly and allow the colocation of servers. They have also noticed the quotation patterns to be more random-walk resembling.

Research gap and hypothesis formulation

Current literature fails either to discuss the impact of HFT on the entire network of recognized financial markets or does not necessarily distinguish the function of the supervised and not supervised market players.

Since modern dematerialized markets allow distant order placement and execution, part of the performance of HFT market participants should be explained by the physical distance between servers of traders and the market (stock exchange). As the licensed companies might have direct access to the recognized financial market and might have inherent credibility due to the supervision processes, we verify whether there are any differences in the performance of licensed vs. non-licensed market participants. Taking the above into consideration, we hypothesize that:

H_{01}: There is a difference in performance between supervised and not supervised financial institutions.

The differentiation between successful and unsuccessful trading strategies relies on their performance. Thus, we analyze the influence of colocation on the performance of market participants, aggregated at their return on assets (RoA). Therefore, we hypothesize that:

H_{02}: RoA is affected by distance to the nearest stock exchange.

Following prior research, we extend the perspective from neighboring financial markets into the whole network of financial markets in Europe. Thus, we formulate our third working hypothesis that:

H_{03}: The geographical position of the financial institution within the net of the European recognized financial markets impacts performance.

Suppose our hypothesis should be confirmed, then there would be a clear message to the financial authorities to adjust the market participant's rules as the sole geographical position would impact the fairness of trading. On the contrary, rejection of the set of hypotheses above would indicate that each stock exchange's local setting plays a substantial role in driving the HFT's transaction.

Methodology and data set

Methodology

Our basic approach is to regress the performance of the financial institution in terms of the distance to the stock exchange. Direct access to the stock server requires licensing, thus, to verify our hypotheses we contrast supervised and non-supervised entities across different financial markets.

This study uses the univariate and multivariate statistical analysis of the archived data. The research applies both the geocoding distance calculation based on the seat of the traders and stock exchange and the regression analysis of the institution's return on equity (RoE). The study follows prior research of Hau (2001) on the German market and Staszkiewicz and Staszkiewicz (2015) and Staszkiewicz (2015a) on the Polish and Central European markets.

The approximation of the distance between any two different locations A and B is given by the following formula:

$$d = \frac{2\pi q R}{360}, \tag{2.1}$$

where: $\pi = 3.1415...$, $R = 6371$ km (average radius of the Earth), and q is the solid angle between points A and B.

Prior studies applied RoE as a measurement, however, the performance measured concerning the equity tends to be endogenous, as the unallocated profit impacts total shareholders' resources, thus we based our approach on RoA. To account for potential biases resulting from not including all possible variables that drive performance, we applied a dynamic panel with the difference and system generalized method-of-moments (GMM) estimators (Roodman, 2009). The application of the GMM was developed by Arellano and Bond (1991), enhanced by Arellano and Bover (1995), and further developed in Blundell and Bond (1998).

The GMM estimator requires two conditions. Firstly, that the over-identifying restrictions are valid. Secondly, it does not allow the presence of second-order serial correlation in the error term. The Hansen test shows the overall validity of the instruments while Arellano and Bond's test verifies the presence of the second-order correlation.

Table 2.1 Summary of definitions of variables and expected direction

Name of the variable	Symbol	Definitions
RoA	Y	RoA is the net profit divided by the total assets (a response variable)
Assets	x_1	Natural logarithm of the total assets
Consol_level	x_2	A factorial variable: (1) Consolidated accounts with no unconsolidated companion; (2) Consolidated accounts with an unconsolidated companion; (3) Unconsolidated accounts with no consolidated companion; (4) Unconsolidated accounts with a consolidated companion
Supervised	x_3	A binary variable, a value of 1 indicates the licensed entity otherwise 0
Cap_Requ	x_4	Relation of the core capital to the total assets
NACE_Rev	x_5	6419 – Other monetary intermediation, 6499 – Other financial service activities, except insurance and pension funding
MIN	x_6	Distance to the closest stock exchange from the seat of the company

Source: own presentation.

The analytical equation of the model of the panel data is shown below:

$$y_{i,t} = \omega y_{i,t-1} + \sum_{j=1}^{k} \beta_j x_{j,i,t} + \sum_{l=1}^{m} \delta_l z_{l,i} + \sum_{r=1}^{f} \gamma_r c_{r,i,t} + \alpha_i + \mu_{i,t}, \qquad (2.2)$$

where: $y_{i,t}$ = response variable - RoA, $x_{j,i,t}$ = independent variables time-variant, $z_{l,i}$ = independent variable time-invariant, $c_{r,i,t}$ = control variables, and $\omega, \beta, \delta, \gamma$ = parameters, α_i = individual effects, $u_{i,t}$ = error term. Table 2.1 presents the definitions of the variables.

Development of the variables in the equation

Many articles explain possible sources of return for an investment company. Part of previous research points out the influence of home bias, regarded as asymmetry of information between local and external market participants (Staszkiewicz, 2015b). The home biases might be attributed to different aspects like market liberalization (Dahlquist & Robertsson, 2004), market size (Portes & Rey, 2005), and investors' perceptions (Brennan et al., 2005). Home bias is additionally supported by the shift from inside trading to market informational efficiency (Halling et al., 2007). Since the relationship between country and return is not unequivocal, it can be treated only as a control variable.

Assets and their volume are also expected to influence the performance of a company. In this regard, there are adverse approaches in the literature. Financial institutions that are subject to independent authority supervision at the same time are obliged to meet certain capital requirements. Therefore, from their perspective, a certain level of assets is expected to be kept to balance their operational risks. However, the research of Teixeira et al. (2014) proved that the banking sector is overcapitalized and that capital requirements have a low impact on the level of capital held by banks.

These findings are also contrary to Mishkin's (2000) claims that bank executives prefer to maintain capital levels lower than required to minimize the cost of capital. However, with that in mind, it is important to include in the model the fact that compared to non-regulated companies – regulated companies are affected by capital requirements. Therefore, the authors included "license" as a binary variable, indicating whether the market participant is or is not a licensed entity.

Fama and French (1993) ascertained the negative relation between size and return and Buchuk et al. (2014) noticed that there is a positive correlation between RoE and the fact that the company is borrowing capital within a capital group. Since the literature shows multiple factors that may influence RoE, in our model they are treated as control variables. The tested variables are the distance of the company seat within one km to the stock exchange and the distance within three km to the stock exchange.

Datasets

We collected data from the Orbis database (Van Dijk, 2020). We based our research on the NACE Rev. 2[1] classification of entities. We examined the population of the entities classified under code numbers 6419 – other monetary intermediation and 6499 – other financial service activities, except insurance and pension funding, which had the seat in the European Union (EU) administrative region. We considered entries with ten years of consecutive reporting history to rectify the noise raised for newcomers and insolvent companies. Our population contains both supervised and unsupervised institutions. We identified the entities subject to the supervision scrutiny by reference to the ESMA registers. We geocoded the addresses of entities with the application of the Google Geocoding API. We also geocoded the unrecognized addressees manually. The data period ranges from 2010 to 2019. The cut-off year of 2010 was taken to avoid the impact of the liquidity crisis 2007–2009. The identification of our population resulted in 4,964 entities. Table 2.2 presents the identification of the population.

From the total population identified, we drew a random sample. Table 2.3 shows the geographical distribution and the structure of the final sample versus the population.

Table 2.2 Usable sample identification

Search step		Search result
Status	Active companies, unknown situation	283,459,876
NACE Rev. 2 (Primary codes only)	6419 – Other monetary intermediation, 6499 – Other financial service activities, except insurance and pension funding	1,716,734
World region/Country/Region in country	EU [27]	144,120
Number of years with accounts	10 years	13,800
Years with available accounts	2010, 2011, 2012, 2013, 2014, 2015, 2016, 2017, 2018, 2019	4,964
Total		4,964

Source: own calculation.

Table 2.3 The geographical distribution of the population and sample with the number of supervised entities in the sample

	Country	Population	Sample	Supervised in sample
PT	Portugal	1		
AT	Austria	17	2	2
BE	Belgium	102	15	7
BG	Bulgaria	45		
CY	Cyprus	1		
CZ	Czech Republic	19	2	2
DE	Germany	5	1	0
DK	Denmark	1		
EE	Estonia	23		
ES	Spain	5	3	1
FI	Finland	812	116	28
FR	France	12	3	0
IE	Ireland	212	32	15
IT	Italy	135	52	16
LT	Lithuania	104	2	2
LV	Latvia	42	4	1
NL	Netherlands	14	1	0
SE	Sweden	3406	146	56
SK	Slovakia	8	1	0
	Total	4964	380	130

Source: own presentation.

Our final usable sample consists of 380 entities and 3,800 firm-yearly observations.

The output data were reviewed for consistency and manual corrections were made for the missing coding. The calculation was performed using the application of the R environment (R Core Team, 2018) and Stata (StataCorp., 2020).

Results

General overview

The available research shows that there is a significant HFT market in Europe. Following this, we understand, that it should be reflected in the performance of investment companies that operate in this market. Therefore, if a company is active in the HFT market in Europe, that fact should be reflected in its RoA. Since the performance of HFT is closely related to the colocation of servers, the lower the distance, the higher the return on HFT activities. Therefore, entities that are licensed market participants should generate statistically important overperformance compared to non-regulated investors.

Descriptive statistics

Table 2.4 presents descriptive statistics.

In general, the majority of the companies report losses, the sample comprises all possible consolidation levels and approximately one-third of the sample relates to the supervised firms. The sample is not homogenous in terms of the capital requirements values.

Multivariate statistics

Below we report the results of the estimation of Equation (2) with an application of the system estimator (GMM). Table 2.5 shows the results of the system estimators.

Table 2.4 Descriptive statistics

	Count	Mean	SD	Min	Max
RoE	3,658	−.5030116	28.61369	−1713.941	61.67882
Assets	3,750	15.68583	2.158306	.6931472	23.74914
Consol_level	3,800	3.063158	.5678131	1	4
Supervised	3,800	.3421053	.4744771	0	1
Cap_Requ	3,740	−1487.004	64,197.53	−3,266,293	1.5
MIN	3,800	117.7404	159.8923	.1080127	968.9037
N	3,800				

Source: own calculation.

Table 2.5 The system estimator results

	RoA			
	B	se	t	P
L.RoA	−.0048863	.1165961	−.041908	.966572
Assets	100.6086	312.1279	.3223312	.7472018
Consol_level	−1,657.305	3,163.966	−.5238061	.6004134
Supervised	2,385.651	3,528.241	.6761587	.4989399
NACE_Rev	.1098518	1.669847	.0657856	.9475485
Cap_Requ	−.0017002	.0043083	−.3946317	.6931147
MIN	16.32827	25.6398	.6368331	.5242335
2010.year	0	-	-	-
2011.year	0	-	-	-
2012.year	−5.390294	17.39304	−.3099111	.7566286
2013.year	−7.188539	24.41637	−.2944148	.768441
2014.year	−12.93544	45.79548	−.282461	.77759
2015.year	−16.87024	57.51939	−.2932966	.7692955
2016.year	−22.37026	71.34475	−.3135516	.7538617
2017.year	−17.22126	52.77464	−.3263169	.7441846
2018.year	−6.059709	27.68973	−.2188432	.8267722
2019.year	−9.336774	32.42388	−.2879598	.7733775
_cons	0	-	-	-
N		3274		
Hansen		16.81		
Sargan		2,279.3		
AR(2) p-value		0.607		

Source: own presentation.

Our results are controlled with the yearly effects, none of the variables in dispute significantly affect the RoA. We also tested the stock exchange's individual effects, shown in Table 2.6.

Appendix 1 presents the definitions of the stock exchange's name abbreviations.

The results do not indicate any specific stock exchange significant effect.

Research gap verification

To avoid the bias of the authors' judgmental selection of papers, scientific sources with substantial impact on the literature were identified by regressing citation counts on prior publications' metadata collected from the Web of Science Core Collection, based on the method developed by Staszkiewicz (2019). We applied this method to the colocation and HFT literature published between January 2015 and June 2020. We verified the research gap with the application of the citation count regression. We enhanced the initial literature review with the Business and Economics perspective and Web of Science Index. Out of the population of 132 papers selected this way, none of the important papers were omitted in our literature review.

Table 2.6 Stock exchange's individual effects

	RoA			
	B	se	t	P
L.RoA	−.4563728	.0276964	−16.47768	0
Assets	221.3951	189.891	1.165907	.2436522
Consol_level	27,193.58	5,658,695	.0048056	.9961657
Supervised	0	-	-	-
NACE_Rev	479.9743	18,305.98	.0262195	.9790822
2010.year	0	-	-	-
2011.year	0	-	-	-
2012.year	−13.43831	12.28758	−1.09365	.2741086
2013.year	−20.71188	17.68398	−1.171222	.2415094
2014.year	−31.30272	28.76113	−1.088369	.2764323
2015.year	−43.56381	37.41446	−1.164358	.2442791
2016.year	−57.55229	51.33885	−1.121028	.2622759
2017.year	−51.80147	42.71453	−1.212736	.2252306
2018.year	−35.3467	24.967	−1.415737	.1568526
2019.year	−44.3002	31.65284	−1.399565	.1616437
WB_AG	0	-	-	-
B_EB	−550.2736	71,869.22	−.0076566	.993891
BL_BSE	0	-	-	-
C_CSE	0	-	-	-
CZ_PSE	−1749.61	29,497.66	−.0593135	.9527024
D_CSE	0	-	-	-
E_NASDAQ	0	-	-	-
F_NASDAQ	−83.62739	12,423.73	−.0067313	.9946293
FR_EURO	0	-	-	-
D_DB	0	-	-	-
G_AE	0	-	-	-
HSE	0	-	-	-
IR_ISE	591.5214	29,382.84	.0201315	.9839385
I_BI	116.7536	25,177.45	.0046372	.9963
LA_NASDAQ	−344.0065	16,701.51	−.0205973	.9835669
LI_NASDAQ	90.84748	-	-	-
LUX_SBL	0	-	-	-
M_MSE	−611.0242	48,770.69	−.0125285	.990004
NL_NYSE	0	-	-	-
PL_WSE	0	-	-	-
PO_ERONEXT	0	-	-	-
RO_BSE	0	-	-	-
SK_BSE	2,163.648	90,661.88	.023865	.9809603
SO	0	-	-	-
ESP_BVB	95.293	2,516.221	.0378715	.9697902
SW__NASDAQ	0	-	-	-
UK_LIFFE	0	-	-	-
UK_LME	0	-	-	-
UK_ICE	0	-	-	-
IR_NASDAQ	−701.5924	2,2168.3	−.0316484	.9747524
NOR_OB	671.1461	31,731.82	.0211506	.9831255
R_ME	0	-	-	-
S_SE	0	-	-	-
U_USE	0	-	-	-

Table 2.6 (Continued)

	RoA			
	B	se	t	P
_cons	−1,875,886	2.85e+07	−.0658719	.9474798
N		3284		
Hansen		35.61		
Sargan		1730.1		
AR(2) p-value		0.397		

Source: own presentation.

Discussion and conclusion

The estimations of ESMA suggest that HFT activities are a significant part of equity trading in Europe. With that in mind, we expected that this fact should be reflected in the return of market participants. Particularly, it should impact the return on their assets, leading to a conclusion that the shorter the distance between market servers and the server of the investment company, the higher the performance of such a company. Therefore, there should be a statistically important correlation between the colocation of servers and the performance of an investment company. Our research proves that there is no such correlation. This stresses the fact that the ESMA perspective, however, relates more to turnover and liquidity than to the number of market participants.

The results of our research show that all three hypotheses formed, should be rejected. We cannot confirm that there is a difference in performance between supervised and not supervised financial institutions. Also, investment company performance measured with RoA is not affected by the physical distance to the nearest stock exchange. Thirdly, the geographical position of the financial institution within the net of the European recognized financial markets does not impact its performance. The distance to exchanges was then not a decision-taker parameter for broker-dealer return.

Although our findings do not confirm any relationship between investment company performance and colocation, they lead us to certain conclusions. Entities that operate a close distance to the market are mainly local investment companies and banks. For such entities, short distances to market servers may not be a sufficient proxy of their HFT capabilities. It is worth mentioning here, that markets of Central and Eastern Europe were heavily covered by the entities with EU passports with the main seats in the UK. Brexit created a chance to change this status quo, opening the gate of opportunities for local financial institutions.

The relationship between the performance of HFT companies and the colocation of trader's and market's servers was however of little coverage. Still, taking into consideration the previous research, the performance of HFT should partly be explained by the physical colocation of servers. However, it is not the only determining element. As our findings do not necessarily comply with prior results (Ivarsson et al., 2017; Kudic et al., 2016; Zubcsek et al.,

2017), this might imply further conclusions that the European markets more prudently apply the rules for the colocation of servers.

Our findings stay in line with the research of Hau (2001) and Staszkiewicz (2015a) in respect of the impact of distance on the performance of Central and Eastern European investment companies. Also, these findings showed that there is no evidence of such a correlation. As our research takes into account both supervised and non-supervised entities and a wider population of investment companies, it can be concluded, that the HFTs in the EU are likely to be dominated by a few market players, like BATS Chi-X Europe (Ibikunle, 2018), who gain a competitive advantage due to technological development and individual access to the trading book building.

The relationship between the colocation of servers and the performance of companies was confirmed for the US market (Shkilko & Sokolov, 2020), but it seems it does not apply identically to the EU markets. This fact leads to the natural question of a difference in price quotations between European and US markets. If the price quotation on European markets allows price volatility on a very distant decimal level, it obviously would give leverage only to a small group of market players. In such a situation, only high-volume transactions would allow outperforming on HFT, as only residual price difference multiplied by assets of large volume would allow for a meaningful return on HFT.

This would result in a high RoE being shared by a very limited group of market participants, therefore potential performance-colocation relationships may not be observable in a large-scale population. In our opinion, the rejection of our testing hypotheses might indicate that the real economy is being diluted within a large group of investment companies, a significant majority of which do not have asset capabilities and technical knowledge to participate in the HFT market at all.

Alternatively, the results might be explained with the identification of the investments institution population. Our research strategy relies on coherent reporting and gathering data in a financial database; however, we cannot exclude the situation that the HFTs traders were misclassified to the high-tech companies instead of the financial institution due to the core activities mismatch.

Our dataset is inherently limited in terms of financial data quality. Throughout the study, we assumed that the potential modification of the audit ports does not significantly impact our findings. We based our assumption on the fact that the modifications themselves are infrequent (Carson et al., 2013).

Another limitation of the study is based on the lack of information regarding the methods of order placement by HFT market participants. Theoretically, the shorter the distance between the broker's server and the market server, the higher the performance rate. However, it also depends on the quality of cable or radio infrastructure that is used as well as on the weather conditions (Shkilko & Sokolov, 2020). The cable connection is constrained by the physical limitation of the possible ground path, on the other hand, the radio connection suffers from weather conditions and surface fluctuation. The last one opens an interesting field for further research.

The equity trading market is fragmented in its latent segment. This is contrary to the HFT market, which may be strongly concentrated and where there is a limited number of participants with assets of significant volume at their disposal. Their possible market advantage relies on these assets as well as on the quality of algorithms used. This may, in turn, lead to the continuous widening of market quotations. From this perspective, legal regulations enforcing the colocation of servers gain new sense in terms of the protection of latent participants.

Acknowledgment

The research was funded by grant no B701084 - Faculty of Economics and Finance, Wroclaw University of Economics and Business, Poland.

Note

1. NACE is derived from the French title "Nomenclature générale des Activités économiques dans les Communautés Européennes" (Statistical classification of economic activities in the European Communities).

References

Aitken, M., Cumming, D., & Zhan, F. (2017). Trade size, high-frequency trading, and colocation around the world. *The European Journal of Finance, 23*(7–9), 781–801. doi: https://doi.org/10.1080/1351847X.2014.917119.

Arellano, M., & Bond, S. (1991). Some tests of specification for panel data: Monte Carlo evidence and an application to employment equations. *The Review of Economic Studies, 58*(2), 277. doi: https://doi.org/10.2307/2297968.

Arellano, M., & Bover, O. (1995). Another look at the instrumental variable estimation of error-components models. *Journal of Econometrics, 68*(1), 29–51. doi: https://doi.org/10.1016/0304-4076(94)01642-D.

Blundell, R., & Bond, S. (1998). Initial conditions and moment restrictions in dynamic panel data models. *Journal of Econometrics, 87*(1), 115–143. doi: https://doi.org/10.1016/S0304-4076(98)00009-8.

Brennan, M., Henrycao, H., Strong, N., & Xu, X. (2005). The dynamics of international equity market expectations. *Journal of Financial Economics, 77*(2), 257–288. doi: https://doi.org/10.1016/j.jfineco.2004.06.008.

Buchuk, D., Larrain, B., Muñoz, F., & Urzúa, I. F. (2014). The internal capital markets of business groups: Evidence from intra-group loans. *Journal of Financial Economics, 112*(2), 190–212. doi: https://doi.org/10.1016/j.jfineco.2014.01.003.

Busch, D. (2016). MiFID II: Regulating high frequency trading, other forms of algorithmic trading and direct electronic market access. *Law and Financial Markets Review, 10*(2), 72–82. https://doi.org/10.1080/17521440.2016.1200333

Van Dijk, B. (2020). *Orbis.* https://orbis.bvdinfo.com/

Carson, E., Fargher, N. L., Geiger, M. A., Lennox, C. S., Raghunandan, K., & Willekens, M. (2013). Audit reporting for going-concern uncertainty: A research synthesis. *Auditing, 32*(SUPPL.1), 353–384. doi: https://doi.org/10.2308/ajpt-50324.

Chlistalla, M. (2011). High-frequency trading. Better that its reputation? *Deutsche Bank Research*.

Conrad, J., Wahal, S., & Xiang, J. (2015). High-frequency quoting, trading, and the efficiency of prices. *Journal of Financial Economics*, *116*(2), 271–291. doi: https://doi.org/10.1016/j.jfineco.2015.02.008.

Dahlquist, M., & Robertsson, G. (2004). A note on foreigners' trading and price effects across firms. *Journal of Banking & Finance*, *28*(3), 615–632. doi: https://doi.org/10.1016/S0378-4266(03)00036-0.

Diaz-Rainey, I., & Ibikunle, G. (2012). A taxonomy of the "dark side" of financial innovation: The cases of high frequency trading and exchange traded funds. *International Journal of Entrepreneurship and Innovation Management*, *16*(1–2), 51–72. doi: https://doi.org/10.1504/IJEIM.2012.050443.

Essendorfer, S., Diaz-Rainey, I., & Falta, M. (2015). Creative destruction in wall Street's technological arms race: Evidence from patent data. *Technological Forecasting and Social Change*, *99*, 300–316. doi: https://doi.org/10.1016/j.techfore.2014.11.012.

Fama, E. F., & French, K. R. (1993). Common risk factors in the returns on stocks and bonds. *Journal of Financial Economics*, *33*(1), 3–56. doi: https://doi.org/10.1016/0304-405X(93)90023-5.

Fičura, M. (2019). Profitability of trading in the direction of asset price jumps - analysis of multiple assets and frequencies. *Prague Economic Papers*, *28*(4), 385–401. doi: https://doi.org/10.18267/j.pep.703.

Francioni, R., Schwartz, R. A., Byrne, J., & Welkoborsky, S. (2017). Equity markets in transition the value chain, price discovery, regulation, and beyond. *Equity Markets in Transition: The Value Chain, Price Discovery, Regulation, and Beyond*, 1–611. https://doi.org/10.1007/978-3-319-45848-9

Frino, A., Garcia, M., & Zhou, Z. (2020). Impact of algorithmic trading on speed of adjustment to new information: Evidence from interest rate derivatives. *Journal of Futures Markets*, *40*(5), 749–760. doi: https://doi.org/10.1002/fut.22104.

Gong, Y., Chen, Q., & Liang, J. (2018). A mixed data sampling copula model for the return-liquidity dependence in stock index futures markets. *Economic Modelling*, *68*(April 2017), 586–598. doi: https://doi.org/10.1016/j.econmod.2017.03.023.

Halling, M., Pagano, M., Randl, O., & Zechner, J. (2007). Where is the market? Evidence from cross-listings in the United States. *Review of Financial Studies*, *21*(2), 725–761. doi: https://doi.org/10.1093/rfs/hhm066.

Hau, H. (2001). Location matters: An examination of trading profits. *The Journal of Finance*, *56*(5), 1959–1983. doi: https://doi.org/10.1111/0022-1082.00396.

Ibikunle, G. (2018). Trading places: Price leadership and the competition for order flow. *Journal of Empirical Finance*, *49*, 178–200. doi: https://doi.org/10.1016/j.jempfin.2018.09.007.

Ivarsson, I., Alvstam, C., & Vahlne, J. E. (2017). Global technology development by colocating R&D and manufacturing: The case of Swedish manufacturing MNEs. *Industrial and Corporate Change*, *26*(1), 149–168. doi: https://doi.org/10.1093/icc/dtw018.

Korajczyk, R. A., & Murphy, D. (2019). High-frequency market making to large institutional trades. *Review of Financial Studies*, *32*(3), 1034–1067. doi: https://doi.org/10.1093/rfs/hhy079.

Kudic, M., Pyka, A., & Sunder, M. (2016). The formation of R&D cooperation ties: An event history analysis for German laser source manufacturers. *Industrial and Corporate Change*, *25*(4), 649–670. doi: https://doi.org/10.1093/icc/dtv047.

Labadie, M., & Lehalle, C.-A. (2010). *Optimal algorithmic trading and market microstructure* (Issue September).

Lenczewski-Martins, C. J. (2017). *Handel o wysokiej częstotliwości na rynku walutowym*. Difin.

MacKenzie, D., Hardie, I., Rommerskirchen, C., & van der Heide, A. (2020). Why hasn't high-frequency trading swept the board? Shares, sovereign bonds and the politics of market structure. *Review of International Political Economy*, 1–25. doi: https://doi.org/10.1080/09692290.2020.1743340.

Marszk, A., Lechman, E., & Kato, Y. (2019). *The emergence of ETFs in Asia-Pacific*. Springer International Publishing. doi: https://doi.org/10.1007/978-3-030-12752-7.

Meyer, D. R., & Guernsey, G. (2017). Hong Kong and Singapore exchanges confront high frequency trading. *Asia Pacific Business Review*, 23(1), 63–89. doi: https://doi.org/10.1080/13602381.2016.1157927.

Mishkin, F. S. (2000). *The economics of money, Banking, and financial markets* (6th ed.). Addison-Wesley series in economics. http://books.google.pl/books?id=1BBmPgAACAAJ.

Portes, R., & Rey, H. (2005). The determinants of cross-border equity flows. *Journal of International Economics*, 65(2), 269–296. doi: https://doi.org/10.1016/j.jinteco.2004.05.002.

R Core Team. (2018). *R: A language and environment for statistical computing*. Foundation for Statistical Computing. http://www.r-project.org.

Raddant, M., & Wagner, F. (2017). Transitions in the stock markets of the US, UK and Germany. *Quantitative Finance*, 17(2), 289–297. doi: https://doi.org/10.1080/14697688.2016.1183812.

Roodman, D. (2009). How to do xtabond2: An introduction to difference and system GMM in stata. *The Stata Journal*, 1, 86–136.

Roqueiro, C. A., Guagliano, C., Guillaumie, C., Nauhaus, S., Winkler, C., & Kern, S. (2016). Order duplication and liquidity measurement in EU equity markets. *ESMA Economic Report*, 1, 1–38.

Shkilko, A., & Sokolov, K. (2020). Every cloud has a silver lining: Fast trading, microwave connectivity, and trading costs. *The Journal of Finance*. doi: https://doi.org/10.1111/jofi.12969.

Staszkiewicz, L., & Staszkiewicz, P. (2015). HFT's potential of investment companies. *Prace Naukowe Uniwersytetu Ekonomicznego We Wrocławiu*, 381, 376–389. doi: https://doi.org/10.15611/pn.2015.381.28.

Staszkiewicz, P. (2015a). High frequency trading readiness in Central Europe. *GSTF Journal on Business Review*, 4(2), 61–67. doi: https://doi.org/10.5176/2010-4804_4.2.371.

Staszkiewicz, P. (2015b). How far is enough for financial markets? *5th Annual International Conference on Accounting and Finance (AF 2015)*, 21–26. doi: https://doi.org/10.5176/2251-1997_AF15.61.

Staszkiewicz, P. (2019). The application of citation count regression to identify important papers in the literature on non-audit fees. *Managerial Auditing Journal*, 34(1), 96–115. doi: https://doi.org/10.1108/MAJ-05-2017-1552.

StataCorp. (2020). *Statistical Software: Release 16.0* (No. 16). Stata Corporation.

Tabuchi, T. (2019). Do the rich and poor colocate in large cities? *Journal of Urban Economics*, 113. doi: https://doi.org/10.1016/j.jue.2019.103186.

Teixeira, J. C. A., Silva, F. J. F., Fernandes, A. V., & Alves, A. C. G. (2014). Banks' capital, regulation and the financial crisis. *The North American Journal of Economics and Finance*, 28, 33–58. doi: https://doi.org/10.1016/j.najef.2014.01.002.

Upson, J., & Van Ness, R. A. (2017). Multiple markets, algorithmic trading, and market liquidity. *Journal of Financial Markets*, *32*, 49–68. doi: https://doi.org/10.1016/j.finmar.2016.05.004.

Van Kervel, V., & Menkveld, A. J. (2019). High-frequency trading around large institutional orders. *Journal of Finance*, *74*(3), 1091–1137. doi: https://doi.org/10.1111/jofi.12759.

Watkins, J. (2014). Regulating HFT "No Easy Task", Says FCA's Wheatley. *Euromoney Institutional Investor*, June 5.

Weller, B. M. (2018). Does algorithmic trading reduce information acquisition? *The Review of Financial Studies*, *31*(6), 2184–2226. doi: https://doi.org/10.1093/rfs/hhx137.

Wurgler, J. (2000). Financial markets and the allocation of capital. *Journal of Financial Economics 58*, 87–214. doi: https://doi.org/10.1093/brain/117.1.117.

Zubcsek, P. P., Katona, Z., & Sarvary, M. (2017). Predicting mobile advertising response using consumer colocation networks. *Journal of Marketing*, *81*(4), 109–126. doi: https://doi.org/10.1509/jm.15.0215.

Appendix 1

Reference entity	Nick
Wiener Börse AG	A_WB
Euronext Brussels SA/NV	B_EB
Българска Фондова Борса — София АД (Bulgarian Stock Exchange — Sofia JSCo)	BL_BSE
Cyprus Stock Exchange	C_CSE
Prague Stock Exchange	CZ_PSE
Copenhagen Stock Exchange AS	D_CSE
NASDAQ OMX Tallinn AS (NASDAQ OMX Tallinn Ltd.) (Estonia)	E_NASDAQ
NASDAQ OMX Helsinki Oy (NASDAQ OMX Helsinki Ltd.)	F_NASDAQ
Euronext Paris	FR_EURO
Deutsche Börse AG	D_DB
Athens Exchange	G_AE
Budapesti Értéktőzsde Zrt. (Budapest Stock Exchange	H_BSE
Irish Stock Exchange Ltd	IR_ISE
Borsa Italiana SpA	I_BI
JSC NASDAQ OMX Riga	LA_NASDAQ
Nasdaq OMX Vilnius	LI_NASDAQ
Société de la Bourse de Luxembourg SA	LUX_SBL
Malta Stock Exchange	M_MSE
NYSE Euronext (International) BV, NYSE Euronext (Holding) BV, Euronext NV, en Euronext Amsterdam NV	NL_NYSE
Giełda Papierów Wartościowych w Warszawie SA (Warsaw Stock Exchange)	PL_WSE
Euronext Lisbon — Sociedade Gestora de Mercados Regulamentados, SA	PO_ERONEXT
S.C. Bursa de Valori București SA (Bucharest Stock Exchange SA)	RO_BSE
Bratislava Stock Exchange	SK_BSE
Ljubljana Stock Exchange (Ljubljanska borza)	SO_LSE
Soc. Rectora de la Bolsa de Valores de Madrid SA	ESP_BVB
NASDAQ OMX Stockholm AB	SW_ NASDAQ
LIFFE Administration and Management	UK_LIFFE
The London Metal Exchange Limited	UK_LME
ICE Futures Europe	UK_ICE
Nasdaq OMX Iceland hf.	IR_NASDAQ
Oslo Børs ASA	NOR_OB

Source: own presentation.

3 Necessity of digitalization in the capital market of developing countries in current pandemic situation

The case of Bangladesh

S. M. Sohrab Uddin, ANM Moinul Islam and Mohammad Robaitur Rahat

Introduction

Digitalization has been recognized as a commonly accepted strategy by a growing number of firms in different sectors for the development of a digitally-enabled business model, which in turn creates more value in the long run (Kane et al., 2019; Liu et al., 2011; Schallmo et al., 2017). The adoption brings drastic changes by leading to a partial or full-fledged technology-driven transformation of not only interactions and communications with major stakeholders including suppliers, employees, customers, and regulators, but also different functional activities of the business firm (Laudon & Laudon, 2019; Soto-Acosta et al., 2016). The ongoing fourth industrial revolution makes digitalization even more inevitable for the business organizations in all countries, irrespective of their stages of development. On the other hand, the capital market, in particular the stock market, helps the business activities by meeting the demand for long-term funds and serves as one of the most liquid markets in an economy. It deals with stocks, bonds, Treasury securities, mortgages, mutual funds, and so on by ensuring the functioning of primary market, where the borrower of long-term funds raises capital, and that of the secondary market, where the investors trade among themselves in the stock exchange. The adoption of digitalization in the stock market, initially in developed countries and later on in emerging economies, brings a paradigm shift by replacing the traditional slow auction-based trading system by faster, accurate, and less risky trading system (Polimenis, 2006). However, the stock market in developing countries requires further digitalization for catching up.

The ongoing coronavirus disease 2019 (COVID-19) pandemic is viewed as one of the biggest crises of all times. According to ADB (2020), the estimated global cost of the current pandemic could be 4.1 trillion USD, much higher than the devastation of earlier epidemics like Influenza, Ebola, and Severe Acute Respiratory Syndrome (SARS). OECD (2020) indicates that the gross

DOI: 10.4324/9781003095354-3

domestic product (GDP) of the most developed nations witnessed an immediate decline of 20 to 25 percent due to the ongoing crisis. Interestingly, the global stock markets observed highly noticeable drop in their market prices as an immediate effect of the pandemic. For instance, the value of the world's largest stock indexes including National Association of Securities Dealers Automated Quotations System (NASDAQ)100, Nikkei225, and Standard & Poor (S&P)500 declined by nearly 30 percent since the beginning of the crisis (Ding et al., 2020).

Even though economic activities halted down to a great extent because of the continuing crisis, consumers prefer to spend more time and money online due to the lockdown and social distancing, which contribute to a higher volume of online trade and consumption (Huang et al., 2020). In addition, digital technology and connectivity have appeared as vital ingredients for fighting against the pandemic and for enhancing resilience within the society and economy as a whole (Okuda & Karazhanova, 2020). This is because firms with the digital transformation uphold some degree of operations and consequent revenue stream in spite of the pandemic, which contributes to more resilient stock prices and stronger market sentiment for these firms. It is, thus, argued that digital transformation will be prominent in the post-COVID-19 era. In order to keep pace with the requirement, stock markets, listed companies, brokerage houses, and merchant banks need to embrace the changes for overturning the confidence of the individual and institutional investors.

In an attempt to foster digitalization in the capital market of Bangladesh, several steps have been taken by Bangladesh Securities and Exchange Commission (BSEC), the regulator of the market, for facilitating the investment process of investors and stakeholders, and for monitoring the market with the modern surveillance system. The traditional cry-out system has already been replaced by the next generation trading system (NGTS) in both the exchanges of the country, namely Dhaka Stock Exchange (DSE) and Chittagong Stock Exchange (CSE). Internet and mobile-based platforms are also available in both exchanges, which are expected to enable investors to put buy-sale orders directly and to get price alerts. The commencement of the operations of Central Depository Bangladesh Limited (CDBL) in 2003 for the electronic possession and settlement of securities is regarded as one of the remarkable steps for the digitalization of the stock market. The establishment of Investment Corporation of Bangladesh (ICB) as the biggest underwriter and fund manager in 1976, and Bangladesh Institute of Capital Market (BICM) in 2010 for enhancing knowledge, skills, and competence of the stakeholders of the capital markets can be considered as other significant initiatives.

The first COVID-19 case in Bangladesh was announced on March 8th, 2020, which caused a huge drop in investors' confidence. The authority set a floor price to prevent the fall in market price, though one of the indexes of DSE, Dhaka Stock Exchange Broad Index (DSEX), fell to 3953.38 points, which has been the lowest in 13 years. In fact, Bangladesh remained as one of the rare countries where the stock markets were closed for more than two months due to the ongoing pandemic before the resumption of operations of the two exchanges on May 31st, 2020. BSEC also intervened in the market by issuing a circular stating that the opening price of the listed security will be set on the average closing price of preceding five trading days and the average price will be considered as the floor price and lower limit of the circuit breaker, which was lifted on June 15th, 2020.

The existing literature focuses on the impact of the pandemic on capital market of Bangladesh. For instance, Aktar et al. (2020) correlate the COVID-19 cases with the stock market return and market capitalization of DSE by observing the data of 43 trading days and conclude that the growth of COVID-19 cases has strong adverse impact on the stock market of Bangladesh. However, there is no such study concentrating on the necessity of digitalization in the capital market of a developing country like Bangladesh. This study aims at evaluating the necessity of digitalization with particular emphasis on current pandemic situation. In particular, event study approach is adopted for testing the significance of various digitalization programs by analyzing whether a particular event generates abnormal return (AR) and cumulative abnormal return (CAR) in the stock market.

The later part of the chapter is divided into five sections. Section two highlights the literature review. Section three presents the data and methodology associated with the study. Section four introduces the overview of the capital market of Bangladesh with particular emphasis on the stock market. Section five provides the findings and corresponding analyses, and the last section concludes the chapter with a few policy recommendations.

Literature review

The term digitalization, is defined by Stolterman and Fors (2004), as the widespread changes in every spheres of human society by applying the blessings of digital technology. Digital transformation, analogous to digitalization, is also described as the capability of transforming current products, services, and operations into digital versions in an effort to take advantage over the previous version (Gassmann et al., 2013; Henriette et al., 2015; Parviainen et al., 2017). In sum, it is the process of altering business operations, products, and services by adopting technologies with a view to minimizing costs, improving turnaround times, and introducing automation instead of manual process (Parviainen et al., 2017). There are nine important technologies such as big data and analytics, autonomous robots, horizontal and vertical system integration, internet of things, cybersecurity, simulation, cloud computing, additive manufacturing, and augmented reality that will play vital role in the future (Lorenz et al., 2015). In order to be recognized as digitalized business, it is highly needed to incorporate either partial or full digital technologies into operational activities (Soto-Acosta, 2020). In particular, digitalization can be adopted in various levels of an organization. Parviainen et al. (2017) state four levels including process level, organizational level, business domain level, and society level. Process level covers the adoption of newer tools and processes by replacing manual systems, organizational level includes the alteration of ways of offering services, business level contains changes in the ecosystem of the business including the value chains, and society level comprises of the change in the society structure and the decision making process.

Organizations get advantages by utilizing the blessings of digitalization in the forms of increased efficiency in utilizing resources, enhancement of productivity, reduction of costs, improvement in satisfaction, and customer loyalty (Loebbecke & Picot, 2015). Bouwman et al. (2019) have proved that the effect of innovation in the business operations is direct and profound on the business performance. It enhances the efficiency in communications with stakeholders, in addition to giving birth to new professions, economic systems, and financial services (Shkarlet et al., 2020). It also helps government and business organizations to be more transparent, along with providing better life to the public and customers with more services (Parviainen et al., 2017). Overall, it is evident that highly digitally transformed sectors achieved two to three times higher growth rates in terms of profitability (Ding et al., 2020). However, dependence on information technologies more than ever can lead to vulnerability in corporate data and fraudulent activities (Shkarlet et al., 2020). Besides, a study made by Massachusetts Institute of Technology (MIT) Sloan Management Review and Deloitte on 4800 participants reports that 76 percent of the participants believe that increasing adoption of technological products disrupt the industry in the future (Kane et al., 2015).

Stock exchanges, previously used to trade stocks through physical interactions of buyers and sellers, now adopt automated or electronic trading in which no physical interaction and manual quotation is necessary (Marynowski et al., 2014). Such adoption expects to enhance the liquidity and informativeness of the market with an opportunity to ensure remote access to investors at a lower cost and higher transparency. It is expected that a higher level of ex-ante transparency reduces the adverse selection problem to a great extent (Pagano & Roell, 1996). In fact, the digitalization of stock market was started in 1987 in the aftermath of stock market crash in the US, which asked for the replacement of people with computers. After that, many stock markets in other countries entered into the age of automated trading. The development was further enhanced with the regulation passed by the US government in 2005 in order to transform the stock exchanges like NASDAQ and New York Stock Exchange (NYSE) into public organizations in an attempt to improve competition in the market and to reduce cost. In 2012, brokerage houses started to provide full-fledged services that include both custodial and clearing duties (Goldenberg, 2017). In addition, financial technologies, popularly known as fintechs, arise as a groundbreaking player in the financial sector of the world market. It brings innovation in the payment systems by introducing mobile banking and blockchain technologies, the methodology of financing process and asset management by using robotics, and the infrastructural systems of the market (Brandl & Hornuf, 2017). Besides, electronic finance is dominating now to diminish the points of mismatch between traditional banks and investment banks, traditional brokerage houses and electronic trading platforms, and the role of different types of financial intermediaries (Lin et al., 2001).

In spite of all these developments, the negative trend created by the pandemic hits the stock market and leads to a decline in the stock prices. According to Yu and Aviso (2020), the stock market has seen the toughest one-day reduction in market indices around the world, causing 80 percent fall in the stock prices. Even countries with highly digitalized stock markets including the USA, Germany, and the UK observed 30 percent, 33 percent, and 37 percent respective fall in the overall stock market index compared to the peak prices. In the same way, developing countries like Brazil and Poland also noticed a respective reduction of 48 percent and 38 percent. This is highly likely as "studies in behavioral finance have shown that investors may overreact in the short term when they become extremely pessimistic during downturns or place too much importance on recent events while ignoring historical data" (Ding et al., 2020, p. 2 of 21). However, a subsequent possible market correction was reported in the stock market. By observing the top 25 most affected countries' stock markets, Phan and Narayan (2020) mention that during the initial stages of the pandemic the stock prices in majority of these countries responded negatively, while with the passage of time, especially when countries observed 100,000 infections and 100 deaths, the reaction in 50 percent of these markets was positive. Nevertheless, the ongoing pandemic has made dramatic changes since the beginning of 2020 by introducing social distancing and lockdown around the world, which forced the businesses to embrace new normal situation such as adopting work from home policy, teleworking, and most importantly, the use of digital technologies in the office (Soto-Acosta, 2020). Stock markets and the listed companies need to embrace the changes fluently in order to overturn the investors' confidence.

The price movement of the stock depends on the reflection of information (Fama, 1970). According to Fama's Efficient Market Theory (1970), the price of any security is the sum of standardized cash flows and it reflects the information about the business. An event related to the stock can alter the performance of the security (Brown & Warner, 1985), and whether a particular event can cause the security to produce AR is needed to be examined (Agrawal & Kamakura, 1995). In this regard, event study method, which states that security price movement will be affected by a particular event as long as efficient market hypothesis works accurately (Liu et al., 2020), has been used by several studies to understand the impacts of various events including mergers and acquisition announcement, dividend declaration, changes in government policy, and so on (MacKinlay, 1997). Dolley (1933) adopts event study for the first time for examining the effect of 95 stock split on the prices. Later on, Gaver et al. (1992) examine the effect of adopting long-term compensation contracts on the stock market, Thompson (1993) employs event studies to come to the conclusion that the agreement between Canada and the US for establishing free trade between them significantly affected the market to generate AR for the manufacturing industry, Wang et al. (2013) conclude that biotechnological companies' stocks enjoyed significant AR due to the emergence of infectious epidemics, and Liu et al. (2020) analyze the impact of COVID-19 outbreak on 21 top stock market indexes.

Data and methodology

Market indicators including beneficiary owner (BO) accounts, market capitalization, stock indexes, issuance of initial public offering (IPO), total number of listed companies, number of mutual funds, debentures, corporate bonds, and so on are analyzed for a period starting from 1991 to 1999 by retrieving the data from BSEC databases.

The impact of the digitalization events on the stock market of Bangladesh is examined through event studies. With an effort to make the stock market more efficient, DSE and CSE were demutualized on November 21st, 2013. Later, DSE inaugurated the NGTS on December 11th, 2014, although CSE initiated the system on October 20th, 2011, which has been regarded as one of the initial steps toward digitalization. In order to make investors more informed about the stock market, DSE introduced mobile app "DSE Info" on November 25th, 2015, and "DSE-Mobile" on March 9th, 2016. DSE also made an agreement with Shanghai-Shenzhen Stock Exchange Consortium by selling 25 percent shares to them. Thus, the demutualization of DSE and CSE, the inauguration of the NGTS in DSE and CSE, the introduction of "DSE Info", the initiation of "DSE-Mobile", and the agreement between DSE and Shanghai-Shenzhen Stock Exchange Consortium are considered as five vital digitalized events. Data relating to all of these events are extracted from the databases of BSEC, DSE, and CSE.

Four representative stock indices from DSE and CSE are used for the event study. DSEX and Dhaka Stock Index 30 (DSE30) are selected from DSE, and Chittagong Stock Exchange Broad Index (CSEX) and Chittagong Stock Index 30 (CSE30) are selected from CSE. DSEX, the major index of the DSE, is selected as a benchmark index. It includes all the shares of the market. In addition, CSEX, the all-share index of CSE, is also adopted as a benchmark index to check the robustness of the findings. In order to perform the event studies, daily closing prices of these indexes have been collected from the databases of DSE and CSE for a period of 21 years starting from January 1st, 2000 to November 15th, 2020. In order to supplement the discussion, additional table and information are also used.

Event studies can be short-term and long-term. If the data are taken on a short-term basis, the study will avail the investor with information regarding current expectation of returns based on any particular event, whereas if data are long-term in nature, the whole study will facilitate to know the ultimate effect of the impact of the event (Jeng, 2015). Therefore, focusing on the long-term nature, this study defines a window of 252 trading days before two days of each of the events. In addition, the T-test is incorporated to test the significance of the output. The following regression model is applied for finding the expected returns of the index:

$$R_{i,t} = \alpha_i + \beta_i R_{mt} + \varepsilon_{i,t} \tag{3.1}$$

where, $R_{i,t}$ refers to the expected returns of the index i, R_{mt} is the normal returns in percentage on day t of the estimated window, and $\varepsilon_{i,t}$ is the statistical error of the index i on day t of the estimated window. The coefficients, α_i and β_i, are obtained from the dependent variable and independent variable. After calculating the coefficients, following formula is incorporated to estimate the expected returns in the event window:

$$E(R_{i,t}) = \alpha_i + \beta_i R_{mt} \qquad (3.2)$$

In order to find out the AR during event window, the following formula is adopted:

$$AR_{i,t} = R_{i,t} - E(R_{i,t}) \qquad (3.3)$$

here,
$AR_{i,t}$ = The AR of the index i on day t within event window
$R_{i,t}$ = The real return of the index i on day t
$E(R_{i,t})$ = The expected return of the index i on day t

The CAR is calculated on the basis of the following formula:

$$CAR_i(t_0, t_1) = \sum_{t=t_0}^{t_1} AR_{i,t} \qquad (3.4)$$

After calculating the AR, the following formula is used to estimate the AR Statistic for testing whether the return is significant or not:

$$\frac{AR_{i,t}}{\text{Standard Error}} \qquad (3.5)$$

The output is tested based on both 99 percent and 95 percent confidence levels.

Overview of the capital market of Bangladesh

BSEC was established in 1993, as per the Bangladesh Securities and Exchange Commission Act 1993. Its main purpose is to serve the best interest of the investors as well as to formulate the rules and procedures for the smooth operations of the market. It regulates two stock exchanges of the country, DSE and CSE; one depository institution, CDBL; and a number of depository participants, and listed securities. CDBL was established in an effort to store and record the accounts and transfer of stocks and securities in the Central Depository System (CDS). The depository participants include 63 merchant bankers, 8 credit rating companies, 48 asset management companies, 11 custodians for mutual funds, 84 trustees for asset backed securities, 6 trustees of alternative, and 18 fund managers as of December 2020.

The capital market of Bangladesh started its journey in 1952 with the intent of having an independent bourse in East Pakistan. As a result of the continuous regional demand, DSE started its operation in the name of East Pakistan Stock Exchange Association Limited in 1962. It took the name Dacca Stock Exchange in 1964. After the independence of Bangladesh in 1971, trading in

Table 3.1 Evolution of capital market of Bangladesh (1954–2020)

Events	Year
Inauguration of DSE	1954
Trading Started in DSE	1956
All Share Price Calculation in DSE	1986
Establishment of BSEC	1993
Establishment of CSE	1995
First Automated and Online Trading System in CSE	1998
Automated Trading in DSE	1998
Depository Act of CDBL	1999
Depository Regulation Act of CDBL	2000
Incorporation of CDBL as Public Limited Company	2000
Electronic Government Securities Registry of CDBL	2003
Initiation of Dematerialization in of CDBL	2004
Internet Based Trading System at CSE	2004
Renovation of DSE All Share Index	2005
Digitalization in Balance Inquiry and Valuation of Portfolio in CDBL	2006
SMS Alert Service of CDBL	2009
Center for Data and Disaster Recovery in CDBL	2009
Introduction of Book Building Methodology at DSE	2010
Achievement of 100 percent Trade Settlement Through CDS of CDBL	2010
First NGTS at CSE	2011
Introduction of Measurement Systems Analysis (MSA) Software at DSE	2012
Introduction of DSEX and DSE30	2013
Demutualization of DSE and CSE	2013
Introduction of DSE Shariah Index	2014
Market Surveillance Software at DSE	2014
NGTS at DSE	2014
Initiation of DSE Mobile	2015
Introduction of New Book Building Software at DSE	2016
Investment from Shanghai-Shenzhen Consortium at DSE	2018
Renovation in Depository System by activating VeDAS Software at CDBL	2018

Source: BSEC (2017).

the exchange was resumed in 1976 after a 5-year suspension. With the initiation of BSEC in 1993 and CSE in 1995, the market started its reign to facilitate the investors and companies. The evolution of the capital market of Bangladesh, including significant digitalization initiatives, is provided in Table 3.1.

Capital market indicators, for example, BO accounts; market capitalization; DSEX and CSEX; DSE and CSE turnovers; total depository participants; and number of IPOs, mutual funds, debentures, corporate bonds, and government treasury bonds are summed up in Table 3.2. BO accounts were about 2.81 million in 2019, which is currently 2.5 million as of December 2020. Market capitalization was only BDT (the currency of Bangladesh) 10.4 billion in 1991, which reached BDT 3998 billion by the end of 2019. It increased significantly in the last three decades and has been showing a positive trend. As the market matures, depository participants have been increasing year by year. In 1991, the number of market participants was too small to support the markets. However, in 2019, there were

Table 3.2 Capital market indicators (1991–2019)

Year/Indicator	1991	1996	2001	2006	2011	2016	2017	2018	2019
BO accounts (in million)	–	–	–	1.25	2.67	3.16	2.93	2.77	2.81
Market capitalization (in billion BDT)	10.4	166.04	67.45	315.5	2737	3185	3801	3847	3998
DSE turnover (in billion BDT)	0.12	30.14	39.86	65.07	3259	1072	1805	1460	1591
CSE turnover (in billion BDT)	–	6.08	14.95	16.75	322	78	118	110	85
DSEX (in points)	296	2300	829	1609	5093	4508	5656	5405	5422
CSEX (in points)	–	1157	1352	3724	17060	13803	17517	16559	16634
Depository participants	–	–	185	200	328	393	402	405	411
IPOs	–	–	9	12	17	11	9	12	13
Mutual fund	–	8	12	13	35	36	35	37	37
Debentures	–	–	8	8	8	8	8	8	8
Corporate bond	–	–	1	1	3	2	2	1	1
Listed companies	138	205	249	310	232	292	297	305	317
Treasury bonds	–	–	84	84	212	221	221	221	221

Source: different annual reports of CDBL.

411 participants. Every year, the market observes a positive trend in terms of listing depository participants. In 2019, 13 companies were enlisted in the market, whereas the number reached 15 by the end of December 2020.

Figure 3.1. shows that the turnover of DSE is far greater than that of CSE. Both markets had the highest turnover in 2011. Although the turnover of DSE is much higher than that of CSE, the CSEX is higher than the DSEX

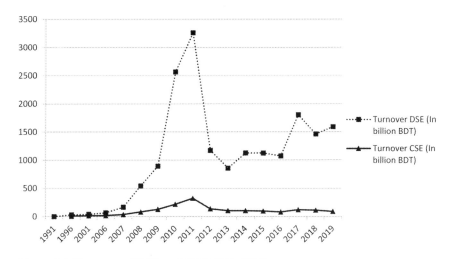

Figure 3.1 Turnover of DSE and CSE (1991–2019).

Source: different annual reports of CDBL.

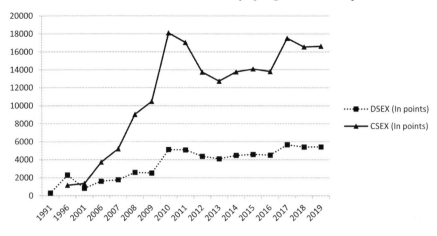

Figure 3.2 The trend of DSEX and CSEX (1991–2019).
Source: different annual reports of CDBL.

(see Figure 3.2.). However, both exchanges observed a huge rise in 2010 in which DSEX rose from 2520 points to 5122 points and CSEX increased from 10477 points to 18116 points. By the end of 2019, DSEX and CSEX stood at 5422 points and 16634 points, respectively.

Findings and analyses

In an effort to find out the impact of the digitalization progresses on the performance of the market, the mean and standard deviation of the indexes of two stock exchanges are calculated and presented in Table 3.3. Returns of both estimation window and event window are taken into consideration.

Demutualization of the stock exchanges was initiated by BSEC in an attempt to make exchanges more efficient. DSE and CSE were demutualized on November 21st, 2013. In Table 3.3., an estimation window from January

Table 3.3 Mean returns and standard deviation before and after the demutualization

Index	Estimation window (Demutualization)			Event window (Demutualization)		
	Trading Days	Mean Returns (%)	Standard Deviation (%)	Trading Days	Mean Returns (%)	Standard Deviation (%)
DSEX	190	0.02	1.38	10	(0.19)	1.51
DSE30	190	(0.004)	1.47	10	0.06	1.64
CSEX	252	(0.03)	1.25	10	(0.17)	1.66
CSE30	252	(0.02)	1.31	10	(0.22)	1.50

Source: Authors' calculation.

Table 3.4 Mean returns and standard deviation before and after the starting of NGTS

Index	Estimation window (NGTS)			Event window (NGTS)		
	Trading days	Mean returns (%)	Standard deviation (%)	Trading days	Mean returns (%)	Standard deviation (%)
DSEX	252	0.06	0.80	10	(0.19)	0.46
DSE30	252	(0.08)	0.93	10	0.16	0.51
CSEX	252	(0.12)	2.52	10	(0.47)	2.72
CSE30	252	(0.07)	2.68	10	(0.20)	2.72

Source: Authors' calculation.

29th, 2013 to November 18th, 2013 is taken for DSE and October 23rd, 2012 to November 18th, 2013 for CSE. Ten trading days after the estimation window is considered as an event window. It is observed that the mean return of DSE30 was increased, although all other indexes showed decreased return after the demutualization. However, standard deviation of returns increased for all the indexes.

NGTS, an intuitive and digital platform, was established by CSE and DSE on October 19th, 2011, and December 11st, 2014, respectively. For estimating mean returns and standard deviation of returns of the index in Table 3.4., the estimation window from September 28th, 2010 to October 17th, 2011 in the case of CSE, and from November 19th, 2013 to December 8th, 2014 in the case of DSE are considered. Event window is taken as trading days immediately after the estimation window. Mean returns of DSE30 were increased during the event window. Risks in indexes represented by the standard deviations, other than CSE30 and CSEX, observed the reduction due to the trading in NGTS.

DSE launched the mobile application, DSE Info, in order to provide information to the investors in an accurate and timely manner. In Table 3.5., the associated mean returns and standard deviation of returns of estimation window and event window are placed. Estimation window is selected from November 9th, 2014 to November 22nd, 2015. Event window is the next ten trading days after the estimation window. DSE Info played a role by

Table 3.5 Mean returns and standard deviation before and after the initiation of DSE info

Index	Estimation window (DSE Info)			Event window (DSE Info)		
	Trading days	Mean returns (%)	Standard deviation (%)	Trading days	Mean returns (%)	Standard deviation (%)
DSEX	252	(0.040)	0.84	10	0.13	0.35
DSE30	252	(0.035)	0.92	10	0.28	0.60

Source: Authors' calculation.

Table 3.6 Mean returns and standard deviation before and after starting of the DSE Mobile

Index	Estimation window (DSE Mobile)			Event window (DSE Mobile)		
	Trading days	Mean returns (%)	Standard deviation (%)	Trading days	Mean returns (%)	Standard deviation (%)
DSEX	252	(0.030)	0.76	10	0.02	0.37
DSE30	252	(0.019)	0.79	10	(0.12)	0.57

Source: Authors' calculation.

showing a positive trend in both DSE30 and DSEX indexes, which resulted in the increased returns and decreased risk.

DSE launched another application, DSE Mobile, on March 9th, 2016 to ensure automated facilities of the exchange for the investors. The mean returns and standard deviation of estimation window are calculated from daily returns of the exchange from February 24th, 2015 to March 6th, 2016. Event window is selected from March 7th, 2016 to March 21st, 2016. Like DSE Info, the adoption of DSE Mobile resulted in increased mean return, except the case of DSE30, and decreased risk, as shown in Table 3.6.

DSE, as per the rules of the Demutualization Act, made an agreement to avail Shanghai-Shenzhen Stock Exchange Consortium to become the strategic partner by selling 25 percent of its outstanding shares. An estimation window from February 9th, 2017 to February 14th, 2018, and event window from February 15th, 2018 to March 1st, 2018 is selected for the impact of the event. Although the consortium has been highly appreciated and expected to bring positive outcome for the market, the other side of the expectation is noticed in Table 3.7, as mean returns slumped to negative with an increased amount of risk denoted by the standard deviation.

Event studies are run to find out the intercepts, slope, R-squared, and standard error by using the least square regression over the estimation window. From Table 3.8., it is clear that the standard error is almost zero in every case, which means that the sample mean and the population mean are closer to each other. R-squared, in case of all events, except the case of

Table 3.7 Mean returns and standard deviation before and after the declaration of the Shanghai-Shenzhen stock exchange consortium

Index	Estimation window (consortium)			Event window (consortium)		
	Trading days	Mean returns (%)	Standard deviation (%)	Trading days	Mean returns (%)	Standard deviation (%)
DSEX	252	0.042	0.59	10	(0.387)	0.84
DSE30	252	0.053	0.56	10	(0.349)	0.90

Source: Authors' calculation.

Table 3.8 Summary of output of event studies

Event	Exchange	Intercept	Slope	R-squared	Standard error
Demutualization	DSE	(0.00009)	0.19738	0.03441	0.01451
	CSE	0.00056	1.02915	0.93564	0.00680
NGTS	DSE	0.00022	1.03157	0.78669	0.00432
	CSE	0.00056	1.02915	0.93564	0.00680
DSE Info	DSE	(0.00002)	0.96137	0.76459	0.00448
DSE Mobile	DSE	0.00007	0.81152	0.60035	0.00502
Consortium	DSE	0.00005	0.06973	0.00534	0.00561

Source: Authors' calculation.

DSE Shanghai-Shenzhen Consortium and the case of DSE demutualization, show higher percentage. It indicates that there is a strong relationship between the event studies' models and the dependent variables, DSEX and CSEX. Positive slopes in case of all events are also observed, which means that the variables are positively correlated.

Table 3.9. reports the impact of demutualization in both DSE and CSE for two consecutive trading days. The results indicate that demutualization was not able to produce significant AR for both exchanges on the event day and the next trading days. Although there was a positive AR on the event day, it was not statistically significant.

The NGTS was brought to the market to make it more efficient and faster than ever. However, the findings indicate that the starting of NGTS in the market would not produce significant AR for the investors. The outcome of event studies of the impact of initiation of NGTS on the market shows that there was slight improvement in the market return in both DSE and CSE. However, they both were insignificant at 1 percent and 5 percent levels, as indicated by Table 3.10.

Table 3.11. shows the impact of introducing DSE Info and DSE Mobile for the investors. According to the table, returns increased on the event day and the following trading day, though AR Statistic indicates that the increased returns in both cases are not significant. It means the increase in returns was not necessarily due to the events.

Table 3.9 Impact of the demutualization

Exchange	Date	AR (%)	CAR (%)	AR Statistic	Significance at 5%	Significance at 1%
DSE	21-Nov-2013	1.37	5.09	0.941	No	No
	24-Nov-2013	(0.65)	4.43	(0.454)	No	No
CSE	21-Nov-2013	(0.09)	0.31	(0.249)	No	No
	24-Nov-2013	(0.11)	0.20	(0.309)	No	No

Source: Authors' calculation.

Table 3.10 Impact of the initiation of NGTS

Exchange	Date	AR (%)	CAR (%)	AR Statistic	Significance at 5%	Significance at 1%
DSE	11-Dec-2014	(0.016)	(0.071)	(0.036)	No	No
	14-Dec-2014	0.006	(0.065)	0.013	No	No
CSE	20-Oct-2011	(0.218)	(0.279)	(0.321)	No	No
	23-Oct-2011	(0.136)	(0.415)	(0.201)	No	No

Source: Authors' calculation.

DSE welcomed the Shanghai-Shenzhen Stock Exchange Consortium in the capital market of Bangladesh. In response to this event, market returns produced fewer negative returns on event day and the following trading day (see Table 3.12.). Event studies indicate that the AR is significant at both 1 percent and 5 percent level on the event day. It means that the event posed an impact on the market. However, AR is not significant on the following trading day.

Based on the above tables and discussions, it is found that only the announcement of the inclusion of Shanghai-Shenzhen Stock Exchange Consortium in DSE had a statistically significant impact on the market. It means that various other digitalized events have yet to generate positive outcome for the two exchanges. Just as evidence, even though total number of BO accounts has reached 2,526,133 as of December 9th, 2020; 3.96 percent and 1.98 percent of the investors in DSE use DSE Info and DSE Mobile, respectively. The statistics are worse in the case of CSE where only 0.04 percent and 0.20 percent of the investors use CSE Cloud and CSE Chitra applications, CSE launched the former on October 3rd, 2015, and the latter on August 5th, 2019. All of these indicate that investors are not well aware of the digital improvement of the market.

Furthermore, 250 sample brokerage houses are selected for identifying whether they are offering websites for their investors or not. Interestingly, brokerage houses are not fully digitalized, as it is found that 42 percent of the houses maintain their websites necessary for the interaction with the investors, whereas the rest do not have basic websites. In addition, all listed companies of banking, financial institutions, food and allied, fuel and

Table 3.11 Impact of DSE info and DSE Mobile

Exchange	Date	AR (%)	CAR (%)	AR Statistic	Significance at 5%	Significance at 1%
DSE	25-Nov-2015	(0.003)	0.09	(0.007)	No	No
	26-Nov-2015	(0.002)	0.07	(0.048)	No	No
DSE	09-Mar-2016	(0.01)	(0.13)	(0.024)	No	No
	10-Mar-2016	0.06	(0.07)	0.124	No	No

Source: Authors' calculation.

Table 3.12 Impact of the Shanghai-Shenzhen consortium's inclusion

Exchange	Date	AR (%)	CAR (%)	AR Statistic	Significance at 5%	Significance at 1%
DSE	19-Feb-2018	(1.62)	(2.35)	(2.893)	Yes	Yes
	20-Feb-2018	(0.25)	(2.59)	(0.4381)	No	No

Source: Authors' calculation.

power, service and real estate, tannery, and telecom sectors have websites from where investors and other stakeholders can get information. However, a significant portion of the companies in various sectors including cement, ceramic, jute, and paper and printing do not have their functional websites. Companies of the other sectors reported in Table 3.13. also fail to ensure the availability of their websites.

Thus, although both CSE and DSE have the automated trading facility, investors have yet to utilize fully by placing orders using the applications from the remote location due to paper-based regulatory practices of BSEC, lack of financial literacy, and many other issues. Moreover, not all investors take advantage of electronic floor trading and application, rather they prefer to visit brokerage houses for placing and executing the orders. It is also found that money transfer process of the exchanges, after completing the share transfer by CDBL, is still accomplished manually.

Table 3.13 Sector-wise distribution of companies not maintaining websites

Sector	Total number of companies	Number of companies not maintaining website
Banking	30	0 (0.00)
Cement	7	2 (28.57)
Ceramic	5	2 (40.00)
Engineering	41	7 (17.07)
Financial institution	23	0 (0.00)
Food and allied	18	0 (0.00)
Fuel and power	20	0 (0.00)
Insurance	48	11 (22.92)
Information technology	10	2 (20.00)
Jute	3	1 (33.33)
Paper and printing	4	2 (50.00)
Chemical and pharmaceuticals	31	5 (16.13)
Service and real estate	4	0 (0.00)
Tannery	6	0 (0.00)
Telecom	2	0 (0.00)
Textile	56	11 (19.64)
Travel and leisure	5	1 (20.00)
Miscellaneous	13	4 (30.77)

Source: Authors' survey.

Note: The figures in parentheses represent the percentage of companies having no website.

Conclusion

Bangladesh, once tagged as a bottomless basket, is classified as one of the next eleven emerging markets with 163 million active mobile phone users. Like other sectors, the capital market has incorporated several technologies such as the electronic trading system, dematerialization of the paper-based shares, mobile applications for transactions, and so on. However, despite being digitized, the stock market suffered during the initial stage of the pandemic, even the trading was surprisingly suspended for more than two months. Keeping the impact of digitalization on the capital market in consideration, this study aimed at evaluating the urgency with particular emphasis on the pandemic situation.

Event study was used to identify whether several events in the market, initiated by the authorities, generate AR for the investors or not. In order to supplement the findings, listed companies and brokerage houses were selected and analyzed for identifying their website availability. The evidence suggests that the demutualization of stock exchanges, the introduction of NGTS, and the development of DSE Info and DSE Mobile do not match the expectation as these events fail to produce significant AR for the investors. Interestingly, only the Consortium of Shanghai and Shenzhen Stock Exchange has a single day significant impact on the returns of the index. It is also noticed that the investors are not well aware of the digital applications provided by the exchanges. This is because only DSE Info application has the highest users whilst others are not installed even in 2 percent of investors' devices. The condition of digitalization in brokerage houses is also unsatisfactory since only 42 percent of the houses maintain their own website. The study also finds that among the listed companies, banks and financial institutions, and companies from the food and allied, service and real estate, fuel and power, tannery, and telecom sectors have their websites. However, the digitalization of their operational activities is subject to further research. All of these indicate that the digitalization adopted in the stock market of a developing country like Bangladesh is partial in nature and accordingly it fails to provide adequate platform for dealing with the adverse situations.

Based on the study, a few policy recommendations can be made. The study indicates that improvement from the side of authorities and exchanges cannot make the market digitized, rather the whole ecosystem is in dire need of technological improvement. Since there is a positive trend in IPOs, listed companies, depository participants, investors, and market capitalization, the authorities need to ensure the adoption of advanced technologies for all stakeholders. In aggregate, it can be concluded that the capital market, in particular the stock market, in Bangladesh requires the adoption of full-fledged digitalization by connecting and involving the stakeholders in the chain for dealing with the sudden and long-lasting unprecedented shock created by the pandemic like COVID-19.

References

ADB. (2020). *Global cost of coronavirus may reach USD 4.1 trillion, ADB says*. Manila: Bloomberg. https://www.bloomberg.com/news/articles/2020-04-03/global-cost-of-coronavirus-could-reach-4-1-trillion-adb-says.

Agrawal, J., & Kamakura, W. A. (1995). The economic worth of celebrity endorsers: An event study analysis. *Journal of Marketing, 59*, 56–62.

Aktar, M., Begum, H., & Sohag, A. (2020). Impact of COVID-19 on stock market in Bangladesh. *IOSR Journal of Economics and Finance (IOSR-JEF), 11*(4), 30–33.

Bouwman, H., Nikou, S., & De Reuver, M. (2019). Digitalization, business models, and SMEs: How do business model innovation practices improve performance of digitalizing SMEs? *Telecommunications Policy, 49*(3). doi: https://doi.org/10.1016/j.telpol.2019.101828.

Brandl, B., & Hornuf, L. (2017). Where did FinTechs come from, and where do they go? The transformation of the financial industry in Germany after digitalization. *SSRN Electronic Journal.* doi:http://dx.doi.org/10.2139/ssrn.3036555.

Brown, S. J., & Warner, J. B. (1985). Using daily stock returns: The case of event studies. *Journal of Financial Economics, 14*, 3–31.

BSEC (2017). *Capital market digitalization.* Dhaka: BSEC.

Ding, D., Guan, C., Chan, C. M., & Liu, W. (2020). Building stock market resilience through digital transformation: Using google trends to analyze the impact of COVID-19 pandemic. *Frontiers of Business Research in China, 14*, 21. doi:https://doi.org/10.1186/s11782-020-00089-z

Dolley, J. C. (1933). Characteristics and procedure of common stock split-ups. *Harvard Business Review, 11*, 316–326.

Fama, E. F. (1970). Efficient capital markets: A review of theory and empirical work. *Journal of Finance, 25*, 383–417.

Gassmann, O., Frankenberger, K., & Csik, M. (2013). *The St. Gallen business model navigator.* The Business Model Navigator.

Gaver, J. J., Gaver, K. M., & Battistel, G. P. (1992). The stock market reaction to performance plan adoptions. *The Accounting Review*, 172–182. https://www.jstor.org/stable/248026.

Goldenberg, T. (2017, November 9). Guest Opinion: The Digital Evolution of Stock Trading. *The Financial Revolutionist.* https://thefr.com/opinion/2017/11/9/guest-opinion-the-digital-evolution-of-stock-trading?rq=tom%20goldenberg.

Henriette, E., Mondher, F., & Boughzala, I. (2015). "The Shape of Digital Transformation: A Systematic Literature Review" (2015). *MCIS 2015 Proceedings. 10.* https://aisel.aisnet.org/mcis2015/10.

Huang, X., Kuijpers, D., Li, L., Sha, S., & Xia, C. (2020). *How Chinese consumers are changing shopping habits in response to COVID-19.* McKinsey & Company.

Jeng, J. L. (2015). *Analyzing event statistics in corporate finance: Methodologies, evidences, and critiques.* New York: Palgrave Macmillan.

Kane, G. C., Palmer, D., Phillips, A. N., Kiron, D., & Buckley, N. (2015). Strategy, not technology, drives digital transformation, becoming a digitally mature enterprise. *MIT Sloan Management Review.* https://sloanreview.mit.edu/projects/strategy-drives-digital-transformation/.

Kane, G. C., Phillips, A. N., Copulsky, J. R., & Andrus, G. R. (2019). *How people are the real key to digital transformation: A Q&A with the authors of "The technology fallacy".* The MIT Press. https://mitpress.mit.edu/blog/how-people-are-real-key-digital-transformation-qa-authors-technology-fallacy.

Laudon, K. C., & Laudon, J. P. (2019). Management Information Systems: Managing the Digital Firm (16th ed.). *New Jersey: Pearson.*

Lin, L., Geng, X., & Whinston, A. (2001). A new perspective to finance and competition and challenges for financial institutions in the internet era. *BIS Papers, Monetary and Economic Department, 7,* 23–35.

Liu, D. Y., Chen, S. W., & Chou, T. C. (2011). Resource fit in digital transformation: Lessons learned from the CBC bank global e-banking project. *Management Decision, 49,* 1728–1742.

Liu, H., Manzoor, A., Wang, C., Zhang, L., & Manzoor, Z. (2020). The COVID-19 outbreak and affected countries stock markets response. *International Journal of Environmental Research and Public Health, 17.* https://doi.org/10.3390/ijerph17082800.

Loebbecke, C., & Picot, A. (2015). Reflections on societal and business model transformation arising from digitization and big data analytics: A research agenda. *Journal of Strategic Information Systems, 24*(3), 149–157.

Lorenz, M., Rüßmann, M., Waldner, M., Engel, P., Harnisch, M., & Justus, J. (2015). Industry 4.0: The future of productivity and growth in manufacturing industries. *The Boston Consulting Group, 9,* 54–89.

MacKinlay, A. C. (1997). Event studies in economics and finance. *Journal of Economic Literature, XXXV,* 13–39.

Marynowski, J. M., Voinescu, C. D., Puscasu, S., & O'Donnell, T. M. (2014). Automated trading system in an electronic trading exchange. *DCFB LLC.* https://patents.google.com/patent/US8725621B2/en.

OECD. (2020). *Evaluating the initial impact of COVID-19 containment measures on economic activity.* Paris: OECD. https://www.oecd.org/coronavirus/policy-responses/evaluating-the-initial-impact-of-covid-19-containment-measures-on-economic-activity-b1f6b68b/.

Okuda, A., & Karazhanova, A. (2020). *Digital resilience against COVID-19.* Bangkok: United Nation ESCAP.

Pagano, M., & Roell, A. (1996). Transparency and liquidity: A comparison of auction and dealer markets with informed trading. *The Journal of Finance, 51*(2). https://doi.org/10.1111/j.1540-6261.1996.tb02695.x.

Parviainen, P., Tihinen, M., Kääriäinen, J., & Teppola, S. (2017). Tackling the digitalization challenge: How to benefit from digitalization in practice. *International Journal of Information Systems and Project Management, 5*(1), 63–77. doi: 10.12821/ijispm050104.

Phan, D. H., & Narayan, P. K. (2020). Country responses and the reaction of the stock market to COVID-19—A preliminary exposition. *Emerging Markets Finance and Trade, 56*(10), 2138–2150. doi: https://doi.org/10.1080/1540496X.2020.1784719.

Polimenis, V. (2006). Trading on the floor after sweeping the book. *Review of Futures Markets, 14*(4), 451–459.

Schallmo, D., Williams, C. A., & Boardman, L. (2017). Digital transformation of business models — Best Practice, enablers, and roadmap. *International Journal of Innovation Management, 21*(1), 1740014. doi: 10.1142/S136391961740014X.

Shkarlet, S., Dubyna, M., Shtyrkhun, K., & Verbivska, L. (2020). Transformation of the paradigm of the economic entities development in digital economy. *WSEAS Transactions on Environment and Development, 16.* 413–422.

Soto-Acosta, P. (2020). COVID-19 pandemic: Shifting digital. *Information Systems Management,* 3–5. doi:10.1080/10580530.2020.1814461.

Soto-Acosta, P., Popa, S., & Palacios-Marqués, D. (2016). E-business, organizational innovation and firm performance in manufacturing SMEs: An empirical study in Spain. *Technological and Economic Development of Economy, 22*(6), 885–904.

Stolterman, E., & Fors, A. C. (2004). Information Technology and the Good Life. *Information Systems Research: Relevant Theory and Informed Practice: 20th Years Retrospective: Relevant Theory and Informed Practice- Looking Forward from a 20-year Perspective on IS Research,* 687-692. Retrieved from http://urn.kb.se/resolve?urn=urn:nbn:se:umu:diva-33145

Thompson, A. J. (1993). The anticipated sectoral adjustment to the Canada – United States free trade agreement: An event study analysis. *The Canadian Journal of Economics, 26*(2), 253–271. https://www.jstor.org/stable/135906.

Wang, Y. H., Yang, F. J., & Chen, L. J. (2013). An investor's perspective on infectious diseases and their influence on market behavior. *Journal of Business Economics and Management, 14,* S112–S117. doi:10.3846/16111699.2012.711360.

Yu, K. D., & Aviso, K. B. (2020). Modelling the economic impact and ripple effects of disease outbreaks. *Process Integration and Optimization for Sustainability, 4,* 183–186.

4 Information and communication technologies versus diffusion and substitution of financial innovations. The case of exchange-traded funds in Japan and South Korea

Adam Marszk and Ewa Lechman

Introduction

Exchange-traded funds (ETFs) are one of the most influential and successful financial products introduced in the last few decades, as evidenced by the rapid growth of their assets and number. They are among the key contributors and, at the same time, the main effects of the rise of the passive investing commenced on the most developed financial markets since 1980s (Anadu et al., 2020). The growth of the ETF markets has been accompanied by the introduction and rapid adoption of the new technologies, in particular information and communication technologies (ICTs), which has led to deep transformation of the financial markets and their digitalization (Asongu & Nwachukwu, 2019; Cheng et al., 2021). Digitalization of the financial markets has resulted in several important developments on the segments of the financial system that are most closely related to the ETF markets such as the introduction and rapid expansion of the automated trading systems based on sophisticated ICT-related technologies, leading to decrease in the trading costs and facilitating gaining access to the markets regardless of the physical location (Aldridge, 2013; Huang et al., 2019).

Another important process is changing position of ETFs in the financial system in terms of their competitors. Initially, due to their roots and the type of managing financial institutions, ETFs were mainly innovative substitutes for various types of mutual funds with the passive investment strategies, offering relative advantages in relation to the conventional funds such as lower costs or higher transparency (Agapova, 2011; Deville, 2008). However, the increasing popularity and heterogeneity of ETFs has made them also alternative solution in relation to quite different type of financial instruments, i.e. stock index derivatives, in particular stock index futures and options (Arnold & Lesné, 2015). The relative strengths of ETFs in comparison to derivatives, such as higher accessibility or open-ended structure linked with no predefined maturity and thus less problematic position

DOI: 10.4324/9781003095354-4

management by the holder (Eurex, 2016), have resulted in some cases in the process of the replacement of the conventional products (i.e. derivatives) by the newer innovative ones (i.e. ETFs). This applies to an increasing range of applications.

Both above-mentioned relationships have previously been rarely verified empirically. Some of the exceptions include our previous studies: Marszk et al. (2019) examined the diffusion of ETFs and the role of ICT in this process in the group of Asia-Pacific economies. Marszk and Lechman (2020) conducted similar analysis for the European countries; however, these studies inspected either different countries or applied slightly varying research methods (as well as time periods considered) than the current analysis. This study addresses the apparent research gap in the assessment of the spread of ETFs with regard to the other index instruments and its factors which comprises its main contribution. The aim of the paper is to verify empirically the diffusion and substitution of ETFs in the market for index financial instruments. More precisely, the detailed aims of the study are twofold:

1 Examination of the relationship between development of the ETF markets (in the context of the other index financial instruments) and adoption of ICT;
2 Assessment of the position of ETFs in relation to the stock index derivatives, i.e. their diffusion and substitution on the financial markets.

The analysis covers two countries: Japan and South Korea – they were selected as countries in the same geographical region, with relatively comparable socio-economic conditions. Moreover, in both countries, the ETF markets are among the most developed in the world. Therefore, they may serve as reference points for the other countries, with less advanced markets for the innovative funds such as the majority of the European economies; the analysis of Japan and South Korea can indicate the possible future trajectories of the substitution between ETFs and competing index financial instruments in the currently less developed European ETF markets. Time period of the study differs in the two parts of the analysis: in the verification of the links between ICT and ETFs we analyze the time period 2004–2019 in order to check the relationships in the possibly largest time period, whereas in the study of the substitution we focus on the time period 2003–2015 which can be characterized as the years of the most dynamic changes on the ETF markets; additionally, in both cases the choice was affected by data availability. Research methods comprise following: country-specific regression models and technological substitution framework.

The rest of this chapter is structured as follows. The next section presents the background of our study, with the focus on the contribution of ICT to the spread of ETFs as well as the comparison of ETFs to stock index derivatives. In the subsequent section data and methodology of our study are described. The results of the study are discussed in the successive section. The final section concludes the chapter with its key insights.

Background

ETFs and adoption of ICT

Adoption of ICT can be regarded as one of the key factors of the development of the ETF markets, regardless of the approach to the measurement of the spread of the innovative funds (i.e. with the use of asset or turnover-based indicators). The influence of ICT on the ETF markets stems from the impact of the new technologies on the financial system and financial markets in particular. Below we discuss some of the main channels of transmission between ICT and ETFs identified in the literature, starting with more general overview of the effects of ICT adoption. Our discussion below is based on the overview presented in Marszk and Lechman (2021).

Diffusion of ICT in the economy should be perceived as substantially contributing to the broadly understood financial development (Kim, 2019). In the context of the ETFs, which are strongly linked to the financial markets, it should be emphasized that the correct functioning of financial markets depends to a large extent on the unrestricted flows of information (Michaelsen, 2020). Consequently, adoption of ICT-based solutions by the market participants and entities related to their infrastructure affects the dissemination of information among the market participants (more recently, increasingly important role is played by various Big Data solutions (Ahmed et al., 2017)), potentially decreasing information asymmetries and time delays (the latter to the extremely low values). Moreover, growing ICT penetration in various countries, and the resulting digitalization of the financial markets decreases the importance of the physical distance and the associated discrepancies in the access to the financial markets in various regions and countries (Bai et al., 2016). In other words, it can boost the decentralization of the financial markets (Klagge & Martin, 2005) and allow market participants to invest into securities (or other types of assets), which they cannot access at their geographical location. Particularly strong influence can be exerted by the high-speed broadband Internet connections with the substantial information-carrying capacity. The negative effects of the diffusion of ICT on the financial systems can include the magnified volatility of financial markets (Pantielieieva et al., 2018), related issue of increased financial instability (Knell, 2015), and gaps in the access to the financial services (i.e. financial exclusion) resulting from differences in the adoption of the new technologies (Cvetanović et al., 2018; Pozzi et al., 2013).

In our study, we concentrate on the comparison of ETFs to the stock index derivatives. Therefore, the main analyzed category of ETFs are passive funds with the exposure to the stock market indexes – such funds constitute the majority of the global ETF market, it applies also to the two examined countries (Japan and South Korea). It means that effects of ICT adoption on the stock markets are of particular importance in this context. Diffusion of ICT can boost the development of the stock markets through the introduction and spread of the digitalized trading and settlement systems which lead to the deep transformation of the stock exchanges (Bhunia & Ghosal, 2011; Diaz-Rainey et al., 2015; Dutta et al., 2017; Nishimura, 2010), acceleration of the dissemination of data, reduction in transaction costs, and improved risk-sharing mechanisms (Hendershott et al., 2011; Thiagarajan et al., 2019).

The exact mechanisms of transmission between diffusion of ICT and development of ETF industry can be divided into two categories, taking into account the relevant side of the ETF market.

On the demand side, we should consider above all the attributes of ETFs which determine their attractiveness for investors and how they are affected by ICT. To begin with, the digitalization of financial markets can result in the decrease of the stock trading and settlement costs and thus lower the overall costs faced by ETF providers and, accordingly, expenses incurred by their users (Al-Busaidi & Al-Muharrami, 2020; Drummer et al., 2017). Another demand-side ICT-related effect is the possibility to provide investors with the continuously updated price of the shares of ETFs and opportunity to act on this information without substantial time delays (Kirilenko et al., 2017). Moreover, important measure considered by investors with regard to passive investments such as the core category of ETFs is their tracking error, representing their performance in mirroring the performance of the tracked (usually stock market) index. In case of majority of ETFs (with the physical structure), their tracking error is minimized in the course of arbitrage operations conducted in relation to the in-kind creation and redemption mechanism of their shares (Chen et al., 2017). The time delays and costs of such transactions are decreased due to the digitalization of the financial markets.

On the supply side of the ETF market, representing the conditions affecting, among other, ETF providers and the market's infrastructure, major effects of ICT adoption are strongly linked to the effects discussed in the preceding paragraph (e.g., impact of ICT on arbitrage operations). However, there are some additional aspects that should be taken into account. First, adoption of ICT is necessary for the dual and cross-listing of ETFs, in particular in case of funds with shares listed in more than one country (Alderighi, 2020). Second, the aforementioned requirement applies also to the funds that are not necessarily listed in more than location but offer exposure to some kind of assets located on other markets; the requirements are particularly high in case ETFs with exposure to some less liquid classes of assets, from markets characterized by high transactional costs (Blitz & Huij, 2012; MacDonald, 2017). Third, profitability of offering ETFs for their providers and thus the decisions to add them to their product range depend on the associated costs which can be limited by adopting the new technologies with regard to, for instance, stock trading or other elements of portfolio management (Li & Marinč, 2018; Schaper, 2012; Schmiedel et al., 2006). Finally, the launch and management of some more exotic types of ETFs (such as synthetic funds, based on derivatives for the tracking mechanism) are linked to even higher requirements in terms of the trading and settlement systems and, accordingly, their digitalization, than in case of physical ETFs (Liebi, 2020; Nwogugu, 2018).

ETFs and other index financial instruments

In our empirical analysis, we regard ETFs as a subset of index financial instruments. We refer thus to the concept of 'equity index arbitrage complex' introduced by Gastineau (2010). It can be understood as a set of instruments linked by the common underlying assets – equity (stock) market indexes, with the possibility to conduct arbitrage operations based on the observed price discrepancies. For the purpose of our analysis, we focus on the following financial instruments within the equity index arbitrage complex: ETFs, stock index futures, and stock index options; the other elements of this complex (such baskets of equities) have been omitted due to lack of data hindering their analysis or due to the high similarity to the selected instruments. From the theoretical perspective of the equity index arbitrage complex, it means that we analyze one type of instrument from each category of the complex, i.e. traditional, symmetric derivatives, and convex derivatives. In our theoretical overview, we focus on the comparisons between ETFs and stock index futures but the discussion to a large extent applies to stock index options as well. Discussion below draws heavily from Marszk and Lechman (2020).

The main common attributes of ETFs and stock index futures comprise following elements (Arnold & Lesné, 2015; Goltz & Schröder, 2011; Liu & Tse, 2017): underlying (tracked) assets (i.e. stock market indexes), trading locations (on-exchange trading available; associated attribute is intra-day pricing), highly limited counterparty risk, high liquidity, and high number of market participants.

There are also certain differences that distinguish ETFs from stock index futures and make either instrument more advantageous for its users in relation to the second one (CME Group, 2016; Eurex, 2016). The key relative advantages of ETFs include following attributes: broader product range (access to investments into stock market indexes of various sectors and countries), higher availability (accessibility), open-ended structure linked with no predefined maturity, and thus less problematic position management by the holder, and less problematic investing into foreign instruments (Chang et al., 2019). The crucial relative benefits of stock index futures are lower capital requirements and easier access to leveraged and short positions. Overall, the relative attractiveness of either instrument stems from a high degree from the rolling costs typical for futures contracts; the exact choice depends on the holding period of the investor (Madhavan et al., 2014).

However, in case of the short or leveraged position, the relative advantages of futures are generally magnified (CME Group, 2016).

ETFs constitute competing financial instruments for stock index derivatives in a number of applications. The most well-grounded choice in the financial industry between ETFs and stock index derivatives refers to the area of risk management by large investors (Gastineau, 2010) and their decisions are based mostly on the cost factor. Relatively more recent applications for which ETFs and stock index derivatives can be regarded as substitutes include other types of risk management operations, not necessarily limited to the largest financial institutions – the increasing popularity of ETFs in this field at the expense of derivatives in many countries is a side-effect of various regulatory changes imposed after the 2008 global financial crisis which made derivatives less cost-effective in relation to ETFs (Arnold & Lesné, 2015; Madhavan et al., 2014). Moreover, the other fields in which the discussed financial instruments may be perceived as substitutes are gaining exposure to the commodities markets (Chang et al., 2019; Kaur & Singh, 2020).

Data and methodology

Empirical approach

Within the methodological framework, aside from standard descriptive statistics and time trends analysis, we use research methods that allow for identification of the role of digital technologies for ETF markets development, and tracing substitution trajectories observed on examined financial markets.

First, to trace if digital technologies diffusion plays a significant role in fostering ETF markets development, we estimate individual country regressions that take the general econometric form:

$$\theta_i = \omega_0 + \omega_{1,i} + \ldots + \omega_{m,i} + \varepsilon_i, \tag{4.1}$$

where i denotes the country and m is the number of explanatory variables.

Second, to trace substitution trajectories we use the technological substitution model framework proposed by Fisher and Pry (1972)[1]. Technological substitution is a process of gradual replacement of 'old' technologies by 'newly emerged' ones. The technological substitution model adopted for the purposes of this analysis demonstrates patterns and over-time dynamics of changing market shares (fractions) between consecutive technologies (Wang & Lan, 2007) – in our case different financial instruments. In this research, we follow the methodological approach offered by Blackman (1971) and Marchetti and Nakicenovic (1979) and we adopt a 3-parameter logistic substitution model that traces the behavior of competing financial instruments to gain higher market share.

Suppose that N_i stands for the users of the two technologies (financial instruments), so that the share of the population having access and using technology i at time t is (Lechman, 2015) $\frac{N_i(t)}{N}$. We assume that the number of users is fixed and each uses one of the two available technologies (Morris & Pratt, 2003), which implies that:

$$f_i(t) + f_j(t) = 1, \qquad (4.2)$$

where i and j are competing technologies. Each examined technology (financial instrument) follows a logistic growth pattern formalized as:

$$f_i(t) = \frac{\kappa}{1 + \exp(-\alpha(t-\beta))}. \qquad (4.3)$$

In further analysis, technology i possesses $(y_i(t))$ share of a given market, and if Fisher-Pry transformation (1972) is applied:

$$y_i(t) = \ln\left[\frac{f_i(t)}{1 - f_i(t)}\right], \qquad (4.4)$$

hence the market share of technology j is expressed as:

$$f_j(t) = 1 - \sum_{j \neq i} f_i(t). \qquad (4.5)$$

In the substitution analysis, it is essential to trace the specific times when substitution phases begin and end. To specify these we follow the approach Meyer et al. (1999), and we calculate:

$$\frac{y_i''(t)}{y_i(t)} \to min., \qquad (4.6)$$

indicating the time when the saturation phase stops. Having only y_i and y_i', we estimate the two parameters of the logistic curve for technology i:

$$\Delta t_i = \frac{\ln(81)}{y_i'(t)} \qquad (4.7)$$

and

$$T_{m_i} = \ln\left[\frac{\left(y_i(t) - \frac{\ln(81)}{\Delta t}\right)}{\frac{\ln(81)}{\Delta t}}\right], \qquad (4.8)$$

where Δt_i indicates the 'takeover' (Fisher & Pry, 1972) and shows the time needed for technology i' to increase its market share from $y_i(t) = 0.1$ to $y_i(t) = 0.9$; while $T_{m_{is}}$ is the specific point in time when the substitution process is half complete.

In our research, we analyze the financial substitution process and we adopt the methodological strategy discussed above. We hypothesize there are at least two competing financial instruments and each possesses a share of financial market in country i. We adjust Eq. (4.2) and define it as:

$$f_i^{\vartheta}(t) + f_i^{\varphi}(t) = 1, \tag{4.9}$$

where

$$f_i^{\vartheta}(t) = \frac{\kappa_i^{\vartheta}}{1 + \exp\left(-\alpha_i^{\vartheta}\left(t - \beta_i^{\vartheta}\right)\right)} \tag{4.10}$$

and

$$f_i^{\varphi}(t) = \frac{\kappa_i^{\varphi}}{1 + \exp\left(-\alpha_i^{\varphi}\left(t - \beta_i^{\varphi}\right)\right)}. \tag{4.11}$$

In Eqs. (4.10–11) i denotes country, ϑ and φ stand for examined competing financial instruments on a financial market in country i.

Data

In our research, we consider two ETF markets: Japan and South Korea. The time period of the regression analysis is 2004–2019, selected in order to check the relationship between ICT and ETFs in the largest time period for which data could be acquired. The time span of the substitution analysis covers the period between 2003 and 2015 which can be characterized as the years of the most dynamic changes on the ETF markets; moreover, exclusively for this time, a well-balanced data set is available.

The most important financial indicators used to achieve the stated aims are the values of turnover (in USD millions) of selected instruments on the stock exchanges in Japan and South Korea: ETFs, stock index options, and stock index futures labeled together as 'index financial instruments.' Our main data source on turnover of equity index instruments is the World Federation of Exchanges database (World Federation of Exchanges, 2020). Supplementary sources, used in case of missing or inconsistent observations, are the datasets and reports of local stock exchanges. For equity index instruments the underlying core indicator is the turnover of ETFs, stock index options, and stock index futures (in millions of US dollars, for international comparability). Our focus is on how ETFs stand in relation to stock index derivatives. Therefore, our primary indicator of ETF market development is the share of ETFs in the total turnover of equity index instruments.

As for ICT indicators in the first part of the analysis, we use two types of data: the number of fixed broadband subscriptions (FBS) per 100 inhabitants; and Internet users (IU), or the 'proportion of individuals who used Internet from any location in the last three months.' All the data on ICT access and use are from the World Telecommunication/ICT Indicators database (June 2019 Edition).

Results

This section describes the results of our empirical research. First, it briefly examines if digital technologies affect the process of financial instruments diffusion. In the second part, it develops and discusses the country-specific financial innovations (ETFs) development pattern and presents basic descriptive statistics for Japanese and South Korean stock exchanges. It should be emphasized that in our study we associate the development of ETF markets in the absolute dimension (i.e. increase in the value of turnover of ETF units (in USD millions)) with their diffusion on the local financial markets. Finally, in the second part, we analyze the process of substitution between ETFs and similar investment options, i.e. stock index futures and options. The increase in the share of ETFs in the total turnover of index financial instruments is the main indicator in the substitution analysis.

ICT versus ETFs: Empirical study

Fast expansion of innovative financial instruments in Japan and South Korea coincides with rapidly increasing deployment of digital technologies, which – to a large extent – precondition the emergence and further propagation of ETF. Between 2004 and 2019 we observe continuous fast shifts regarding two seminal ICT core indicators – fixed broadband networks and Internet users. Fixed broadband penetration rates grew from 15.2% to 31.1% and from 24.6% to 40.3% in Japan and South Korea accordingly. Similarly, Internet user's penetration rates went up to 93.2% in Japan and 92.8% in South Korea. The latter shows that access to ICT in both countries became ubiquitous in 2019. In the first step of our analysis, we test whether ICT diffusion and growing access to and use of digital technologies is statistically associated with ETF propagation on financial markets. Table 4.1. summarizes respective country-level estimates for Japan and South Korea. Our estimates unequivocally speak in support of our hypothesis that novel solutions offered by digital technologies enhance emergence and development of innovative financial instruments. Estimated coefficients of the lagged value of Internet users are stable, positive, and statistically significant in all three specifications for Japan and for South Korea.

Diffusion and substitution of ETFs: Empirical study

In the first years, the sizes of both ETF markets were minimal. The lowest value of turnover in ETFs in Japan was observed at the beginning of the time period analyzed, i.e. in January 2003; in South Korea, the minimum turnover was c. $111 million in February 2005 (see Figures 4.1. and 4.2.).

Table 4.1 ETF shares versus Internet users: Country-specific models, 2004–2019 (annual series)

	\multicolumn{6}{c}{$LnETFshare_{(i,y)}$}					
	OLS	IV 2SLS	IV 2SLS	OLS	IV 2SLS	IV 2SLS
	\multicolumn{3}{c}{Japan}	\multicolumn{3}{c}{South Korea}			
$LnIU_{(i,y-1)}$	**2.72**	**2.82**	**2.65**	14.5	14.5	15.6
	[0.01]	**[0.91]**	**[0.88]**	[1.73]	[1.65]	[1.68]
R^2	0.41	0.41	0.41	0.85	0.85	0.83
Instrument: $LnFBS_{(i,y-1)}$	No	No	Yes	No	No	Yes
Instrument: $LnIU_{(i,y-2)}$	No	Yes	No	No	Yes	No
# of observations	15	15	15	15	15	15

Source: Authors' estimations. Note: robust SE in square brackets below coefficients. Constants included but not reported. Statistically significant results in bold.

Between 2011 and 2013 the turnover in ETF shares on the South Korean stock exchange was the highest among all Asia-Pacific countries, even though the values of assets under management (AUM) or fund flows lagged behind Japan and China. Overall, the diffusion of ETFs was more pronounced in Japan: in 2003–2015 the mean turnover value in Japan was $9.5 billion versus $5.3 billion in South Korea. The highest values of turnover in ETFs were reached in September 2015 in Japan, and in South Korea in August 2011 (see Figures 4.1. and 4.2.).

However, these results should be interpreted carefully as at those points in time the whole market for index financial instruments reached its record high level in both countries. More meaningful analysis is possible by considering the shares of ETFs – in both countries, the ETF markets reached the highest levels of their development at the end of the 2003–2015 time period (in Japan in October 2015, and in South Korea in July 2014), which indicates growing popularity – this process is analyzed in detail in the next paragraphs. ETFs were the only category of instruments whose market share grew in 2003–2015; the shares of both stock index futures and options declined. In terms of market share, Japan exceeded South Korea by c. 0.3 pp (1.4% versus 1.1%). In Japan, the ETF market consisted mostly of equity ETFs whereas in South Korea their share, while still the highest, was substantially lower. The largest ETFs in South Korea in the time period analyzed were funds tracking the main index of the Korean exchange, KOSPI 200, and the situation was similar in Japan. Therefore, the underlying assets were the same as for stock index options and futures. The leading index financial instrument category in the whole time period considered was stock index futures, both in terms of turnover and their share in the total market – in Japan, their maximum share exceeded 99% in December 2007 and in South Korea 97% in March 2010. This situation was similar to the one observed in majority of other economies.

ICT verus diffusion and substitution 67

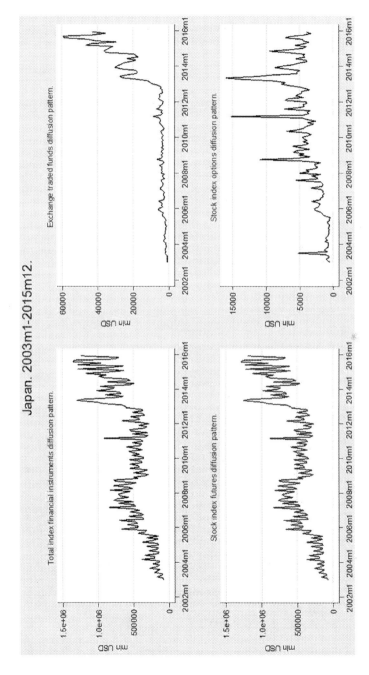

Figure 4.1 Total index financial instruments, exchange-traded funds, stock index options, and stock index futures diffusion patterns in Japan (million USD). Monthly data for 2003–2015.

Source: Authors' elaboration in STATA software.

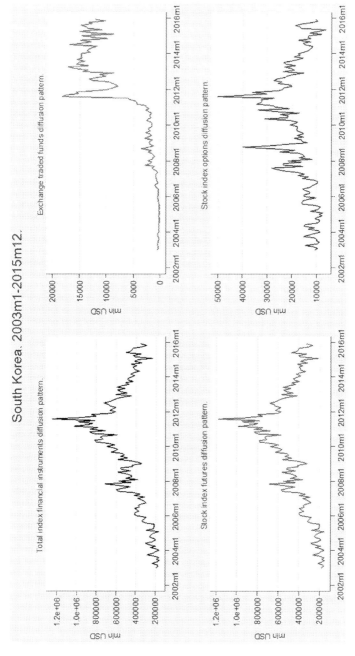

Figure 4.2 Total index financial instruments, exchange-traded funds, stock index options, and stock index futures diffusion patterns in South Korea (million USD). Monthly data for 2003–2015.

Source: Authors' elaboration in STATA software.

Table 4.2 Changes of market shares in the total turnover of index financial instruments in Japan and South Korea. 2003–2015

	Japan			South Korea		
Time	ETFs [%]	Stock Index Options [%]	Stock Index Futures [%]	ETFs [%]	Stock Index Options [%]	Stock Index Futures [%]
2003m12	.70	.31	98.99	.20	5.25	94.55
2004m12	.63	.24	99.14	.11	3.28	96.62
2005m12	.86	40	98.74	.16	3.41	96.43
2006m12	.43	.28	99.29	.19	3.27	96.54
2007m12	.34	.26	99.40	.34	3.55	96.11
2008m12	.74	.69	98.58	.44	5.07	94.49
2009m12	.68	.77	98.55	.24	2.81	96.95
2010m12	.90	.49	98.61	.29	2.96	96.75
2011m12	.79	.93	98.29	1.82	3.94	94.24
2012m12	1.03	1.12	97.86	1.94	3.41	94.64
2013m12	2.96	.85	96.19	3.01	3.46	93.53
2014m12	2.98	.57	96.45	2.97	3.27	93.76
2015m12	3.46	.32	96.22	3.43	2.98	93.59

Source: Authors' elaboration.

The remainder of this section presents the results of the analysis of financial substitution process traceable on the Japanese and South Korean stock exchanges between 2003 and 2015. Tables 4.2. and 4.3. summarize changes in index financial instrument market shares and changes in market shares of ETFs *versus* options considered as total market, in both cases using monthly time series.

Table 4.3 Changing market shares of ETFs versus options considered as total market. Japan and South Korea. 2003-2015

	Japan		South Korea	
Time	ETFs [%]	Stock Index Options [%]	ETFs [%]	Stock Index Options [%]
2003m12	69	31	4	96
2004m12	73	27	4	96
2005m12	68	32	5	95
2006m12	61	39	5	94
2007m12	56	44	8	91
2008m12	52	48	8	92
2009m12	47	53	8	92
2010m12	65	35	9	91
2011m12	46	54	32	68
2012m12	48	52	36	64
2013m12	78	22	47	53
2014m12	84	16	48	52
2015m12	92	8	54	46

Source: Authors' calculations.

As preliminary evidence, in Table 4.2. we briefly discuss shifts in market shares regarding ETFs, stock index options, and stock index futures. Both in Japan and South Koreas fast expansion of ETFs during the period examined is visible, as this category of index instruments was gradually gaining market shares. In Japan, the absolute change in market share was 2.76 pp., while in South Korea the change is 3.23 pp. On the Japanese stock exchange, the growth of this financial innovation parallels a decrease of stock index futures. At the same time, despite several observed changes, the market share of stock index options remained relatively stable between 2003 and 2015. On the contrary, on the South Korean stock exchange, the fast development of ETFs was accompanied by falling market shares of stock index options while the market shares of stock index futures remained relatively unchanged (see Table 4.2.). Hence, a preliminary conclusion may be drawn that in Japan ETFs are gradually gaining market share at the expense of stock index futures, while in South Korea it is at the expense of stock index options. As demonstrated in Table 4.2., in both countries between 2003 and 2015 a huge part of the index financial instruments market belonged to stock index futures. Bearing this in mind, we argue that the process and patterns of financial substitution should be analyzed mostly between exchange-traded funds and stock index options, which we label below as 'Selected Index Financial Instruments.' With this aim, we assume that ETFs and stock index options constitute a separate hypothetical market, and the process of financial substitution is limited to gradually changing market shares between the two index instruments. Put differently, we assume that ETFs as financial innovations are invading the stock exchanges and this generates competition between ETFs and stock index options, eventually leading to increases in the market shares of ETFs.

Table 4.3. shows market shares of ETFs and stock index options in the turnover of selected index financial instruments in Japan and South Korea over the period 2003–2015. It shows that in both Japan and South Korea ETFs as financial innovations are rapidly invading the financial market at the expense of stock index options. In South Korea, however, this change seems to be more radical, as the absolute change (in pp.) between December 2003 and December 2015 was c. 50 pp., while in Japan it was only 23 pp. Despite this, on the Japanese stock exchanges, the role of ETFs in challenging stock index options seems to be more significant. In Japan between 2003 and 2015 the maximum share of ETFs was 91% in December 2015 while the relevant value in South Korea was much lower, reaching 63% in May 2015. Figures 4.3. and 4.4. show the financial substitution effects encountered in the two economies and Table 4.4. summarizes the results from the financial substitution models estimated. Consecutive Figures 4.3. and 4.4 visualize the process of gradual 'switching' from stock index options into ETFs in both examined economies. The process of substitution has taken place at a rather limited rate and during some periods it has been random. On both stock exchanges, ETF and stock index options have competed to win the market share.

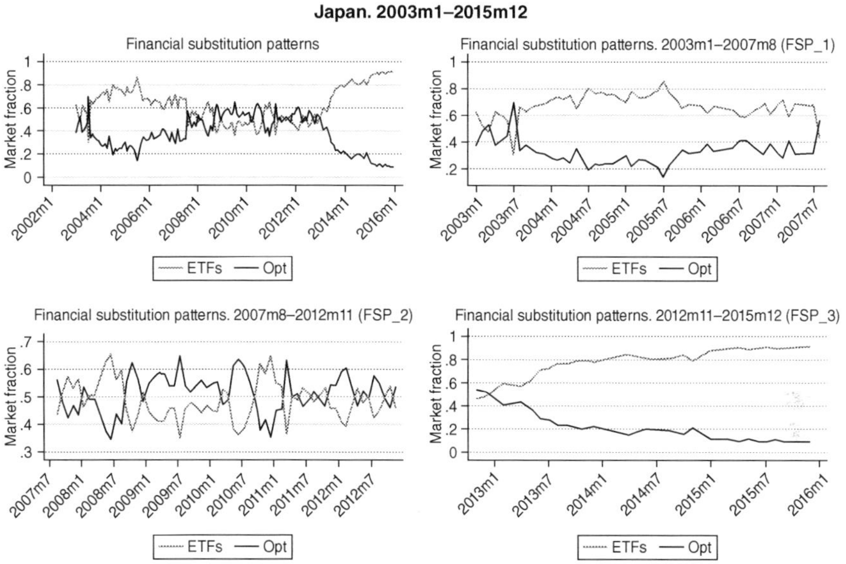

ICT verus diffusion and substitution 71

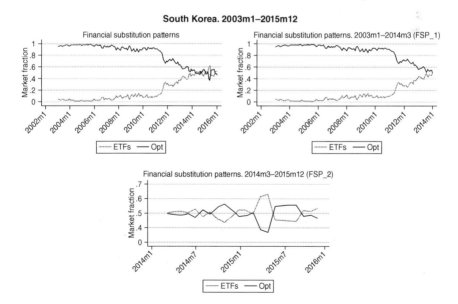

Figure 4.3 Financial substitution patterns. ETFs versus stock index options in Japan. Monthly data for 2003–2015.

Source: Authors' elaboration in STATA software.

Figure 4.4 Financial substitution patterns. ETFs versus stock index options in South Korea. Monthly data for 2003–2015.

Source: Authors' elaboration in STATA software.

Table 4.4 Financial substitution model estimates. Japan and South Korea, 2003–2015

	Japan		South Korea	
	Exchange-traded funds *versus* stock index options			
	Full sample estimates			
Tm_i^δ	−60.2	Substitution not definite.	148.4^T / 135^E	Substitution reported.
Δt_i^δ	1 028		146.5	
	Sub-samples estimates			
Tm_i^δ	2003m1 to 2007m8 (Stage_1_Jap) −480.4	Substitution not definite. Multiple takeovers reported	2003m1 to 2014m3 (Stage_1_Kor) 150.3^T / 135^E	Substitution reported.
Δt_i^δ	3 019.8		149.2	
Tm_i^δ	2007m8 to 2012m11 (Stage_2_Jap) 58.5	Substitution trajectories are random	2014m3 to 2015m12 (Stage_2_Kor) 122.3	Substitution trajectories are random.
Δt_i^δ	2 282.8		10 050	
Tm_i^δ	2012m11 to 2015m12 (Stage_3_Jap) 114.4^T / 121^E	Substitution reported	-	-
Δt_i^δ	71.2		-	

Source: Authors' elaboration. Note: misspecifications in italics; Tm_i^δ – time (month) when financial substitution is half complete (^{T} – theoretical/modelled time of substitution; ^{E} – empirical month of substitution); Δt_i^δ – takeover time (specific number of months).

In Japan, the process of *'ETFs to stock index options'* financial substitution yields special interest. Preliminary examination of data uncovers that the switching process between different types of financial instruments may be perceived as rather random and unclear. If we consider the full-time series analyzed (January 2003 – December 2015) no rigid conclusions can be drawn as the financial substitution is not definite. Moreover, the parameters estimated (Tm_{Jap}^δ and Δt_{Jap}^δ) using financial substitution model are statistically insignificant. More detailed examination of the financial substitution patterns in Japan shows that there are three phases of the process. We divide the full-time series into three stages:

- Stage_1_Jap: January 2003 – August 2007;
- Stage_2_Jap: August 2007 – November 2012;
- Stage_3_Jap: November 2012 – December 2015.

Table 4.4 demonstrates the financial substitution model estimates for each financial substitution phase separately. During the initial stage of the substitution process, our empirical results indicate that in this period ETFs may be regarded as the losing index financial instrument. The financial substitution patterns are revealed as parallel but at the end of the first stage ETFs lose their winning market position and are substituted by stock index options – in August 2008 the share of ETFs was at 47%. The estimated parameters regarding initial stage are statistically insignificant, which may be a consequence of relative instability of substitution patterns during this period. During the second stage of the substitution process, the substitution trajectories are totally random and multiple 'takeovers' are traced. Between August 2007 and November 2012, we observe multiple switching between ETFs and stock index options, and they 'lose and win' the leading market position. This random walk of ETFs and stock index options again results in statistically insignificant financial substitution model estimates. Finally, during the third, final, stage (November 2012 – December 2015) the substitution patterns change sharply. From November 2012 onwards ETFs steadily gain market share, while stock index options – lose. In this stage the substitution patterns constantly diverge, revealing the process of ETF market invasion at the expense of stock index options. The values of the market shares in November 2012 were following: $ETFs^{Jap}\_share\_SIFI = 43\%$ and $Opt^{Jap}\_share\_SIFI = 57\%$ but in December 2015 the respective values were at following levels: $ETFs^{Jap}\_share_{SIFI} = 92\%$ and $Opt^{Jap}\_share_{SIFI} = 8\%$. ETFs have totally taken over the market for selected index financial instruments in Japan by the end of 2015. According to the financial substitution model estimates presented in Table 4.4., Tm^{δ}_{Jap} = month 114.4 (June 2012) (modelled) and Tm^{δ}_{Jap} = month 121 (January 2013) (empirical). This is the time when the process of financial substitution is half complete, hence $f^{\delta}_{Jap}(t) = f^{\theta}_{Jap}(t) = 0.5$. Moreover, the 'take-over' time is estimated as $\Delta t^{\delta}_{Jap} = 71.2$, representing the number of months necessary for the market share of the invading innovative index financial instrument (ETFs) to grow from 10% to 90%.

In case of the second country, South Korea, the substitution process differs compared to that identified in Japan. At the beginning of the period examined, $ETFs^{Kor}\_share\_SIFI$ was about 4.5%, a minimal share of the market. However, from 2003 onwards we observe a gradual yet negligible growth in the ETF market share, still remaining below 10% until the beginning of 2011. From mid-2011 we observe an abrupt shift. In June 2011 $ETFs^{Kor}\_share\_SIFI$ was 14% but in October 2011 $ETFs^{Kor}\_share\_SIFI$ = 33%. Then, in July 2014 it reached 53% and achieved its peak at 63% in May 2015. The parameters from the financial substitution model estimates are statistically significant: Tm^{δ}_{Kor} = month 148 (April 2015) (modelled) and Tm^{δ}_{Kor} = month 135 (March 2014) (empirical). These indicate the time when the process of financial substitution was half complete, when $f^{\delta}_{Kor}(t) = f^{\theta}_{Kor}(t) = 0.5$. Δt^{δ}_{Kor} = 146 months is the number of months needed for $f^{\delta}_{Kor}(t)$ to pass from 10% to 90%. Similar to Japan, distinct phases may be traced for Korea, namely:

- Stage_1_Kor: January 2003 – March 2014;
- Stage_2_Kor: March 2014 – December 2015.

The first stage is characterized by an initial slow growth of the ETF market share, which – as already noted – began to abruptly increase in mid-2011. However, during the whole first phase, we observe that $ETFs^{Kor}\_share\_SIFI < Opt^{Kor}\_share\_SIFI$, while March 2014 is the first month when the ETF market share exceeded the respective value for stock index options. The parameters estimated for the time series covering this first phase are statistically significant, and differ only slightly from the estimates returned from the full sample – see Table 4.4. However, during the second stage, the financial substitution patterns are random and characterized by multiple 'takeovers,' which indicates that between March 2014 and December 2015 ETFs and stock index options were alternately gaining and losing the dominant market position. In the second stage the averages of $Opt^{Kor}\_share\_SIFI$ and $ETFs^{Kor}\_share\_SIFI$ are 49.7% and 50.3% respectively. We can therefore claim that the two market shares were equal between March 2014 and December 2015.

Conclusions

The purpose of this paper was to present in-depth insights into the development of selected financial instruments traded on the stock exchanges in Japan and South Korea, focusing on the development patterns of ETFs. We claim and then provide evidence for the linkages between ETFs and ICT – we show that the emergence and then fast propagation of the innovative financial instruments is preconditioned and strongly determined by digital technologies deployment in both countries. As briefly discussed, both in Japan and South Korea, digital technologies were diffusing at high pace and provided solid background for the emergence of new financial instruments.

In our work, we have concentrated on the potential substitution between ETFs and stock index derivatives which remains an understudied issue in the academic literature. The results of the analysis show that both in Japan and South Korea the local ETF market has been developing (i.e. diffusion of ETFs has occurred) in terms of turnover and of the share in the total market for index financial instruments. One of the key factors in the ETF market development in both economies was the launch of leveraged and short ETFs (subcategories of synthetic ETFs which offer investors modified returns), which soon gained high popularity. These contributed significantly to the diffusion of ETFs in relation to index derivatives as they diminish the key advantages of futures or options in comparison to ETFs.

We have also checked substitution between ETFs and stock index options. The process of 'switching' from stock index options into ETFs was to some extent confirmed for both countries. However, the process of substitution has taken place at a rather limited rate and during some periods it has been random.

Acknowledgment

This chapter is a result of scientific project no. 2015/19/D/HS4/00399 financed by the National Science Centre, Poland.

Note

1. See also Kucharavy and Guio (2011).

References

Agapova, A. (2011). Conventional mutual index funds versus exchange-traded funds. *Journal of Financial Markets, 14*(2), 323–343.

Ahmed, M., Choudhury, N., & Uddin, S. (2017). Anomaly detection on big data in financial markets. In *2017 IEEE/ACM international conference on advances in social networks analysis and mining (ASONAM)* (pp. 998–1001). IEEE.

Al-Busaidi, K. A., & Al-Muharrami, S. (2020). Beyond profitability: ICT investments and financial institutions performance measures in developing economies. *Journal of Enterprise Information Management, 34*(3), https://doi.org/10.1108/JEIM-09-2019-0250.

Alderighi, S. (2020). Cross-listing in the European ETP market. *Economics Bulletin, 40*(1), 35–40.

Aldridge, I. (2013). *High-frequency trading: A practical guide to algorithmic strategies and trading systems.* John Wiley & Sons.

Anadu, K., Kruttli, M., McCabe, P., & Osambela, E. (2020). The shift from active to passive investing: Risks to financial stability? *Financial Analysts Journal, 76*(4), 23–39.

Arnold, M., & Lesné, A. (2015). *The Changing Landscape for Beta Replication – Comparing Futures and ETFs for Equity Index Exposure.* State Street Global Advisors.

Asongu, S. A., & Nwachukwu, J. C. (2019). ICT, financial sector development and financial access. *Journal of the Knowledge Economy, 10*(2), 465–490.

Bai, J., Philippon, T., & Savov, A. (2016). Have financial markets become more informative? *Journal of Financial Economics, 122*(3), 625–654.

Bhunia, A., & Ghosal, A. (2011). An impact of ICT on the growth of capital market-empirical evidence from Indian stock exchange. *South Asian Journal of Marketing & Management Research, 1*(3), 1–10.

Blackman, A. W. Jr (1971). A mathematical model for trend forecasts. *Technological Forecasting and Social Change, 3*, 441–452.

Blitz, D., & Huij, J. (2012). Evaluating the performance of global emerging markets equity exchange-traded funds. *Emerging Markets Review, 13*(2), 149–158.

Chang, C. L., Liu, C. P., & McAleer, M. (2019). Volatility spillovers for spot, futures, and ETF prices in agriculture and energy. *Energy Economics, 81*, 779–792.

Chang, C. L., McAleer, M., & Wang, C. H. (2018). An econometric analysis of ETF and ETF futures in financial and energy markets using generated regressors. *International Journal of Financial Studies, 6*(1), 2.

Chen, J., Chen, Y., & Frijns, B. (2017). Evaluating the tracking performance and tracking error of New Zealand exchange traded funds. *Pacific Accounting Review, 29*(3), 443–462.

Cheng, C. Y., Chien, M. S., & Lee, C. C. (2021). ICT diffusion, financial development, and economic growth: An international cross-country analysis. *Economic Modelling, 94*, 662–671.

CME Group. (2016). *The Big Picture: A Cost Comparison of Futures and ETFs.* https://www.cmegroup.com/trading/equity-index/report-a-cost-comparison-of-futures-and-etfs.html

Cvetanović, S., Ribać, S., & Cvetanović, D. (2018). Financial innovations as a possible sourc e of economic instability. *Knowledge International Journal*, *26*(1), 253–259.

Deville, L. (2008). Exchange traded funds: History, trading and research. In M. Doumpos, P. Pardalos, & C. Zopounidis (Eds.), *Handbook of financial engineering* (pp. 67–98). Springer US.

Diaz-Rainey, I., Ibikunle, G., & Mention, A. (2015). The technological transformation of capital markets. *Technological Forecasting and Social Change*, *99*, 277–284.

Drummer, D., Feuerriegel, S., & Neumann, D. (2017). Crossing the next frontier: The role of ICT in driving the financialization of credit. *Journal of Information Technology*, *32*(3), 218–233.

Dutta, S., Essaddam, N., Kumar, V., & Saadi, S. (2017). How does electronic trading affect efficiency of stock market and conditional volatility? Evidence from Toronto stock exchange. *Research in International Business and Finance*, *39*, 867–877.

Eurex (2016). *Futures or ETFs? – Not as simple as yes or no*. https://www.eurex.com/ec-en/find/news/futures-or-etfs-140344

Fisher, J. C., & Pry, R. H. (1972). A simple substitution model of technological change. *Technological Forecasting and Social Change*, *3*, 75–88.

Gastineau, G. L. (2010). *The exchange-traded funds manual*. John Wiley & Sons.

Goltz, F., & Schröder, D. (2011). Passive investing before and after the crisis: Investors' views on exchange-traded funds and competing index products. *Bankers, Markets & Investors*, *110*, 5–20.

Hendershott, T., Jones, C. M., & Menkveld, A. J. (2011). Does algorithmic trading improve liquidity? *The Journal of Finance*, *66*(1), 1–33.

Huang, B., Huan, Y., Xu, L. D., Zheng, L., & Zou, Z. (2019). Automated trading systems statistical and machine learning methods and hardware implementation: A survey. *Enterprise Information Systems*, *13*(1), 132–144.

Kaur, P., & Singh, J. (2020). Price formation in Indian gold market: Analysing the role of gold exchange traded funds (ETFs) against spot and futures markets. *IIMB Management Review*, *32*(1), 59–74.

Kim, H. M. (2019). *Globalization of international financial markets: Causes and consequences*. Routledge.

Kirilenko, A., Kyle, A. S., Samadi, M., & Tuzun, T. (2017). The flash crash: High-frequency trading in an electronic market. *The Journal of Finance*, *72*(3), 967–998.

Klagge, B., & Martin, R. (2005). Decentralized versus centralized financial systems: Is there a case for local capital markets? *Journal of Economic Geography*, *5*(4), 387–421.

Knell, M. (2015). Schumpeter, Minsky and the financial instability hypothesis. *Journal of Evolutionary Economics*, *25*(1), 293–310.

Kucharavy, D., & De Guio, R. (2011). Logistic substitution model and technological forecasting. *Procedia Engineering*, *9*, 402–416.

Lechman, E. (2015). *ICT diffusion in developing countries: Towards a new concept of technological takeoff*. Springer.

Li, S., & Marinč, M. (2018). Economies of scale and scope in financial market infrastructures. *Journal of International Financial Markets, Institutions and Money*, *53*, 17–49.

Liebi, L. J. (2020). The effect of ETFs on financial markets: A literature review. *Financial Markets and Portfolio Management*, in press.

Liu, Q., & Tse, Y. (2017). Overnight returns of stock indexes: Evidence from ETFs and futures. *International Review of Economics & Finance*, *48*, 440–451.

MacDonald, M. (2017). International capital market frictions and spillovers from quantitative easing. *Journal of International Money and Finance*, *70*, 135–156.

Madhavan, A. N., Marchioni, U., Li, W., & Du, Y. (2014). Equity ETFs versus index futures: A comparison for fully funded investors. *Institutional Investor Journal*, *5*(2), 66–75.

Marchetti, C., & Nakicenovic, N. (1979). *The dynamics of energy systems and the logistic substitution model*. Laxenburg: International Institute for Applied Systems Analysis.

Marszk, A., & Lechman, E. (2020). Application of diffusion models in the analysis of financial markets: Evidence on exchange traded funds in Europe. *Risks*, *8*(1).

Marszk, A., & Lechman, E. (2021). Reshaping financial systems: The role of ICT in the diffusion of financial innovations – Recent evidence from European countries. *Technological Forecasting and Social Change*, *167*.

Marszk, A., Lechman, E., & Kato, Y. (2019). *The emergence of ETFs in Asia-Pacific*. Springer International Publishing.

Meyer, P., Yung, J. W., & Ausubel, J. H. (1999). A primer on logistic growth and substitution: The mathematics of the loglet lab software. *Technological Forecasting and Social Change*, *61*(3), 247–271.

Michaelsen, M. (2020). Information flow dependence in financial markets. *International Journal of Theoretical and Applied Finance (IJTAF)*, *23*(05), 1–34.

Morris, S. A., & Pratt, D. (2003). Analysis of the Lotka–Volterra competition equations as a technological substitution model. *Technological Forecasting and Social Change*, *70*(2), 103–133.

Nishimura, K. G. (2010). *Electronic trading and financial markets*. Bank of Japan.

Nwogugu, M. I. (2018). *Indices, index funds and ETFs*. London: Palgrave Macmillan.

Pantielieieva, N., Krynytsia, S., Khutorna, M., & Potapenko, L. (2018). FinTech, transformation of financial intermediation and financial stability. In *2018 International scientific-practical conference problems of infocommunications. Science and technology (PIC S&T)* (pp. 553–559). IEEE.

Pozzi, F., Di Matteo, T., & Aste, T. (2013). Spread of risk across financial markets: Better to invest in the peripheries. *Scientific Reports*, *3*(1), 1–7.

Schaper, T. (2012). Organising equity exchanges. *Information Systems and E-Business Management*, *10*(1), 43–60.

Schmiedel, H., Malkamäki, M., & Tarkka, J. (2006). Economies of scale and technological development in securities depository and settlement systems. *Journal of Banking & Finance*, *30*(6), 1783–1806.

Thiagarajan, R., Lacaille, R. F., Im, H., & Wang, J. (2019). The need for speed: Does high-frequency trading make or break equity markets? *The Journal of Index Investing*, *10*(2), 6–23.

Wang, M. Y., & Lan, W. T. (2007). Combined forecast process: Combining scenario analysis with the technological substitution model. *Technological Forecasting and Social Change*, *74*(3), 357–378.

World Federation of Exchanges (2020). *WFE Database*. https://www.world-exchanges.org/our-work/statistics

Part 2:
FinTech: Selected issues

5 FinTechs, BigTechs and structural changes in capital markets

Janina Harasim

Introduction

The financial industry has experienced many waves of technological innovation. While these have been shifting the balance in the financial system from banks towards financial markets and specialized players, the overall structure of the financial industry with banks at its core has remained remarkably robust (Philippon, 2015). However, the ongoing changes in the financial industry appear to be more fundamental than previous ones and may have considerable impact on competition and the market structure. There is a growing body of literature confirming that technology can impact not only features of financial services (such as speed, transparency, cost, and security) but also the market structure, especially on the supply side, i.e., the organization of financial service providers (Alt et al., 2018; Boot et al., 2020; He et al., 2017).

The rapid development of technology can affect the market structure in the financial services industry in a multitude of ways. However, when analyzing competition, the entry of technology firms (usually referred as "FinTech") into the provision of financial services cannot be neglected. There is some evidence that their dynamic expansion, supported by certain regulatory initiatives (e.g., PDS2, "regulatory sandboxes") may lead to ground-breaking changes in the market structure, which could have significant implications for competition in the financial industry as well as for the position of incumbent institutions.

The potential impact of FinTech development on competition and market structure is increasingly more often analyzed, but the vast majority of studies focus on its consequences for banks, their market position, and strategy (Alt et al., 2018; Bank for International Settlements, 2018, 2019; European Banking Authority, 2018; Financial Stability Board, 2019; Frost et al., 2019; Navaretti et al., 2018; Petralia et al., 2019; Stulz, 2019) To date, researchers have paid only limited attention to the analysis of the impact of technology companies on competition in financial markets. Therefore, the considerations set out in this chapter fit into the gap existing in the literature.

DOI: 10.4324/9781003095354-5

This chapter aims at exploring some theoretical issues associated with the impact of technology companies on competition and the market structure in the financial industry. To significantly contribute to the present state of knowledge, attention is focused on analyzing structural changes taking place in capital markets. This chapter begins with the explanation, supported by the industrial organization theory (IO), how technology affects the market structure in the financial industry, especially market imperfections and market contestability. The next section shows the impact of FinTechs and BigTechs on competition in the financial industry. Contrary to most previous studies, it has been assumed that their impact should be analyzed separately due to the significant differences between them regarding their size, scale of activity, specific features, and the extent to which the assets and features of both complement or substitute those of incumbents. The next two parts focus on those capital market segments that have most been influenced by digitalization, i.e., the stock market and the asset management and mutual funds industry. In the case of the stock market more attention has been paid to electronic trading and FinTech solutions transforming the organization of securities trading. In the second case, it is shown how digital platforms have been changing the structure of the asset management and mutual funds industry.

General impact of technology on the market structure in the financial industry

In order to explain how technology could affect the market structure in the financial services industry, it is necessary to remind ourselves of traditional theories of intermediation. These are built on the notion that financial intermediaries serve to reduce market imperfections: information asymmetry (which helps minimize problems of moral hazard and adverse selection), communication frictions (by facilitating match-making among interested parties), and decrease in transaction costs (Allen & Santomero, 1997). However, in recent decades, there have been significant changes that are difficult to reconcile with the traditional theories. Scholtens and Van Wensveen (2003) noticed that as developments in information technology, deregulation, deepening of financial markets tend to reduce transaction costs and market imperfections, the financial intermediation theory fails to provide a satisfactory understanding of the existence of traditional financial intermediaries.

Given that, there is a need to explain how technology may affect market structure and financial intermediation using other theoretical basis. Useful guidance on this topic is provided by industrial organization economics (IO), called sometimes "the economics of imperfect competition." According to IO, technology can affect any of the basic determinants of the market structure (see Table 5.1.).

First, technology can undermine the need for intermediaries by altering market imperfections found in the financial system. The proliferation of the

Table 5.1 Technology impact on the market structure in the financial services industry

Determinant	Impact direction	Examples
Market imperfections		
Information asymmetry	↘	Proliferation of internet (wide and cheap access to information) Automated credit scoring
Communication frictions	↘	Digital platforms – two-sided and multisided (crowdfunding and peer-to-peer platforms, comparison sites for financial products)
Transaction costs	↘	Online and mobile payments Blockchain, robo-advising, smart contracts
Market contestability	↗	The factors mentioned above, back-office automation, the ability to source IT infrastructure through cloud computing services
Integration level of traditional financial intermediaries		
Vertical	↘	Loss of customer interface (e.g., APIs in payment services)
Horizontal	↘	Specialized new entrants (including FinTechs), high cross-selling potential of digital platforms

Source: own study.

internet lowers information asymmetry, making information more available and cheaper since vast amounts of data can be acquired at low cost through web-scraping. This reduces the information gap and increases both market contestability and efficiency of financial markets (Bai et al., 2016; Boot et al., 2020; Gao & Huang, 2020). There is also evidence that automated credit scoring or internal ratings used by platforms, based on non-financial data about customers, performs as well or even better than traditional credit scores in assessing borrower/default risk (Frost et al., 2019; Hau et al., 2019). Most technological innovations have decreased transaction costs, and digital platforms have reduced communication frictions as they more effectively match savers and borrowers (peer-to-peer and crowdfunding platforms) or buyers and sellers (digital marketplaces), consolidate information (comparison sites for financial products), and enable peer-to-peer (P2P) communication (social media).

Second, by enhancing economies of scale and reducing transaction costs and information asymmetry, technological innovations, in general, lower barriers to entry that may increase competition and market contestability. He et al. (2017) provide many examples of the ways that technology can promote market contestability, e.g., they claim that back-office automation allows firms to reduce fixed costs. Boot et al. (2020) highlight another example – according to them the ability to source IT infrastructure through the cloud considerably lowers the barriers to entry, thus increasing market contestability.

Third, technology can affect the level of horizontal and vertical integration of incumbents, especially banks, which are typically vertically and horizontally integrated financial intermediaries. The vertical integration arises from the strategic advantage of relying on core competencies to compete in upstream segments or control upstream activity. This means that banks directly interact with customers in their core maturity transformation business (i.e., when raising deposits and making loans). However, the rise of digital platforms fundamentally changes the way goods and services are distributed and poses a severe threat to banks. Platforms can capture most existing rents and lots of customer data by intercepting the customer interface from banks. As a consequence, banks can lose their position of "first point of contact" for financial services and face the risk of vertical disintegration (Boot et al., 2020).

Horizontal integration comes from economies of scope which means that banks (e.g., through cross-selling) can provide multiple services that do not directly rely on a balance sheet (e.g., payments, advisory services, asset/wealth management, or insurance), using information on savers and borrowers and their behavior. However, such financial services can also be provided by non-bank specialized providers (especially FinTech firms), which can outperform banks in terms of speed, convenience and price. The degree of banks' horizontal integration could also be damaged by the high cross-selling potential of digital platforms, which can offer financial services (complementary to their offer) based on their deep knowledge of user's behavior.

Thus, according to IO, the impact of modern technologies on competition and the structure of the financial industry should be generally positive. However, is it in fact the case? Does the ongoing digitalization also bring about threats to competition? Does it only change products and processes or does it also affect the market structure? Crémer et al. (2019) argue that traditionally understood competition – with a large number of firms competing – is often not feasible in the digital economy, which seems to be confirmed by IO theory. This is probably due to the increasing opportunities created by modern technologies and emergence of entities that utterly transform the way in which products and services, including financial ones, are structured, provisioned, and consumed. The technologies with the greatest impact on the financial industry include application programming interfaces (APIs), artificial intelligence (AI) and machine learning (ML), data analytics, distributed ledger technology (DLT)/blockchain, cloud services and mobile technology, and those entities who can best exploit their potential are technology companies, called FinTechs.

Entry of FinTechs and BigTechs into finance and their impact on competition

Even though FinTech is a buzzword in the financial industry in recent years, it has not been clearly defined yet. On the basis of the current ways of understanding the term "FinTech," Harasim and Mitręga-Niestrój (2018) distinguished two approaches to apprehend it: objective (functional) and subjective (institutional).

In the first of them, FinTech is broadly understood as the use of innovative technologies in order to provide financial services more effectively (Arner et al., 2015; Financial Stability Board, 2017; Lee & Kim, 2015). In the second approach, FinTech is understood more narrowly as the sector created by non-traditional providers of financial services, using innovative technologies to more effectively provide existing services or/and create new ones, which enables the delivery of new value to customers (Harasim & Mitręga-Niestrój, 2018, p. 173). However, only the latter approach allows to measure the development of the FinTech sector and to assess how it affects competition in the financial industry.

In most studies to date, all technology companies operating in the financial sector were included in the FinTech sector. However, this is not a homogeneous group of entities as it encompasses both small innovative technology companies, often start-ups which will be called FinTechs, and the technology giants, known as BigTechs. While the activity of FinTechs is closely related to the provision of financial services, BigTechs provide primarily non-financial services. The dominant areas of BigTechs' activity are social media, search engines, and e-commerce, but their main revenues streams come from targeted advertising. They are large companies, highly capitalized, with the cutting-edge technologies, usually operating on a global or international scale. They are present in all regions of the world, but the largest BigTechs come from the United States and China. In the first case, they are Google, Apple, Facebook, and Amazon, collectively referred to as GAFA, and in the second, Baidu, Alibaba, and Tencent referred to as BAT.

Taking into account the differences between various technology companies, it is reasonable to distinguish between two main types of tech firms:

- FinTechs, which are usually small technology firms focused on the development of products and/or process innovations in the financial services industry, with special emphasis on improving user's experience.
- BigTechs, i.e., large technology companies with an established market position that mainly offer non-financial goods and services (both tangible and digital) via digital platforms, which enter into finance to complement their own offer and gather additional customer data.

Assessing the impact of FinTechs and BigTechs on the shape of financial industry is not easy due to the lack of precise identification criteria (for both),[1] and the relatively short time elapsed since the first financial services were offered by them (for BigTechs). Nevertheless, it is possible to identify the main opportunities and threats related to their expansion into finance (see Figure 5.1.), as most of them have a significant impact on competition and the market structure.

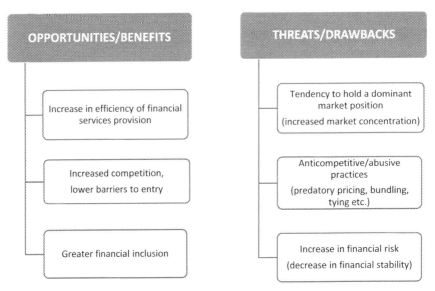

Figure 5.1 Opportunities and threats connected with the entry of FinTechs and BigTechs into finance.

Source: own study.

The opportunities shown in Figure 5.1. are interrelated. The main sources of the competitive advantage of technology companies over incumbents are low transaction costs and low costs of collecting, processing, and analyzing customer data. As a result, they are able to provide financial services in a more effective way, and also offer them to people for whom they were previously unavailable, thus increasing the level of financial inclusion. The undisputed advantages of their expansion into finance are also higher quality of financial services and efficiency of their provision, faster innovation development, increased market competition, and lower barriers to entry.

Although most of the opportunities and threats listed in Figure 5.1. are connected with the expansion of both BigTechs and FinTechs, it should be emphasized that the impact of BigTechs on competition in the financial sector is much greater than that of Fintechs. This difference arises from a much larger scale of BigTechs' activity, their distinctive platform-based business model, and the fact that their features and resources rather substitute those of incumbents. For this reason, when assessing the impact of technology companies on competition and market structure, FinTechs and BigTechs should be treated separately.

The general impact of FinTechs on competition should be more positive than that of BigTechs. Taking into account that FinTechs are generally small young start-ups, and that their resources and features largely complement those of incumbents, the likelihood that they would choose collaboration with traditional market players is greater than that they would compete with them. The fundamental advantage of FinTechs over incumbents is that they are operated as leaner and more agile businesses. Their high-tech capabilities enable them to respond to changing customer expectations in a quicker and more flexible manner, and moreover, they can do it at a low cost, using transparent pricing. They also have the ability to attract talented young people and create innovative solutions which improve user's experience. For these reasons, FinTechs can become a valuable intermediary between incumbents and customers by providing advanced technology solutions that allow financial services and the way they are delivered to be improved, making them more convenient and better suited to satisfying customer preferences.

Positive impact of BigTechs on competition is most evident only in the short term. In the long term, negative effects may prevail, which is mainly related to the BigTech's business model and the features of the platforms they use.

The platform-based business model exploits the most important characteristics of the digital economy: the key role of data, network effects, rapidly growing economies of scale, and economies of scope. BigTechs collect vast amounts of non-financial data through multi-sided platforms which enable direct interactions among a large number of users (buyers and sellers). The large stock of user data enables the use of bigdata analytic tools, such as AI/ML, to enhance existing services that exploit natural network effects and to foster further user activity. Offering financial services can complement and reinforce BigTechs' ecosystem, as payment or lending services generate additional customer data. Having access to new sources of information about customers, in particular data on their financial situation and spending habits, BigTechs can better target advertising and boost the sales of their own products/services. Combining their cutting-edge technology with rich financial and consumer habit information and a stronger customer focus, BigTechs have the communication and informational capacity to compete, and possibly even outperform incumbents in financial services provision.

However, over time, digital platforms may strive to create and maintain dominant market power by maximizing network effects and economies of scale and scope, which subsequently may lead to an increase in market concentration (Evans & Schmalensee, 2007; Fraile Carmona et al., 2018; Rochet & Tirole, 2003; Tucker, 2019). This is because the same features that bring benefits in the short term can generate new risks associated with their market power in the long run. Digital platforms tend to establish captive ecosystems[2] which negatively affect competition. Once such a system is established, potential competitors have little room to build and develop rival platforms. Moreover, by consolidating their dominant position, leading platforms may raise entry barriers excluding competitors from the market (lock-out effect).[3] On the other hand, they can exert their market power to increase user switching costs (lock-in effect), i.e., making it more difficult to change the provider.

Apart from the risks associated with the abuse of market power, BigTechs may use many anti-competitive practices, such as: tying and bundling products,[4] cross-subsidization,[5] and misuse of customer data (Bank for International Settlements, 2019). The first one reduces the price transparency of the offer and of the provider's cost structure and can be perceived as a particular form of price discrimination. The last one is associated with the informational advantage of BigTechs which can be used not only to reduce costs and increase market efficiency but also to apply price discrimination (Bar-Gill, 2019). In extreme cases, this can lead to the exclusion of some customers from accessing particular services. The activity of BigTechs may also generate many risks, including the threat to financial stability (systemic risk), however, this problem goes beyond the scope of this study.

Which of the described effects of BigTechs' expansion will prevail: positive or negative, depends essentially on what is the main driver of their expansion into finance. If the competitive advantage of BigTechs over incumbents, e.g., lower transaction costs, access to better information, and superior technology is a key driver of their entry, this can bring greater efficiency to the provision of financial services and greater financial inclusion. On the other hand, if such an entry is driven primarily by a desire to create and maintain market power (due to network and synergy effects) as well as regulatory arbitrage and additional risk-taking, the consequences of their expansion may be mainly negative and less desirable in welfare terms.

Due to the fact that BigTechs address their services primarily to individuals, and the core financial products they offer, so far, are payments and loans, they pose the greatest threat to banks. However, taking into account the rapid pace of their expansion, the question arises whether they may also threaten the position of traditional financial intermediaries operating on financial markets? There is also a question about the role of FinTechs in financial markets – do the solutions they provide only improve products and processes as well as increase the efficiency of markets or do they significantly change their structure?

An in-depth analysis of the existing literature allowed to identify those financial market segments that changed the most due to digitalization. The first segment is the stock market, and the second is the asset management and mutual fund industry.

FinTech and structural changes on the stock market

Traditionally, the key intermediaries in the primary markets were merchant banks and underwriters and in the secondary markets – stock exchanges and stockbrokers who above all provided liquidity. As the services they offered were relatively costly, their provision was rather limited for both individuals investing and smaller companies raising capital. With the development of technology, capital markets have moved from a traditional specialist model to a technology-driven model where liquidity is primarily provisioned by the buy-side.

Modern technologies have changed the entire securities value chain, but not all of its components have been digitized to the same extent. They heavily influenced trading (price discovery and order execution) and post-trade processes (clearing and settlement, servicing, and administration), and had only limited impact on the front end (client coverage and sales) – see Table 5.2.

Technological changes in the capital market considerably accelerated after the financial crisis. The resulting increased regulatory and capital requirements weakened the position of incumbents and challenged their business models, facilitating the entry of FinTechs into the market. FinTechs have the flexibility, customer proximity, and technology understanding necessary to address business challenges across the entire value chain of capital markets. They provide solutions that (Deutsche Börse & Celent, 2016):

Table 5.2 Digitalization in the stock market

Time period	Trading		Settlement
	Organization of trading venues	Price discovery and order execution	
1971		First fully automated stock trading in National Association of Securities Dealers Automated Quotations (NASDAQ)	-
The 80's	Regional stock exchanges	Open outcry trading floors Designated Order Turnaround (SuperDOT trading system launched by NASDAQ (1984) Electronic trading introduced in London Stock Exchange (1986)	No fixed settlement period
The 90's	Consolidation of the regional stock exchanges	Electronic trading introduced in Borsa Italiana (1994), Toronto Stock Exchange (1997), and Tokyo Stock Exchange (1999)	T+5 settlements Electronic stock registers and dematerialization
From 2000	Fragmentation of trading venues	Internet-based stock trading Algorithmic trading High Frequency Trading (HFT)	Competition between clearing houses
From 2010	-	Electronic trading introduced in New York Stock Exchange (2014) Smart contracts	Clearing house inter-operability T+2 settlements DLT technology (blockchain)

Source: own study.

- Improve the market infrastructure (efficient and intelligent platforms for trading and clearing, new assets classes, API, and cloud services used to seamlessly manage market infrastructure).
- Enable post-trade digitization (automation of compliance, regulatory, collateral management, and securities lending processes, innovative solutions to manage risk attribution and reporting processes).
- Facilitate investment decision-making (robo-advisors, software, online and mobile tools enabling the creation of individual investment strategies).
- Create alternative funding opportunities (lending and other funding platforms).

Electronic trading systems, which have already been introduced on many exchanges (not only stock but also derivatives and commodity exchanges) and other trading venues, facilitate algorithmic and high-frequency trading. In 2015, HFT was reported to account for approximately 55% of trading volume in the US equity markets, and between 23% and 43% of value traded, or 58% and 76% of orders, in the European equity markets (Balp & Strampelli, 2018, p. 3). These technologies created capabilities that no human trader could ever offer, such as assimilating and integrating vast quantities of data and executing thousands of trades at a nanosecond speed with no human intervention (Chaboud et al., 2014; Johnson et al., 2013). As a result, automated high-frequency traders have largely replaced human ones, i.e., the market-making activities traditionally performed by broker-dealers.

HFT impacted not only organization of trading on the stock markets, but also market efficiency and the level of centralization of stock trading. However, this impact is assessed in an ambiguous way. Jain (2005), as well as Hendershott and Moulton (2011), are of the opinion that HFT enhances market efficiency, making stock markets more efficient. On the other hand, Garvey and Wu (2010) or Balp and Strampelli (2018) deem that permissible by regulations two-tiered access to information creates an unfair advantage for HFT and in consequence, can threaten stock markets' long-term efficiency. There is also more and more evidence that algorithmic trading has accelerated the speculative behavior of the market participants (Hasbrouck & Saar, 2013; Riordan & Storkenmaier, 2012). The development of algorithmic trading, including HFT, increased the centralization of trading on exchanges, as the central servers turned out to be more powerful and sophisticated to cope with massive data flows (Geranio, 2016). Thus, centralization of trading resulting from the technological advances, combined with multilayered market infrastructure, neither facilitated access to investment for individuals nor the ability of smaller firms to raise and access capital, but rather additionally hindered them.

The technology which can decentralize trading on the capital market is DLT more commonly known as the blockchain (the latter is in fact a type of DLT). DLT allows for transactions and data to be recorded, shared, and synchronized across a distributed network of different network participants and offers unique benefits in terms of consensus, efficiency, and security (Casey et al., 2018; World Bank, 2017). DLT has great potential to change the way the capital market works. Not only could it facilitate access to the market for smaller investors/firms, but also reduces transaction costs (by streamlining processing and eliminating intermediate steps) and capital costs (by shortening settlement time and more efficient use of collateral), level of risk (credit risk, settlement risk, operational risk, cyber risk, and even systematic risk) (HSBC Securities Services, 2019), and increases market transparency by potentially eliminating the burdens of regulatory reporting and discouraging market abuse (Innovate Finance, 2016).

DLT has many potential applications, as it can be applied to the entire securities value chain, beginning with listing (issuing), through trading, clearing, and settlement up to reporting for OTC securities and derivatives markets. Many large financial institutions, but also FinTechs, are experimenting with DLT and blockchain. The most well-known example is the R3 consortium formed mainly by banks in 2016, which created an open-source distributed ledger platform Corda and helps develop blockchain technology. Blockchain is also used by institutions related to capital markets in many countries, e.g., The Directorate of Defense Trade Controls (DTCC) in the United States is rebuilding its credit default swaps processing platform with blockchain, the Australian and Toronto Stock Exchanges are using blockchain to replace legacy settlement systems, and the Tel Aviv Stock Exchange is working on putting collateral management on a ledger (Accenture, 2018).

However, after the initial enthusiasm with which blockchain was approached by the financial industry, there is more and more skepticism about the possibility of achieving the expected benefits of using DLT (Lee, 2018).[6] The widespread deployment of this technology is hampered by existing regulations which are not adapted to the use of DLT in the financial sector (including competition law), the lack of common standards and interoperability, insufficient skills and knowledge for firms to develop, operate, and monitor DLT effectively (HSBC Securities Services, 2019; Innovate Finance, 2016). Furthermore, Ellul et al. (2020) note that the limited ability for software and data errors to be rectified which result from decentralized nature of DLT pose regulatory challenges to providing protection for the various users and stakeholders of this technology.

While FinTechs provide many technological solutions implemented on capital markets, BigTechs have not been very active in this market segment so far. This does not mean, however, that their expansion has no impact on the capital market. It is indirect in nature and results mainly from their rapidly growing market value and noticeable activity in the area of mergers and acquisitions. The market capitalization of American BigTechs is greater than that of the largest global financial institutions, such as JP Morgan or Bank of America (Frost et al., 2019). In mid-2020, the total market capitalization of five American BigTechs – Apple, Amazon, Microsoft, Alphabet

(Google), and Facebook – amounted to almost USD 6.9 trillion, and their weighted share in the S&P 500 index exceeded 25%. COVID pandemic further strengthens their market power and impact on the stock market – in the first half of 2020, their revenues and year-to-date price returns were growing steadily compared to the first half of 2019 (Ali, 2020). Additionally, BigTechs have taken over many small innovative companies in recent years. As a result, regulators in the United States and China, at the end of 2020, launched antitrust probes into tech giants (GAFA and Alibaba respectively) complaining that they restrict competition and hinder the development of innovation by buying startups in order to keep them from becoming competitors (Zhu et al., 2020).

The rise of digital platforms in the asset management and mutual funds industry

The asset management and mutual funds industry is the second segment that has considerably changed with the digitalization.

Traditional wealth/asset managers (i.e., private banks, bank brokers, registered investment advisors) serve all customer segments with investible capital, i.e., ultra-high net worth, high net worth, and mass affluent customers. The latter segment is the largest, but for a long time, it did not have access to individual advice and a personalized offer. The development of technology has enabled this group of underserved customers to use more sophisticated investment opportunities, taking advantage of social trading tools and platforms and retail algorithmic trading (World Economic Forum, 2015). The first one offers less-experienced investors the opportunity to gain experience and understanding, e.g., by participating in copy trading which allows them to simply replicate the portfolios of top-performing traders (e.g., eToro, Estimize, Stocktwits). The second solution enables investors with limited technical knowledge to create, backtest, and deploy trading algorithms and share them with others (Streak, Quantopian & Zipline, Numerai). These solutions delivered mainly by FinTechs are the easiest and quickest ways to maximize returns. They are also cost-effective – unlike traditional investment management, most social trading platforms do not require a minimum investment threshold to get started.

However, the real breakthrough that changed the structure of the asset management and mutual funds industry was the rise of digital platforms. Evans and Gawer (2016) in their in-depth study divided digital platforms into four types: transaction, innovation, integrated, and investment platforms. The largest number of platforms identified by them, as many as 160 out of 176, belonged to the first type. Transaction platforms enable highly efficient matching between different types of users, and/or the platform provider itself. By maximizing network effects as well as increasing economies of scale, they may significantly impact the structure of the financial markets. Transaction platforms operate in various segments of the financial markets

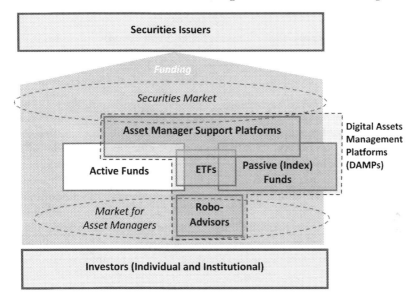

Figure 5.2 Digital platforms in asset management[7].
Source: Haberly et al. (2019, p. 171).

(e.g., the foreign exchange market - Forex or FX), however, their impact on the market structure has been particularly visible in the asset management and mutual funds industry in recent years. The platforms operating in those market segments were called DAMPs (digital asset management platforms) by Haberly et al. (2019). They distinguished four of their types: index funds, EFTs, asset manager support platforms, and robo-advisors (see Figure 5.2.).

Index funds and Exchange Traded Fund (ETFs) both are passively managed investment vehicles designed to mimic the performance of other assets (Marszk & Lechman, 2019). Investing in those funds through the platforms is more accessible and cheaper than in mutual funds due to the low entry thresholds, lower taxation, and relatively low management fees. Index funds and ETF platforms have dramatically enhanced the market functional efficiency. The rise of ETF platforms has also changed the market structure as ETFs can be bought and sold just like regular stocks throughout the trading day, with prices fluctuating constantly as opposed to mutual funds, which are only priced at the end of the day.

Both described types of platforms can be defined as product-driven transaction platforms as opposed to asset manager support platforms, which are rather process-driven as they provide services to both active and passive managers, including portfolio risk management, trading optimization and execution, and regulatory compliance support. By using sophisticated data-driven analytics, they increase both the fundamental valuation efficiency and functional efficiency of the securities market. The robo-advisors' platforms can, in turn, be referred to as customer-driven transaction platforms as they generally operate in the retail market, where they offer high-value advisory services on portfolio allocation based on automated analysis (D'Acunto et al., 2019). Due to the fact that they boost all aspects of market efficiency in a complementary way, they are most similar to platforms operating outside the financial sector.

As demonstrated by Haberly et al. (2019), the entry of platforms significantly increased the level of concentration of the global asset management industry – the three largest passive management companies, i.e., BlackRock, Vanguard, and State Street, controlled in 2016 53% of the global index fund market and as much as 82% of the ETF market in terms of assets under management (AUM) while the actively-managed funds segment remains fragmented with the 10 largest managers worldwide having 27% of market share (and 3 largest companies having only 10% of market share). This concentration was also high in the robo-advising segment, where Vanguard Personal Advisor has half the size of the market share of the next nine companies representing mainly FinTech sector (such as Betterment, Wealthfront, Personal Capital, or Acorns)

Haberly et al. (2019) also note that, like other digital platforms, DAMPs do not deploy so much leverage technology to enhance their competitiveness within markets, as to radically restructure the market itself. However, unlike them, DAMPs were not introduced from the outside, but they have mostly been developed endogenously by leading financial asset management firms. As a result, instead of weakening the position of incumbents, DAMPs reinforced it.

So far, most BigTech companies do not offer asset management services which are complex financial products. Providing them requires risk management skills, as well as knowledge and experience in dealing with regulations, which are not strong points of tech giants. Only Chinese BigTechs offer investment services – in 2011, Alibaba Group launched the Yu'e Bao platform, and six years later, Tencent launched the LiCaitong platform. However, they mainly create opportunities for short-term investments in money market funds – offering such an opportunity allows BigTechs to manage surplus cash in online and mobile payment accounts of platform users. The Yu'e Bao fund offered to AliPay users became in 2018 the largest money market fund in the world in terms of AUM, however, recently its assets have decreased substantially (by almost 40%) because of tighter regulation in China and growing competition from higher-yielding (but risky) wealth management products.

While some money market funds are offered by Chinese BigTechs, mutual funds, in general, are increasingly distributed in China, as in the United States and many other countries, via digital stand-alone platforms. According to Cerulli Associates, in mid-2020, online platforms accounted for 24.7% of the total AUM of mutual funds in China (Acosta, 2020). Nonetheless, recently the Chinese BigTechs have created the possibility for their users to purchase mutual funds directly from asset management firms which can open accounts on platforms operated by them. An example of such a solution is the Caifuhao platform launched by the Alibaba Group in 2017, which is an open marketplace for third-party financial institutions not only Chinese, but also the largest foreign asset managers, such as Vanguard, Schroders, Alliance Bernstein, and Fidelity.

In China, mutual funds are available not only via online platforms but also via mobile applications. As shown by Hong et al. (2020), this impacts the structure of the mutual fund industry as well as the behavior of investors and fund managers. They proved, *inter alia*, that organizational cohesiveness of large fund families, after joining the top platforms, weakens as platforms level the playing fields for all funds. The ability to purchase funds directly via mobile apps results in strong amplification of performance chasing and significant increase in performance sensitivity for both equity and mixed funds. Not having access to professional advice, individual investors often rely on simple performance rank lists displayed in their mobile apps. As a result, their investment decisions are based on similar information mainly regarding past performance, which makes their reactions synchronized. This synchronized performance chasing gives the rise of the amplified performance chasing, which in turn, creates incentives for fund managers to increase risk-taking in order to enhance the probability of getting into the top rank of funds.

To conclude, digitalization and the entry of technology companies have been constantly changing the market structure and competition in the financial industry. This can be observed not only in banking industry but also in capital markets. The stock market has been moving from a traditional specialist model to a technology-driven model. Technology solutions provided mainly by FinTechs have allowed electronic trading as well as automation of clearing and settlement. Electronic trading systems have facilitated the development of algorithmic trading, including HFT, which has increased the level of centralization of trade. This in turn, instead of the expected lowering of entry barriers for smaller investors and smaller firms seeking capital, increased them even more. Although the technology made it possible to reduce transaction costs, but did not eliminate the information asymmetry, as HFT traders using collocation services have an information advantage over other traders. In asset management and mutual funds industry, the main catalyst for structural changes was the rise of digital platforms. They are gaining importance in distribution of index funds and ETFs increasing the concentration of the global market of passively managed funds, while those of actively managed funds remain fragmented. Interestingly, the digital asset management platforms were created by the leading incumbent institutions, which allowed them to reinforce their market position thus increasing market contestability. On the other hand, the development of platforms, especially robo-advisors ones, facilitated access to passive investment for individual investors by reducing transaction costs and communication frictions. However, the issue of reducing information asymmetry remains debatable. It might seem that due to the increasing access to information, this asymmetry has decreased, but in fact, it is rather the opposite. As most investment products are complex, analyzing and using abundant information concerning them to optimize investment decisions lies beyond the capabilities of an average investor. As a result, in the case of online robo-advisors' platforms, it is the algorithms that steer customer choices within a limited, profiled offer. By contrast, investors, who have mobile access to funds, are mainly guided by rankings which makes their decisions more speculative.

Digitalization in capital markets is driven primarily by FinTech solutions that change not only products and processes but also the structure of the market. FinTechs collaborate with incumbents and strengthen their position in the specific market niches, such as robo-advising. This may be somewhat surprising that BigTechs have a very limited interest in entering this market segment. This can be explained by relatively weak complementarity between their core activities and investment services. In addition, providing them requires risk management skills, as well as knowledge and experience in dealing with regulations, which are not strong points of BigTechs. Although Chinese BigTechs enter the asset management segment, they are not in a position to threaten incumbents. However, it should be stressed that the expansion of BigTechs on the capital market is often hampered by regulators, not only in the United States, but also in China.

The changes taking place in capital markets confirm that the greatest challenge for competition is the platform-based business model based on network effects and economies of scale and scope. In capital markets, this business model is not introduced from the outside, as in banking, but come from inside as it is applied by incumbents to reinforce their market position. Although stand-alone platforms developed in the asset management and mutual funds industry entail a lesser risk of distorting competition than those contained in captives' ecosystems built by BigTechs, they also represent a significant challenge for competition policy. Running them in digital economy requires not only other tools but also a different scale as most platforms operate on a transnational or even global scale. As a consequence, there is a need for better coordination of regulatory framework and other measures taken as part of competition policy, on the one hand, to ensure a level playing field for all market players, and on the other, to effectively respond to attempts to exercise the dominant market power. Additionally, the tools used must not contradict the main objective of competition policy in the digital economy which should be the promotion of innovations.

Notes

1. It is particularly difficult to identify companies that belong to the FinTech sector. Many institutions and consulting companies, such as the EBA, FSB, IMF, European Commission, EY, Deloitte, Capgemini and Efma, Accenture, Roland Berger, try to estimate the size of this sector, however, using very different data collection methodology and different identification criteria.

2. This means that the products they offer are most often compatible with other products sold on the same platform, but not compatible with products/services sold on other platforms.
3. According to Shapiro and Varian (1999), in the markets with network effects, pioneer companies can count on a first-mover advantage consisting of quickly acquiring a large number of customers, which will make the entry of later competitors onto the market significantly more difficult.
4. *Bundling* occurs when two products are only sold jointly, making it impossible to acquire the products individually. *Tying* refers to a situation where some of the products in the package may be bought individually, whereas others can be purchased in a package only; however, the price of the package is lower than when buying individual products separately.
5. *Cross-subsidization* occurs when the profits from one activity are used to pay for another activity that is less efficient or even unprofitable, in order to eliminate competition. Cross-subsidization may be combined with the use of price discrimination.
6. Despite this fact, Lee (2018) thinks that DLT in their current form can be utilized to correct some market imperfections by improving trade transparency and making the system more secure, and, at the same time, more cost-efficient for the participants.
7. Reprinted from *Geoforum*, 106 (2019), Haberly, D., MacDonald-Korth, D., Urban, M., & Wójcik, D., Asset Management as a Digital Platform Industry: A Global Financial Network Perspective, pp. 167–181, Copyright (2019), with permission from Elsevier.

References

Accenture (2018). *Capital Markets Vision 2022. Relevance*, Value and Growth in the Digital Era. https://capitalmarketsblog.accenture.com/capital-markets-2022-overview

Acosta, F. N. (2020). *China's online fund platforms a key distribution channel*. Fund Selector Asia. https://fundselectorasia.com/chinas-online-fund-platforms-a-key-distribution-channel/

Ali, A. (2020). *The stocks to rule them all: Big Tech's might in five charts*. Visual Capitalist. https://www.visualcapitalist.com/the-stocks-to-rule-them-all-big-techs-might-in-five-charts/

Allen, F., & Santomero, A. (1997). The theory of financial intermediation. *Journal of Banking and Finance*, *21*(11–12), 1461–1485. doi: https://doi.org/10.1016/s0378-4266(97)00032-0.

Alt, R., Beck, R., & Smits, M. (2018). FinTech and the transformation of the financial industry. *Electronic Markets*, *28*(3), 235–243. doi: https://doi.org/10.1007/s12525-018-0310-9.

Arner, D. W., Barberis, J., & Buckley, R. P. (2015). The evolution of fintech: A new post-crisis paradigm? *SSRN Electronic Journal*. doi: https://doi.org/10.2139/ssrn.2676553.

Bai, J., Philippon, T., & Savov, A. (2016). Have financial markets become more informative? *Journal of Financial Economics*, *122*(3), 625–654. doi: https://doi.org/10.1016/j.jfineco.2016.08.005.

Balp, G., & Strampelli, G. (2018). Preserving capital markets efficiency in the high-frequency trading era. *SSRN Electronic Journal*. doi: https://doi.org/10.2139/ssrn.3097723.

Bar-Gill, O. (2019). Algorithmic price discrimination when demand is a function of both preferences and (mis)perceptions. *University of Chicago Law Review, 86*(2). https://www.jstor.org/stable/26590554.

Bank for International Settlements (2018). *Sound practices: Implications of fintech developments for banks and bank supervisors.* Basel Committee on Banking Supervision (BCBS), February. https://www.bis.org/bcbs/publ/d431.htm.

Bank for International Settlements (2019). *Big tech in finance: Opportunities and risks.* In: Annual Economic Report, 55–79. https://www.bis.org/publ/arpdf/ar2019e3.htm.

Boot, A., Hoffmann, P., Laeven, L., & Ratnovski, L. (2020). Financial intermediation and technology: What's Old, What's New?, *IMF Working Papers, 20*(161). doi: https://doi.org/10.5089/9781513552491.001.

Casey, M., Crane, J., Gensler, G., Johnson, S., & Narula, N. (2018). The impact of blockchain technology on finance: A catalyst for change. *Geneva Reports on the World Economy 21*, International Center for Monetary and Banking Studies (ICMB). https://voxeu.org/content/impact-blockchain-technology-finance-catalyst-change.

Chaboud, A. P., Chiquoine, B., Hjalmarsson, E. & Vega, C. (2014). Rise of the machines: Algorithmic trading in the foreign exchange market, *The Journal of Finance, 69*(5), 2045–2084. doi: https://doi.org/10.1111/jofi.12186.

Crémer, J., De Montjoye, Y. A., & Schweitzer, H. (2019). *Competition policy for the digital era: Final report.* Luxembourg: European Commission, Publications Office of the European Union. doi: https://doi.org/10.2763/407537.

D'Acunto, F., Prabhala, N., & Rossi, A. G. (2019). The promises and pitfalls of robo-advising. *The Review of Financial Studies, 32*(5), 1983–2020. doi: https://doi.org/10.1093/rfs/hhz014.

Deutsche Börse & Celent. (2016). *Future of Fintech in Capital Markets.* June 20. https://www.deutsche-boerse.com/resource/blob/37024/ed055219caeb553f439 50609d29e1bb3/data/future-of-fintech-in-capital-markets_en.pdf

Ellul, J., Galea, J., Ganado, M., Mccarthy, S., & Pace, G. J. (2020). Regulating blockchain, DLT and smart contracts: A technology regulator's perspective. *ERA Forum, 21*, 209–220. doi: https://doi.org/10.1007/s12027-020-00617-7.

European Banking Authority (2018). *Report on the impact of FinTech on the incumbents credit institutions business models,* July. https://www.eba.europa.eu/file/28458

Evans, D. S., & Schmalensee, R. (2007). The industrial organization of markets with two-sided platforms. *Competition Policy International, 3*(1), 151–179. https://econpapers.repec.org/article/cpicpijrn/3.1.2007_3ai=4907.htm.

Evans, P. C., & Gawer, A. (2016). *The Rise of the Platform Enterprise: A Global Survey,* The Emerging Platform Economy Series No. 1, The Center for Global Enterprise. https://www.thecge.net/archived-papers/the-rise-of-the-platform-enterprise-a-global-survey/

Financial Stability Board (2017). *Financial Stability Implications from FinTech, Supervisory and Regulatory Issues that Merit Authorities' Attention.* June. https://www.fsb.org/wp-content/uploads/R270617.pdf.

Financial Stability Board (2019). *FinTech and market structure in financial services: Market developments and potential financial stability implications,* February. https://www.fsb.org/wp-content/uploads/P140219.pdf.

Fraile Carmona, A., González-Quel Lombardo, A., Rivera Pastor, R., Tarín Quirós, C., Villar García, J. P., Ramos Muñoz, D., & Castejón Martín, L. (2018). *Competition issues in the area of financial technology (FinTech),* Directorate-General for

Internal Policies, July. https://www.europarl.europa.eu/RegData/etudes/STUD/2018/619027/IPOL_STU(2018)619027_EN.pdf.

Frost, J., Gambacorta, L., Huang, Y., Song Shin, H., & Zbinden, P. (2019). BigTech and the changing structure of financial intermediation, *Economic Policy*, *34*(100), 761–799. doi: https://doi.org/10.1093/epolic/eiaa003.

Gao, M., & Huang, J. (2020). Informing the market: The effect of modern information technologies on information production. *Review of Financial Studies*, *33*(4), 1367–1411. doi: https://doi.org/10.1093/rfs/hhz100.

Garvey, R., & Wu, F. (2010). Speed, distance, and electronic trading: New evidence on why location matters. *Journal of Financial Markets*, *13*(4), 367–396. doi: https://doi.org/10.1016/j.finmar.2010.07.001.

Geranio, M. (2016). *Evolution of the exchange industry: From dealers' clubs to multinational companies.* Springer International Publishing.

Haberly, D., MacDonald-Korth, D., Urban, M., & Wójcik, D. (2019). Asset management as a digital platform industry: A global financial network perspective, *Geoforum*, *106*, 176–181. doi: https://doi.org/10.1016/j.geoforum.2019.08.009.

Harasim, J., & Mitręga-Niestrój, K. (2018). FinTech – Dylematy definicyjne i determinanty rozwoju. *Prace Naukowe Uniwersytetu Ekonomicznego we Wrocławiu*, *531*, 169–179. doi: https://doi.org/10.15611/pn.2018.531.15.

Hasbrouck, J., & Saar, G. (2013). Low-latency trading. *Journal of Financial Markets*, *16*(4), 646–679. doi: https://doi.org/10.1016/j.finmar.2013.05.003.

Hau, H., Huang, Y., Shan, H., & Sheng, Z. (2019). How fintech enters China's credit market, *AEA Papers and Proceedings*, *109*, 60–64. doi: https://doi.org/10.1257/pandp.20191012.

He, D., Leckov, R. B., Haksar, V., Mancini Griffoli, T., Jenkinson, N., Kashima, M., Khiaonarong, T., Rochon, C., & Tourpe, H. (2017). Fintech and financial services: Initial considerations. *IMF Staff Discussion Notes*. June. https://www.imf.org/en/Publications/Staff-Discussion-Notes/Issues/2017/06/16/Fintech-and-Financial-Services-Initial-Considerations-44985

Hendershott, T., & Moulton, P. C. (2011). Automation, speed, and stock market quality: The NYSE's hybrid, *Journal of Financial Markets*, *14*(4), 568–604. doi: https://doi.org/10.1016/j.finmar.2011.02.003.

Hong, C. Y., Lu, X. & Pan, J. (2020). FinTech platforms and mutual fund distribution, *NBER Working Papers* 26576, National Bureau of Economic Research, Inc. doi: https://doi.org/10.3386/W26576.

HSBC Securities Services (2019). *Distributed Ledger Technology in the capital Markets. Game changers - Future Trends in Securities Services*, March. https://www.gbm.hsbc.com/game-changers-future-trends-in-securities-services/distributed-ledger-technology.

Innovate Finance (2016). *Blockchain, DLT and the Capital Markets Journey Navigating the Regulatory and Legal Landscape,* October. https://www.innovatefinance.com/reports/blockchain-dlt-and-the-capital-markets-journey-navigating-the-regulatory-and-legal-landscape/.

Jain, P. (2005). Financial market design and equity premium: Electronic versus floor trading, *The Journal of Finance*, *60*(6), 2955–2985. doi: https://doi.org/10.1111/j.1540-6261.2005.00822.x.

Johnson, N., Zhao, G., Hunsader, E., Qi, H., Johnson, N., Meng, J., & Tivnan, B. (2013). Abrupt rise of new machine ecology beyond human response time, *Scientific Reports 3*(1), 2627,1–7. doi: https://doi.org/10.1038/srep02627.

Lee, J. (2018). Distributed ledger technologies (Blockchain) in capital markets: Risk and governance, *SSRN Electronic Journal*. doi: https://doi.org/10.2139/ssrn.3180553.

Lee, T., & Kim, H. W. (2015). An exploratory study on Fintech industry in Korea: Crowdfunding case. *2nd International conference on Innovative Engineering Technologies (ICIET'2015) August 7–8, 2015 Bangkok (Thailand)*. doi: https://doi.org/10.15242/iie.e0815045.

Marszk, A., & Lechman, E., (2019). *Exchange traded funds in Europe*. Elsevier: Academic Press.

Navaretti, G. B., Calzolari, G., Mansilla-Fernandez, J. M. & Pozzolo, A. F. (2018). Fintech and banking. Friends or foes? *SSRN Electronic Journal*. doi: https://doi.org/10.2139/ssrn.3099337.

Petralia, K., Philippon, T., Rice, T., & Veron, N. (2019). Banking disrupted. Financial intermediation in an era of transformational technology, *Geneva Report on the World Economy, 22*. https://voxeu.org/content/banking-disrupted-financial-intermediation-era-transformational-technology.

Philippon, T. (2015). Has the US finance industry become less efficient? On the theory and measurement of financial intermediation. *American Economic Review*, *105*(4), 1408–38. doi: https://doi.org/10.1257/aer.20120578.

Riordan, R., & Storkenmaier, A. (2012). Latency, liquidity and price discovery. *Journal of Financial Markets*, *15*(4), 416–437. doi: https://doi.org/10.1016/j.finmar.2012.05.003.

Rochet, J. C., & Tirole, J. (2003). Platform competition in two-sided markets. *Journal of the European Economic Association*, *1*(4), 990–1029. doi: https://doi.org/10.1162/154247603322493212.

Scholtens, B., & Van Wensveen, D. (2003). The theory of financial intermediation: An essay on what it does (not) explain. *SUERF Studies, SUERF - The European Money and Finance Forum*, No 1. August. https://ideas.repec.org/b/erf/erfstu/23.html.

Shapiro C. & Varian H. R. (1999). *Information Rules: A Strategic Guide to the Network Economy*, Boston, Massachusetts: Harvard Business School Press. https://doi.org/10.1080/00220489909595956

Stulz, R. M. (2019). Fintech, Bigtech, and the future of banks. *Journal of Applied Corporate Finance*, *31*(4), 86–97. doi: https://doi.org/10.1111/jacf.12378.

Tucker, C. (2019). Digital data, platforms and the usual [Antitrust] suspects: Network effects, switching costs, essential facility. *Review of Industrial Organization* *54*(4), 683–694. doi: https://doi.org/10.1007/s11151-019-09693-7.

World Bank (2017). Distributed Ledger Technology (DLT) and Blockchain. FinTech Note, No 1. https://openknowledge.worldbank.org/handle/10986/29053.

World Economic Forum (2015). *The Future of Financial Services. How disruptive innovations are reshaping the way financial services are structured, provisioned and consumed*, An Industry Project of the Financial Services Community prepared in collaboration with Deloitte. Final Report, June. http://www3.weforum.org/docs/WEF_The_future__of_financial_services.pdf.

Zhu, J., Wu, K., Leng, Ch. (2020). China launches antitrust probe into tech giant Alibaba. Reuters. https://www.reuters.com/article/us-china-antgroup/china-launches-antitrust-probe-into-tech-giant-alibaba-idUSKBN28Y05T.

6 Critical success factors for FinTech

Anna Karmańska

Introduction

For the last few decades, the financial system has been experiencing enormous transformation given the rapid implementation of new technology on a global scale (Chen et al., 2019; Werth et al., 2019; Zavolokina et al., 2017). FinTechs disrupted the traditional banking by offering customer-friendly and efficient financial services. FinTech is an umbrella term and refers to innovative financial services and products delivered via new technology (Nicoletti, 2017). The COVID-19 crisis has had a profound impact on this sector over the last couple of months. Financing brought the worst results of the first quarter of 2020 for FinTech deals since 2016 and for funding since 2017 (CBInsights, 2020). On the other hand, FinTechs have a competitive advantage over traditional institutions due to low-cost communication channels and limited need for physical infrastructure and hence low fixed overheads. Through the innovative use of emerging technologies: cloud computing, robotic process automation (RPA), chatbots, artificial intelligence (AI), machine learning (ML), open application programming interfaces (APIs), an Internet of things (IoT), blockchain FinTechs enable greater efficiency, agility and accuracy. Nevertheless, it should be stated that the technology itself does not provide any advantage alone, but combined with other available resources (organizational, environmental, strategic), it can create business value (Zavolokina et al., 2017). It is important to explore key factors influencing the success; therefore, the main objective of this chapter is an identification of the critical success factors (CSFs) for FinTech. Furthermore, only limited researches address the CSFs for FinTech, this study contributes toward filling the gap.

The study consists of four sections. The first is introduction. The second section is devoted to the literature review. The third section presents the research methodology and results of the study. The summary and conclusion depict findings, research implications as well as its limitations.

DOI: 10.4324/9781003095354-6

Literature review

FinTechs

Digital and mobile payments are the most popular FinTech service. 96% of global consumers are aware of e-payments and 75% uses them (EY, 2019), but FinTechs also deliver value to customers in other areas (FinTech Poland, 2016):

- Data analysis, including, but not limited to: database creation and management, support in gathering specialized information, customer identification, financial offer adjustment, alternative credit score calculation methods, document automation in the cloud.
- Financial platforms: non-bank lending providers, online currency exchanges, mobile banking solutions, consultancy through the comparison of market offers.
- Crowdfunding (a funding practice by financing a project from a large number of people) and peer-to-peer (P2P) lending.
- Management (applications for individuals, households and enterprises to help them budget as well as manage financial decisions, online factoring, platforms to exchange electronic documents, comparison engines, online debt collection).
- Investment used to help investors in the process of buying, selling and managing assets and securities for wealth creation, examples: robo-advice, digital investment management.
- Blockchain and cryptocurrency based on encryption technologies and distributed data structures.
- TechInsurance (digital brokers, P2P insurance).
- Other, for example: security (identify verification, risk assessment, fraud detection).

In the opinion of Diemers et al. (2015) an ecosystem, created by FinTech, includes five elements: the FinTech start-ups (service providers), technology developers, government (legislation), financial customers and the traditional financial institution. Gomber et al. (2018) identified in FinTechs three new forces, which changed the financial market. The first force is technological innovation which is the main engine behind industrial transformation and economic growth. The second force – a process disruption – creates new products and business models. Moreover, the mainstream of financial products has become more fully digitalized and offered through platforms. The emergence of new technologies transforms the traditional financial services. And finally, the third force is business transformation, which enables financial services to operate in new and completely different ways to those of bricks and mortar banking.

KPMG's (2018) FinTech Pulse report stated that FinTech investment more than doubled globally in 2018 and this sector accounted for nearly half out of USD 256 billion invested in venture capital (VC).

In spite of substantial funding, not every start-up succeeds, therefore, researchers and practitioners try to investigate why certain FinTechs fail while others are successful. Pursuant to Shafer et al. (2005) the success of for-profit organizations is directly related to their ability to both create value and capture returns from that value. Many authors suggested success criteria, e.g. time, cost and user specification. For instance, Chow and Cao (2008) proposed four success attributes: quality (delivering good product or project outcome), scope (meeting all requirements and objectives), time (delivering the products to meet the deadline) and cost (meet the requirements in terms of cost and effort). Similarly, according to Wateridge (1998), a successful project: meets user's requirements; achieves purpose; meets timescale; meets budget; makes users happy and meets quality.

The theory of critical success factors is used to identify key elements which contribute to favorable outcomes and hence can significantly improve the chance for success. The critical success factors (CSFs) can be defined as activities required for ensuring the achievement of the business mission and its success (Nicoletti, 2017). The notion was introduced by Rockart (1979) and later developed (Bullen & Rockart, 1981) to help senior executives define their information needs for the purpose of managing organizations. CSFs were defined as the few key areas of activity in which favorable results were absolutely necessary for a particular manager to reach their goals. The literature indicated five major types of CSFs, namely: industry CSFs – the structure of a particular industry; strategy CSFs – competitive strategy, industry position, geographical factors; environmental CSFs – related with fluctuations in a national economy, politics; temporal CSFs – related with problems or challenges to the organization critical for a particular period of time caused by unusual event; and management CSFs (Bullen & Rockart, 1981). Rockart designated the interview method as the most successful in drawing out CSFs. Furthermore, other research methods can be used, such as the literature review, case studies, multivariate analysis, questionnaires, scenario analysis (Olszak & Ziemba, 2012).

Critical success factors for FinTechs

Over the last years, FinTechs have received considerable attention from academics but the literature has mainly focused on their business value (Jinasena et al., 2020). A noticeable research gap in CSFs for the sector still exists in the literature. A review of the existing studies related to 'FinTechs', 'critical success factors', 'determinants', in three bibliographic databases: ProQuest, Emerald Management and the ISI Web of Knowledge confirmed the paucity of the literature. Moreover, the prior research on CSFs for FinTechs mostly focuses on specific FinTech sectors such as: crowdfunding, P2P lending, mobile payments, while only a few studies have investigated the FinTech market in its entirety (Haddad & Hornuf, 2019). An example of general study can be the research conducted in Germany by Werth et al.

(2019), who analyzed the material from semi-structured interviews with ten managers of FinTechs as well as eight venture capitalists (VC). The FinTechs represented three different business models: personal finance (digital bank), digital payments (cryptocurrency payment provider and alternative lending), financing (bank-as-a-platform). The researchers reported a variety of factors vital to the success from the point of view of an entrepreneur and VC. The qualitative data from interviews identified nine CSFs, which applied to general ventures, namely: team, entrepreneur, capital, product/market fit, idea and execution, pivoting, continuous learning, customer acquisition, internationalization and networking. Moreover, the authors designated six factors that were specific to FinTech, i.e., technological advantage, regulatory knowledge, business-to-business (B2B) focus, incumbent partnerships, growth potential, exit options for VCs.

Another similar research was conducted in Indonesia, which ranks sixth on the list of the top countries of Internet users. Hermawan et al. (2019) analyzed the results of interviews with managers of three FinTechs: Taralite (P2P lending), Futoready (InsureTech) and KUDO (e-payments). The informants indicated five CSFs, in turn: funding, technological development, customer experience, organizational culture and government regulation. The literature has also highlighted the economic and technological determinants of the emergence of the global FinTech market. Haddad and Hornuf (2019) analyzed the data source from the CrunchBase database, which contained detailed information on FinTech startup formations and their financing. For the sample, the authors identified 7,353 FinTech startups with 1,177 observations for the 11-year period from 2005 to 2015 covering 107 countries. The authors estimated a negative binomial regression model with a dependent variable – the number of FinTech startup formations in a given year and country. Their findings suggested that economies witnessed more FinTech startup formations when the country was well-developed, which was measured by GDP per capita, and venture capital was readily available. Moreover, the number of secure Internet servers, mobile telephone subscriptions, and the available labor force had a positive impact. The authors also confirmed the hypothesis that the more difficult it was for companies to access loans, the higher was the number of FinTech startups.

Scholars also consider that the FinTechs advancement is primarily driven by human nature, namely behavior and attitude. The technology acceptance model (TAM) proposed by Davis (1989) is often used in the literature to explain the adoption of FinTechs. The theory posits two main factors, particularly: an individual's perceived usefulness as the degree to which a consumer believes that using the technology will enhance the performance and perceived ease of use – the degree to which a consumer believes that using the technology will be free of effort. In the light of this theory, Singh et al. (2020) explored the FinTech adoption among customers by quantitatively investigating the main drivers in three attribute dimensions: behavioral, technological and adoption. The authors analyzed the data collected from 439 active Internet users through a digital survey. In order to classify the constructs and explore the relationships, the researchers applied structural equation modeling and multi-group analysis. As an adoption attribute, the actual use was postulated, that is, the frequency and an approximate number of times a FinTech service was used in a given period. As behavioral attributes, the authors pointed out the perceived usefulness and the perceived ease of use. Technological attributes comprised of responsiveness, which referred to the user perception of the effectiveness and excellence of service offered online as well as security as users' belief about the safety of the transactions. Their results revealed that perceived usefulness was the key factor that positively influenced the intention to use FinTechs, while the perceived ease of use was the second significant factor. Security was considered more important technological attribute while deciding on the perception of FinTech use.

In contrast, Wang et al. (2019) investigated the customer retention in FinTech on the basis of the monetary fund YuEbao. In the study, a survey questionnaire was deployed (288 users) and a partial least squares structural modeling was used. The findings revealed that customers' continuance intention of FinTech was trust in service and structural assurance, which referred to legal regulations. The trust could be boosted by the system quality – reliability, usability, response time, availability of the system and subjective norm, which reflected social pressure. Therefore, it is imperative for FinTechs to offer customers high-quality products and focus on security.

As financial innovations were changing the economic landscape, new FinTech business models were also subject of interest. Roeder et al. (2018), took into account components of a FinTech business model, which had the highest impact on venture success. The study was based on six dimensions of FinTech business models proposed by Eickhoff et al. (2017), namely:

- Dominant technology component as the driver for the IT-based business model.
- Value proposition, which identifies the value the company creates for its ecosystem (customers, partners etc.).
- Delivery channel, which explains how the products and services are distributed to the customers.
- Customers, which describes to whom the company intends to offer its products and services.
- Revenue stream, which shows how the company generates revenue from its products or services.
- Product/service offering, which describes what the company offers to its customers.

The researchers examined a set of 221 companies from the CrunchBase (more than 50% were from the United States) and the empirical results showed that the component 'Product/Service Offering' was the most influential determinant of the success of FinTechs. The multiple regression analysis showed significant relationships between the three characteristics of this dimension, such as credit lending, financing and information aggregation, and the aggregated funding per company.

According to Leong et al. (2020), FinTechs promoted and contributed to sustainable development. Sustainable development is a concept defined by The World Commission on Environment and Development (i.e., The Brundtland Commission) as 'development that meets the needs of the present without compromising the ability of future generations to meet their own needs (United Nations General Assembly, 1987).

The collection of papers also explored factors for expansion success in emerging economies. For example, Yermack (2018) conducted research on CSFs for FinTech in Sub-Saharan Africa. Africa has the lowest penetration rate of the Internet users in the world – only 42.2%, in Sub-Saharan common law countries, the rate is equal to 38.5% but in Civil law ones only 21.8% (Internet World Stats). Therefore, the author indicated an infrastructure of electric power, telecommunications, internet providers as the main CSF for FinTechs. The other important CFS is a legal system, thanks to better investor protection and lower cost of capital FinTech firms are more extensively developed in countries with a common law legal system, compared to those with a civil law. Meantime Hammerschlag et al. (2020) explored FinTechs intra-Africa expansion. Based on the material of semi-structured interviews at 14 African FinTechs the authors came to the conclusion that the success was measured by customer volume and their behavior and by financial results. From a tech business perspective, frequency of use is the most important metric of success. Furthermore, low-income customers are price-sensitive, FinTech products should therefore be affordable.

FinTechs grow also rapidly in Islamic countries, where innovations are permissible if they are Shariah-complaint. Alam et al. (2019) claimed that the main reason for the growth is high (1.8 billion people) and fast-growing Muslim population. In addition, the median age of Muslims is 24 years of age compared to 32 globally and 15 of the top 50 countries with the highest smartphone penetration belong to Islam economies. Moreover, the researchers consider that Islamic FinTechs are closer to the spirit of Shariah because they must be transparent and beneficial for both parties. For example, P2P lending, which offers remittance, mobile wallets and crowdfunding, meets the needs of the population, especially when it is not possible to transact with conventional banks. The authors indicated neutrality as the next factor, which contributed to the success of FinTechs, because standardized contracts offered via technology mitigate the risk of some financial services.

Chinese FinTech industry has experienced outstanding growth over the past decade. Referring to analysis the phenomenon Sheng et al. (2017) specified five key success factors for FinTechs, particularly:

- Data affluence, i.e., access to large amounts of proprietary data and ability to derive needed information from them.

- Monetization of large customer base.
- Availability of proprietary and comprehensive products to satisfy their customers' need.
- Strong financial service and risk management knowledge.
- 'Fin plus tech' organization and culture.

Central and Eastern Europe became the fastest emerging start-up ecosystem and with USD 1.8 billion invested, 2019 was a new record VC investment in the region's history (Polish Development Fund, Dealroom.co, 2020). Poland has become a regional leader in Central East Europe in technologically advanced, pioneering solutions in the banking sector (Deloitte, 2016). According to the Polish FinTech Map prepared by the website Cashless.pl and the FinTech Poland Foundation (2020), there were 200+ FinTechs companies in Poland in 2019. The dynamic growth of the sector is evidenced by the fact that 70 new projects were launched on the Polish market that year. Based on interviews with experts from 20 FinTechs and 13 banks, the Foundation for Financial Innovation FinTech Poland (2016) prepared a report, in which the experts identified determinates of the success. The first CSF was strong and innovative banking sector as well as worldwide trend of decreasing customer loyalty to traditional banking. The experts claimed that FinTechs were able to respond in a far more flexible manner, using the agile approach instead of waterfall one. The strong point of FinTechs was also their capacity to focus on the customers' needs and quickly set up the optimal conditions for implementing services on foreign markets. The organizational aspect also played an important role as FinTechs with a proper organizational mark-up had a great potential for growth. According to experts, the creativity of people, considerable potential of human resources and IT companies, and hence the capacity for international expansion are also crucial for FinTechs' success. FinTech start-ups are not cheap businesses, another very important aspect is therefore access to the capital and a possibility to exit for VC. At an early stage, a FinTech start-up does not generate revenue, but it needs budget for developing products and customer acquisitions. Due to complexity and dynamics of FinTechs, current legal frameworks are not sufficient. According to EY research (2020) conducted among 596 big Polish enterprises, 91% of respondents still believed that the law was not able to keep pace with the development of new technology and postulated to change the regulations, especially in the areas of cybersecurity, data protection, intellectual property protection and investments in new technologies. In the opinion of experts, knowledge of legal provisions and significant regulatory changes contribute to the FinTechs success. Especially the implementation of the directive on payment services (PSD2) directive contributed to opening up of public data and as well as various initiatives facilitating FinTechs adopted by Polish Financial Supervision Authority, for example a program innovation hub, providing a dedicated point of contact for firms to raise inquiries with competent authorities or the Regulatory Sandbox – a tool for testing new innovative financial solutions in accordance with the law pursuant to a plan agreed and monitored by a competent authority.

Although many factors, such as: access to financing and technology, large customer base are the same for all organizations, it is difficult to indicate one-size-fits-all success formula due to increasing complexity of the FinTech industry. The literature explored specific CSFs for more homogeneous business models: mobile payments, crowdfunding and P2P lending.

For instance, Lee and Teo (2015) used case studies as a research methodology for the mobile payment sector. Based on the analysis of successful FinTechs (M-PESA from Kenya and Alibaba from China), the authors identified five success factors. The attributes were termed as the LASIC principle from the initials of the list: (1) Low margin, (2) Asset light, (3) Scalable, (4) Innovative, and (5) Compliance Easy.

The LASIC principles were also used to build a CSF model for FinTechs by Nicoletti (2017). Based on a previous single research, which highlighted the importance of each of these factors, the author proposed the CLASSIC model. The new model expanded the LASIC components presented by Lee and Teo (2015) and modified one factor of the LASIC model, Asset light, to Agility. Agility is defined as the ability to thrive in an environment of continuous and often unanticipated change. The author also added two essential CSFs, mentioned in the initials first C – Customer centricity, that is, creating a positive customer experience at all the physical or virtual contact points, while simultaneously adding value to the organization and (second) S – Security management as the identification of organization's assets (including information assets), followed by implementation of policies for protecting them.

Pursuant to Leong et al. (2020) various FinTech sectors were shaped by considerably different factors. For instance, the existence of links to a personal page in the social media and number of friends or followers are considered to be critical for crowdfunding. In investments, robo-advisors are used to provide automated financial advice and their driving factors include: automation, personalization, accessibility (24/7), simplification, visualization, service quality, competitiveness on pricing. The authors also focused on the importance of collaboration and partnership between traditional financial institutions and FinTechs.

Felipe and Ferreira (2020) scrutinized success factors of the equity crowdfunding campaigns. Equity crowdfunding seeks investment from a group of people to finance startups, instead of an angel investor or other private-sector investment to attain the financial goal of the ventures. The sample covered 99 startup financing campaigns in Brazil from 2014 to 2017 and the logistic regression with marginal effects and a dummy for time fixed effects were used. The research results indicated that the probability and speed of success of the startup financing were positively affected by the following determinants: the financial goal, the venture category, advisor participation, the campaign duration, and the type of equity offered to the investor.

Meanwhile, Yeh and Chen (2020) developed a predictive model based on machine learning algorithms to predict the success of crowdfunding FinTech projects. Based on the campaign data from Indiegogo, an international crowdfunding platform, the researchers analyzed 4,474 samples from the period between 2015 and 2017. The authors considered that social media activity measured as the number of entrepreneur's social network ties (Facebook fans), human capital of funders (experience) measured as the number of other projects in which an entrepreneur raised money before lead to successful fundraising.

Another example is a segment of loan services. Contreras Pinochet et al. (2019) analyzed P2P lending in Brazil to verify which factors influence individuals to use services offered by FinTechs. The authors discovered that especially young people were interested in new technologies implemented by FinTechs since services were rendered at reduced cost and without bureaucracy. Their results indicated that the following aspects: trust, personal innovation, perceived utility, ease of use and social influence as well as the privacy and transactional distance explained 41.5 percent of the propensity to use services from lending FinTechs in Brazil.

Methodology, research findings and discussion

This study contributes to the literature mainly by exploring CSFs for FinTechs. This section focuses on addressing the following questions:

Q1: What are the CSFs for FinTechs?
Q2: Is there a relationship between the factors?

Based on the above research questions the researcher poses the following hypotheses:

H1: CSFs for FinTech are high-quality products, collaboration, low margins, customer base as well as, broad spread of Internet, management, and cooperation.
H2: There is a positive association between success factors for FinTechs.

Table 6.1. presents a summary of the factors which determine the success of FinTechs based on the academics' and experts' viewpoint.

The data for this study were collected using a structured questionnaire in August, November and December 2020. The survey was conducted by the electronic distribution of a questionnaire to potential participants using social media and groups devoted to survey exchanges. The target respondents were users of FinTechs. The sample comprised of 403 FinTech users: 200 from Poland and 203 international from the following countries: Armenia, Australia, Austria, Bangladesh, Belgium, Brazil. Canada, China, Denmark, Egypt, Ethiopia, France, Germany, Greece, Hong Kong,

Table 6.1 CSFs for FinTech

Number	Critical Success Factor	Source citing CSF
CSF_1	Entrepreneur	Werth et al. (2019)
CSF_2	Financing, funding, capital	Haddad and Hornuf (2019); Hermawan et al. (2019); Werth et al. (2019)
CSF_3	Teamwork	Werth et al. (2019)
CSF_4	Product/market fit	FinTech Poland (2016); Werth et al. (2019)
CSF_5	Good idea and execution, high quality	Sheng et al. (2017); Wang et al. (2019); Werth et al. (2019)
CSF_6	Continuous learning	Werth et al. (2019)
CSF_7	Internationalization	FinTech Poland (2016); Werth et al. (2019)
CSF_8	Customer acquisition	FinTech Poland (2016); Roeder et al. (2018); Werth et al. (2019)
CSF_9	Networking	Werth et al. (2019)
CSF_10	Technological advance	Roeder et al. (2018); Haddad and Hornuf (2019); Hermawan et al. (2019); Werth et al. (2019)
CSF_11	Knowledge of government regulations	Lee and Teo (2015); Hermawan et al. (2019); Nicoletti (2017); Yermack (2018)
CSF_12	Building offer B2B	FinTech Poland (2016); Werth et al. (2019)
CSF_13	Cooperation and partnership with traditional banking	FinTech Poland (2016); Leong et al. (2020); Werth et al. (2019)
CSF_14	High growth potential	Roeder et al. (2018); Werth et al. (2019)
CSF_15	Exit options for venture capital	Werth et al. (2019)
CSF_16	Loss of trust in traditional financial services	FinTech Poland (2016); Hermawan et al. (2019)
CSF_17	Strong and innovative banking sector	FinTech Poland (2016)
CSF_18	Digitalization, personalization, automation, big data, data mining	FinTech Poland (2016); Hermawan et al. (2019)
CSF_19	Decision-based on data	Hermawan et al. (2019); Sheng et al. (2017)
CSF_20	Access to large customer base	Alam et al. (2019); Hermawan et al. (2019); Roeder et al. (2018); Sheng et al. (2017)
CSF_21	Millennials are very familiar with Internet, social media and FinTechs	Alam et al. (2019); Hermawan et al. (2019)
CSF_22	Changes in the legal environment (PSD2, API banking, opening public services and data)	FinTech Poland (2016); Yermack (2018)
CSF_23	Agility, quick modification of strategy	Lee and Teo (2015); FinTech Poland (2016); Nicoletti (2017)
CSF_24	Low margin and costs	Lee and Teo (2015), Nicoletti (2017)
CSF_25	Broad spread of the Internet and mobile devices	Alam et al. (2019);), Hermawan et al. (2019); Yermack (2018)

Table 6.1 (Continued)

Number	Critical Success Factor	Source citing CSF
CSF_26	Access to comprehensive services without time and location restrictions	FinTech Poland (2016); Roeder et al. (2018); Sheng et al. (2017)
CSF_27	Customer centricity	FinTech Poland (2016); Hermawan et al. (2019); Nicoletti (2017); Roeder et al. (2018); Werth et al. (2019)
CSF_28	Risk and security management	Nicoletti (2017); Sheng et al. (2017); Wang et al. (2019)
CSF_29	High organizational culture	FinTech Poland (2016); Hermawan et al. (2019); Sheng et al. (2017)
CSF_30	Promotion of sustainable development	Leong et al. (2020)

Source: own elaboration based on analyzed sources.

Hungary, India, Ireland, Israel, Italy, Japan, Latvia, Lithuania, Malaysia, Malta, Mongolia, Pakistan, Philippines, Portugal, Serbia, Singapore, South Africa, South Korea, Spain, Sweden, Switzerland, Taiwan, Thailand, the Netherlands, Ukraine, the United Kingdom, the United States of America, and Vietnam. The questionnaire items consisted of four demographics, such as: gender, age, education and place of residence. The demographic characteristics of the respondents are presented in Table 6.2. Out of 403 respondents, 317 (79%) were in the age group of less than 30 years. This observation

Table 6.2 Distribution of the sample members

Characteristics	Demographic profile	Number of respondents	Frequency %
Gender	Male	113	28
	Female	266	66
	Not specified	24	6
Age	Up to 20 years	27	7
	21–30 years	290	72
	31–45 years	49	12
	46–60 years	12	3
	Not specified	25	6
Education level	Elementary	5	1
	Secondary	37	9
	High	295	73
	Not specified	66	17
Place of residence	Rural	40	10
	Medium or small city	195	48
	Capital or large city	140	35
	Not specified	28	7

Source: own elaboration based on analyzed data.

Table 6.3 FinTech products used by the sample members

FinTech products	Number of respondents	Frequency %
Digital and mobile payments	353	88
Data analytics	119	30
Financial platforms	142	35
Crowdfunding/P2P lending	65	16
Investments	105	26
Blockchain and cryptocurrency	57	14
Finance Management	131	33
InsurTechs	94	23

Source: own elaboration based on analyzed data.

is in line with the demographic of FinTechs' users based on 22,535 online interviews from 20 markets (EY, 2017) as 25 to 34-year-old consumers were most likely to use FinTech, while older consumers had already established long-standing relationships with traditional providers before the arrival of FinTech. A variety of studies provided evidence for existing a strong relationship between age and FinTechs' use. For instance, the rate for users of mobile payments under 25 years (51%) was almost 11 times as high as the rate for those 65 and older (Li et al., 2020).

The next question of the questionnaire concerned FinTech products used by respondents, more than one could be selected. Table 6.3. displays the results.

Money-related services, including electronic payments, are the largest group in terms of users' interest (88%). Financial platforms are used by 35% of respondents and 33% of them take advantage of personal and business finance management services respectively. Another group of FinTech services is related to data analytics, used by 30% of respondents. 26% of respondents use investment management. These are followed by InsurTechs (23%), crowdfunding and P2P lending –16%, and finally, blockchain and cryptocurrency (14%).

The subsequent items of the questionnaire measured the users' attitudes to rate the degree to which they agree or disagree with a statement towards CSFs for FinTech and the items were developed using a Likert scale. The endpoints anchored at 1 'strongly disagree', whereas 5 meant 'strongly agree' with the affirmative.

The study employed the quantitative research methodology with the support of the SPSS software. First, the Cronbach's alpha coefficient was calculated for the entire scale which finally consisted of 30 items. This coefficient, which provides an overall assessment of a measure's reliability and internal consistency, is high (0.954).

Next, the frequencies and volatility measures were calculated. The statistics are presented in Table 6.4., including responses to the items of the questionnaire and ranks using the sum of positive answers (4–5).

Table 6.4 Frequency of answers and descriptive statistics

	Frequency					Mean	Median	Mode	Std. deviation	Skewness	Sum	Rank
	Strongly agree (5)	Agree (4)	Neither agree nor disagree (3)	Disagree (2)	Strongly disagree (1)							
CSF_1	133	173	68	17	12	3.99	4.00	4	.968	−1.049	1607	12
CSF_2	133	185	65	12	8	4.05	4.00	4	.888	−1.040	1632	5
CSF_3	150	140	83	23	7	4.00	4.00	5	.982	−.807	1612	18
CSF_4	184	150	41	18	10	4.19	4.00	5	.962	−1.367	1689	2
CSF_5	181	148	49	13	12	4.17	4.00	5	.969	−1.358	1682	3
CSF_6	145	158	66	25	9	4.00	4.00	4	.987	−.960	1614	14
CSF_7	125	150	100	22	6	3.91	4.00	4	.951	−.618	1575	20
CSF_8	131	172	72	20	8	3.99	4.00	4	.940	−.915	1607	15
CSF_9	147	158	71	19	8	4.03	4.00	4	.954	−.952	1626	13
CSF_10	190	148	45	10	10	4.24	4.00	5	.923	−1.438	1707	1
CSF_11	138	154	78	23	10	3.96	4.00	4	.994	−.882	1596	17
CSF_12	106	130	122	35	10	3.71	4.00	4	1.028	−.437	1496	28
CSF_13	113	162	89	30	9	3.84	4.00	4	.989	−.706	1549	21
CSF_14	149	160	65	22	7	4.05	4.00	4	.952	−.964	1631	9
CSF_15	79	144	134	36	10	3.61	4.00	4	.980	−.368	1455	29
CSF_16	82	119	117	63	22	3.44	3.00	4	1.139	−.305	1385	30
CSF_17	103	163	99	29	9	3.80	4.00	4	.976	−.638	1531	23
CSF_18	143	170	60	19	11	4.03	4.00	4	.969	−1.098	1624	7
CSF_19	147	146	74	27	9	3.98	4.00	5	1.010	−.878	1604	16
CSF_20	143	171	63	20	6	4.05	4.00	4	.918	−.961	1634	6
CSF_21	167	141	71	16	8	4.10	4.00	5	.959	−1.015	1652	10
CSF_22	101	147	124	22	9	3.77	4.00	4	.962	−.496	1518	27
CSF_23	129	178	71	15	10	4.00	4.00	4	.933	−1.006	1610	11
CSF_24	109	153	103	32	6	3.81	4.00	4	.972	−.530	1536	24
CSF_25	179	148	51	18	7	4.18	4.00	5	.936	−1.198	1683	4
CSF_26	153	158	72	15	5	4.09	4.00	4	.902	−.893	1648	8
CSF_27	120	159	99	18	7	3.91	4.00	4	.934	−.668	1576	19
CSF_28	125	134	115	25	4	3.87	4.00	4	.958	−.438	1560	25
CSF_29	115	134	117	26	11	3.78	4.00	4	1.018	−.554	1525	26
CSF_30	121	147	91	36	8	3.84	4.00	4	1.019	−.632	1546	22

Source: own elaboration based on analyzed data.

The respondents most often agree with the statement that technological advance is critical for the success of FinTechs (84% of positive answers). Subsequently, the respondents indicated CSFs for product/market fit (83%) and good idea, execution, high quality (82%). On the other hand, the users least often indicated the loss of trust in traditional financial services (50%), exit options for VC (55%) and building B2B offer (59%).

For further analysis, the factor analysis was performed to group similar variables into dimensions. This statistic technique is used to reduce a large number of variables into fewer latent factors of composite constructs and involves a three-step process. Initially, determining the proper number of factors requires the transformation of the data into orthogonal variables using the eigenvectors of the matrices of the original data. Kaiser's criterion requires choosing only the factors that have eigenvalues greater than 1. Another – graphical criterion – Cattell's scree plot involves the determination of the substantial drop in the magnitude of eigenvalues.

The next step requires computing the factor loadings, i.e., regression coefficients between items and factors which express the relationship of each variable to the underlying factor. For this purpose, the principal axis of factoring procedure was used as it is appropriate when attempting to identify latent constructs rather than simply reducing the data and it does not require meeting the assumption that the distribution of variables is normal. Finally, the factor rotation was employed to achieve a simple structure in order to improve interpretability of factor loadings through reducing small loadings. Non-orthogonal rotations are more universal as they permit correlation among factors, therefore the rotation Promax with Kappa (4) was used.

Table 6.5. shows two tests that indicate the suitability of the data for factor detection. The Kaiser-Meyer-Olkin Measure of Sampling Adequacy is a statistic that indicates the proportion of variance in variables that might be caused by underlying factors. A high value (close to 1.0) generally indicates sufficient items for each factor. Meanwhile, Bartlett's test of sphericity examines the hypothesis that the correlation matrix is an identity matrix, which would indicate that variables are unrelated and therefore unsuitable for structure detection. A small value (less than 0.05) of the significance level suggests that the factor analysis is useful.

The Pattern Matrix (see Table 6.6.) displays the items and factor loadings for the rotated factors, with loadings less than 0.40 omitted to improve clarity. Only four factors with eigenvalues greater than 1 account for most of the variation, which confirms the scree plot (see Figure 6.1.).

Table 6.5 KMO and Bartlett's test

Kaiser-Meyer-Olkin Measure of Sampling Adequacy.		.961
Bartlett's Test of Sphericity	Approx. Chi-Square	6391.810
	Df	435
	Sig.	.000

Source: own elaboration based on analyzed data.

Table 6.6 Pattern matrix

	Factor			
	1	2	3	4
CSF_6	.783			
CSF_4	.718			
CSF_5	.695			
CSF_3	.672			
CSF_7	.589			
CSF_9	.529			
CSF_8	.481			
CSF_10	.457			
CSF_11	.414			
CSF_25		.803		
CSF_26		.635		
CSF_21		.623		
CSF_20		.542		
CSF_24		.455		
CSF_28			.763	
CSF_29			.705	
CSF_30			.550	
CSF_19			.497	
CSF_15				.756
CSF_16				.643
CSF_12				.443
CSF_13				.442
Variance explained	12.966	1.724	1.117	1.091
% variance explained	43.221	5.746	3.723	3.636
Cumulative % variance explained	43.221	48.967	52.690	56.326

Source: own elaboration based on analyzed data.

The first factor, which accounts for 43.221% of the variance, reflects a FinTech **product**. The factor has strong loadings on the items: product/market fit (CSF_4), good idea, execution and high quality (CSF_5) continuous learning (CSF_6), teamwork (CSF_3), networking (CSF_9) and internationalization (CSF_7). All the aspects are necessary for FinTechs to make a product a success. The second factor accounts for 5.746% of the variance and reflects a **customer base**. The factor has strong loadings on access to customer base (CSF_20), the millennials as a generation which is familiar with the Internet and FinTechs (CSF_21), broad spread of the Internet and mobile devices (CSF_25) and thus access to comprehensive services without time and location restrictions (CSF_26), cost-effectiveness (CSF_24). The third factor, which accounts for 3.723% of the variance, reflects **management** of FinTechs, in which risk and security management (CSF_28) along with organizational culture (CSF_29) and promotion of sustainable development (CSF_30) play the significant role. The last factor emphasizes the **cooperation** aspects, especially with banks and VC and explains 3.636% of the variance. The factor has strong loadings on the items exit options for VC

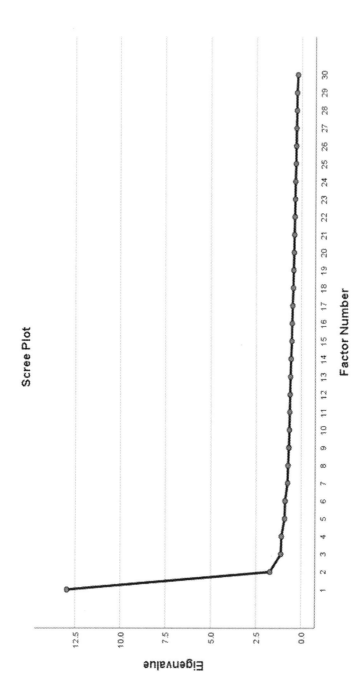

Figure 6.1 Scree plot.
Source: own elaboration based on analyzed data.

Table 6.7 Correlations

		factor score 1	factor score 2	factor score 3	factor score 4
factor score 1	Pearson correlation	1	.844**	.728**	.708**
	Sig. (2-tailed)		.000	.000	.000
factor score 2	Pearson correlation	.844**	1	.743**	.720**
	Sig. (2-tailed)	.000		.000	.000
factor score 3	Pearson correlation	.728**	.743**	1	.793**
	Sig. (2-tailed)	.000	.000		.000
factor score 4	Pearson correlation	.708**	.720**	.793**	1
	Sig. (2-tailed)	.000	.000	.000	

**. Correlation is significant at the 0.01 level (2-tailed)
Source: own elaboration based on analyzed data.

(CSF_15) and loss of trust in traditional financial services (CSF_16), cooperation with banks (CSF_13) and building B2B offer (CSF_12).

Next, the Pearson product-moment correlation coefficient was employed to measure the correlation of linear association between factor scores computed by SPSS. The results (see Table 6.7.) indicated that the correlations between all the factors were strong and positive (significant at 0.01 level).

Summary and conclusion

Based on the outcomes, it is possible to answer the research questions and confirm the two hypotheses. As mentioned above, the factor analysis performed on 30 elements identified 4 factors that together explained 56.326% of the variance. According to the data that have been conveyed, the success of FinTech does not derive from the use of technology *per se*, but from the users' point of view, the most important for FinTechs is a delivered product/service, which explained 43.221% of the variance. Good idea, a high-quality product that can satisfy the market is a must. A competitive FinTech landscape makes users' expectations for services not only remain high, but they are continually growing. To be successful, FinTechs have to adopt a continuous learning approach. Moreover, the respondents emphasize that teamwork, networking and internationalization play a significant role. In the Polish FinTech ecosystem, more and more start-ups are global born, i.e., implemented global-oriented business model (Polish Development Fund, Dealroom.co, 2020). The second factor is related to customer base and explained 5.746% of the variance. It is well known that FinTech is an industry designed to deliver high-volume and low-margin services (Deloitte, 2016). Therefore, a large customer base, especially young people who are naturally adept with technology and ability of FinTechs to adapt to the millennials' needs and expectations, determines the success, in conjunction with high internet penetration rate – by 2019, the share of EU – 27 households with internet access had risen to 90%, some 26% higher than in 2009 (Eurostat, 2020). The third factor refers to management and high organizational culture. In the opinion of Duerr et al. (2018), organizational culture – common values shared by individuals within an organization – is supposed to be a prerequisite to the successful development of digital innovations. The usage of emerging technologies brings risks to consumers and also financial stability; hence it is crucial for FinTechs to manage the risk in a proper way.

The last factor represents cooperation and accounts for 3.636% variance. In the opinion of respondents, customers put their trust in FinTechs over traditional banks. The global financial crisis in 2007–2009, which led to large losses and the collapse of established banks, shattered the trust of customers worldwide (Wewege & Thomsett, 2020). Collaboration between FinTechs and banks is essential, to both partners. The partnership takes different forms from direct cooperation contracts, through labs, to investment or acceleration programs (FinTech Poland, 2016). The findings are proved by the opinion of users; an example can be the following statement of a respondent from South Africa: 'I work in a traditional bank and have personally worked with FinTechs. Very effective partnership in my view between agility, latest technology and established customer base, legal, compliance frameworks. There is some culture clash but I believe traditional banks are aware of the need to disrupt and will accommodate if there is some compromise both ways'. The interaction for both parties can be beneficial. An example can be Millennium Goodie. It is a free mobile application and website offering access to information about coupons, discounts, promotions and events in shopping centers. It was launched by the Millennium Bank at the end of 2016 as an internal start-up and since the time it has been downloaded more than 1 million times. In order to support purchasing process, the platform uses the Microsoft Azure cloud infrastructure and technologies, such as: image recognition, voice search, geolocation, and a recommendation engine based on machine learning. This FinTech is characterized by growth potential as evidenced by the numbers, for instance, in March 2020, the users generated a record number of 180 thousand cashback transactions (five-fold increase compared to March 2019) with a total value of 17.5 million PLN. This translates into a dynamic increase in revenues of the FinTech (4.846 thousand PLN in 2018, 7.489 thousand PLN in 2019), and net profit (2018: 96 thousand PLN, 2019: 305 thousand PLN). In the future, it is planned to sell bank products using the application (ISBnews, 2020).

The conclusion can also be drawn that correlations between four factors were strong and positive.

The respondents also identified other CSFs not mentioned in the questionnaire, that is, due to mobility, digitalization, interaction and personalization FinTechs delivered a better-quality user experience, user interface friendliness for all age range while compared to traditional banking. In addition, FinTechs are characterized by the ability to see and react to industry paradigm shifts.

These research findings contribute to the literature and practice in several ways. First, they provide CSFs for FinTechs. Second, they can be useful for scholars and practitioners to understand the reasons of success or failure of financial innovation projects.

The identification of CSFs provides important basis for further surveys aimed at barriers of FinTechs. However, the findings have to be seen in the light of some limitations. The main one is the fact that the research concerns on demand-side – the user level success factors. It would be advisable to identify also the provider-level success factors. Additionally, more detailed analyses would be expected, and it would be possible to perform thorough analyses on CSFs for specific sectors of FinTech.

References

Alam, N., Gupta, L., & Zameni, A. (2019). *Fintech and Islamic finance: Digitalization, development and disruption*. Springer International Publishing. doi: https://doi.org/10.1007/978-3-030-24666-2.

Bullen, C. V., & Rockart, J. F. (1981). A Primer on Critical Success Factors. No 1220-81. Report (Alfred P. Sloan School of Management. Center for Information Systems Research) ; no. 69., Working papers, Massachusetts Institute of Technology (MIT), Sloan School of Management, https://EconPapers.repec.org/RePEc:mit:sloanp:1988.

Cashless.pl. (2020). *Map of Polish FinTech*. https://www.cashless.pl/system/uploads/ckeditor/attachments/2258/mpf2020b.pdf.

CBInsights. (2020). *The State of Fintech Q1'20 Report: Investment & Sector Trends to Watch*. https://www.cbinsights.com/research/report/fintech-trends-q1-2020/

Chen, M. A., Wu, Q., & Yang, B. (2019). How valuable is FinTech innovation? *The Review of Financial Studies*, *32*(5), 2062–2106. doi: https://doi.org/10.1093/rfs/hhy130.

Chow, T., & Cao, D. B. (2008). A survey study of critical success factors in agile software projects. *The Journal of Systems and Software*, *81*(6), 961–971. doi: https://doi.org/10.1016/j.jss.2007.08.020.

Contreras Pinochet, L. H., Diogo, G. T., Lopes, E. L., Herrero, E., & Bueno, R. L. P. (2019). Propensity of contracting loans services from FinTech's in Brazil. *International Journal of Bank Marketing*, *37*(5), 1190–1214. doi: https://doi.org/10.1108/ijbm-07-2018-0174.

Davis, F. D. (1989). Perceived usefulness, perceived ease of use, and user acceptance of information technology. *MIS Quarterly: Management Information Systems*, *13*(3), 319. doi: https://doi.org/10.2307/249008.

Deloitte. (2016). *FinTech in the CEE region. Charting the course for innovation in financial services technology*. https://www2.deloitte.com/ce/en/pages/about-deloitte/articles/fintech-cee-region.html.

Diemers, D., Lamaa, A., Salamat, J., & Steffens, T. (2015). *Developing a FinTech ecosystem in the GCC*. Retrieved from http://www.strategyand.pwc.com/media/file/Developing-a-FinTech-ecosystem-inthe-GCC.pdf.

Duerr, S., Holotiuk, F., Wagner, H. T., Beimborn, D., & Weitzel, T. (2018). What is digital organizational culture? Insights from exploratory case studies.HICSS *Proceedings of the 51st Hawaii International Conference on System Sciences.*, DOI: 10.24251/HICSS.2018.640

Eickhoff, M., Muntermann, J., & Weinrich, T. (2017). What do FinTechs actually do? A Taxonomy of FinTech Business Models. *ICIS 2017 Proceedings*. International Conference on Information Systems 2017, Seoul, South Korea

Eurostat. (2020). *Digital economy and society statistics – households and individuals*. https://ec.europa.eu/eurostat/statistics-explained/index.php/Digital_economy_and_society_statistics_-_households_and_individuals.

EY. (2017). *Global FinTech Adoption Index 2017*. Retrieved from: https://assets.ey.com/content/dam/ey-sites/ey-com/en_gl/topics/banking-and-capital-markets/ey-fintech-adoption-index-2017.pdf?download

EY. (2019). *Global FinTech Adoption Index 2019*. Retrieved from: assets.ey.com/content/dam/ey-com/en_gl/topics/banking-and-capital-markets/ey-global-FinTech-adoption-index.pdf

EY. (2020). *Law Report Compass Law and Innovation. 2020 challenges*. Retrieved from ey.com/pl_pl/law/raport-ey-law-compass-prawo-i-innowacje-wyzwania-2020

Felipe, I. J. S., & Ferreira, B. C. F. (2020). Determinants of the success of equity crowdfunding campaigns. *Revista Contabilidade & Finanças, 31*(84), 560–573. doi: https://doi.org/10.1590/1808-057x202010460.

Foundation for Financial Innovation Fintech Poland with the support of Obserwatorium. biz and the Center for New Technologies Law of the Faculty of Law and Administration of the University of Warsaw. (2016). *FinTech in Poland – barriers and opportunities, Retrieved from:* fintechpoland.com/wp-content/uploads/2020/02/FinTech-Poland-report-2016.pdf.

Gomber, P., Kauffman, R. J., Parker, C., & Weber, B. W. (2018). On the FinTech revolution: Interpreting the forces of innovation, disruption, and transformation in financial services. *Journal of Management Information Systems: JMIS, 35*(1), 220–265. doi: https://doi.org/10.1080/07421222.2018.1440766.

Haddad, C., & Hornuf, L. (2019). The emergence of the global fintech market: Economic and technological determinants. *Small Business Economics, 53*(1), 81–105. doi: https://doi.org/10.1007/s11187-018-9991-x.

Hammerschlag, Z., Bick, G., & Da Silva Luiz, J. (2020). Intra-Africa expansion and business success for fintech firms: Why adapting marketing strategies is crucial. *Strategic Direction, 36*(8), 13–15. doi: https://doi.org/10.1108/sd-05-2020-0107.

Hermawan, A., Septiawan, B., & Febriani, N. (2019). Critical success factors for financial technology startup company. *Inter-University Forum for Strengthening Academic Competency At: Bandung, Indonesia*.

Internet World Stats. (n.d.). Retrieved August 31, 2020, from http://www.internetworldstats.com.

ISBnews. (2020). *Millennium: Użytkownicy goodie cashback otrzymali już prawie 5 mln zł zwrotu*. https://www.money.pl/gielda/millennium-uzytkownicy-goodie-cashback-otrzymali-juz-prawie-5-mln-zl-zwrotu-6497012877080705a.html.

Jinasena, D. N., Spanaki, K., Papadopoulos, T., & Balta, M. E. (2020). Success and failure retrospectives of FinTech projects: A case study approach. *Information Systems Frontiers: A Journal of Research and Innovation*. doi: https://doi.org/10.1007/s10796-020-10079-4.

KPMG. (2018). *The Pulse of Fintech 2018: Global Report on Fintech Investment Trends*. https://home.kpmg/au/en/home/insights/2017/04/pulse-of-fintech.html.

Lee, D. K. C., & Teo, E. G. S. (2015). Emergence of FinTech and the LASIC principles. *SSRN Electronic Journal*. doi: https://doi.org/10.2139/ssrn.2668049.

Leong, K., Sung, A., & Teissier, C. (2020). Financial technology for sustainable development. In *Encyclopedia of the UN sustainable development goals* (pp. 1–13). Springer International Publishing.

Li, B., Hanna, S. D., & Kim, K. T. (2020). Who uses mobile payments: FinTech potential in users and non-users. *Journal of Financial Counseling and Planning*, *31*(1), 83–100. doi: https://doi.org/10.1891/jfcp-18-00083.

Nicoletti, B. (2017). *The future of FinTech: Integrating finance and technology in financial services* (1st ed.). Springer International Publishing.

Olszak, C., & Ziemba, E. (2012). Critical success factors for implementing business intelligence systems in small and medium enterprises on the example of upper Silesia, Poland. *Interdisciplinary Journal of Information Knowledge and Management*, *7*, 129–150. doi: https://doi.org/10.28945/1584.

Polish Development Fund, Dealroom.co. (2020). *Polish and CEE tech ecosystem outlook*. https://blog.dealroom.co/wp-content/uploads/2020/07/Polish-and-CEE-tech-ecosystem-outlook-Final-rev1.pdf.

Rockart, J. F. (1979). Chief executives define their own data needs. *Harvard Business Review*, *57*(2), 81–93.

Roeder, J., Rodríguez Cardona, D., Palmer, M., Werth, O., Muntermann, J., & Breitner, M. H. (2018). Make or break. Business model determinants of FinTech venture success. *Proceedings of the Multikonferenz Wirtschaftsinformatik, Lüneburg, Germany*.

Shafer, S. M., Smith, H. J., & Linder, J. C. (2005). The power of business models. *Business Horizons*, *48*(3), 199–207. doi: https://doi.org/10.1016/j.bushor.2004.10.014.

Sheng, C., Yip, J., & Cheng, J. (2017). *FinTech in China, Hitting the Moving Target, Oliver Wyman*. Retrieved from: https://www.oliverwyman.com/content/dam/oliver-wyman/v2/publications/2017/aug/Fintech_In_China_Hitting_The_Moving_Target.pdf.

Singh, S., Sahni, M. M., & Kovid, R. K. (2020). What drives FinTech adoption? A multi-method evaluation using an adapted technology acceptance model. *Management Decision*, *58*(8), 1675–1697. doi: https://doi.org/10.1108/md-09-2019-1318.

United Nations General Assembly. (1987). *Report of the world commission on environment and development: Our common future*. Oslo, Norway: United Nations General Assembly, Development and International Co-operation: Environment.

Wang, Z., Guan, Z., Hou, F., Li, B., & Zhou, W. (2019). What determines customers' continuance intention of FinTech? Evidence from YuEbao. *Industrial Management + Data Systems*, *119*(8), 1625–1637. doi: https://doi.org/10.1108/imds-01-2019-0011.

Wateridge, J. (1998). How can IS/IT projects be measured for success? *International Journal of Project Management*, *16*(1), 59–63. doi: https://doi.org/10.1016/s0263-7863(97)00022-7.

Werth, O., Rodriguez, D., Nowatschin, J., Werner, M., Guhr, N., & Breitner, M. (2019). Challenges of the Financial Industry – An Analysis of Critical Success Factors for FinTechs. *Conference: Proceedings of the 25th Americas Conference on Information Systems (AMCIS) at: Cancún, Mexico*.

Wewege, L., & Thomsett, M. C. (2020). *The digital banking revolution: How fintech companies are transforming the retail banking industry through disruptive financial innovation*. De Gruyter. doi: https://doi.org/10.1515/9781547401598.

Yeh, J. Y., & Chen, C. H. (2020). A machine learning approach to predict the success of crowdfunding fintech project. *Journal of Enterprise Information Management*, *ahead-of-print(ahead-of-print)*. doi: https://doi.org/10.1108/jeim-01-2019-0017.

Yermack, D. (2018). FinTech in Sub-Saharan Africa: What has worked well, and what hasn't. *SSRN Electronic Journal.* doi: https://doi.org/10.2139/ssrn.3240899.

Zavolokina, L., Dolata, M., & Schwabe, G. (2017). FinTech transformation: How IT-enabled innovations shape the financial sector. In S. Feuerriegel & D. Neumann (Eds.), *Enterprise applications, markets and services in the finance industry. financeCom 2016. Lecture notes in business information processing* (Vol. *276*). Springer International Publishing.

7 Systemizing the impact of fintechs on the efficiency and inclusive growth of banks' services
A literature review

Piotr Łasak and Marta Gancarczyk

Introduction

Unbanked people and organizations with limited access to basic banking services can be found even in the most developed economies. The fintech transformation of banking services has opened opportunities to increase the efficiency of banks, but also to alleviate social exclusion from financial institutions (Loo, 2019; Economist, 2018). Within the wave of the sharing economy, the banks and fintech-based businesses compete but also join their efforts to provide both the most complex services for demanding customers and to increase the access to finance for earlier excluded entities.

The literature on financial technologies and fintech-based enterprises affecting the efficiency and growth of financial and banking services has been recently advanced (Arslanian & Fisher, 2019; Hill, 2018; Nicoletti, 2017, Scardovi, 2017). Nevertheless, this literature predominantly comprises selected empirical evidence and practitioners' perspectives on individual ICT technologies, while theory-driven categorizations and evaluations of the fintech impact are rare (Kaur et al., 2017; Zhao et al., 2019). Moreover, the fintech consequences are focused on the operational use of information and communication technologies (ICT) in some of the banking areas (Bilan et al., 2019; Hayen, 2016; Wonglimpiyarat, 2019). There is still a research gap as to a comprehensive view of banks' activities affected by different categories of fintechs that generate efficiencies as well as expansion towards underserved customers and markets (Tanda & Schena, 2019). Many economies, especially developing countries, are rapidly heading towards broader application of ICT, which contributes to transformations of their financial systems, as well as financial inclusion or exclusion of social groups and enterprises (Chatterjee, 2020; Frost, 2020; Lechman, 2015; Marszk et al., 2019; Mehrotra, 2019a). The evaluations of these economic and social impacts from ICT innovations are underexplored. Against the above background and research gaps, the aim of this paper is to identify and systemize the impact channels of financial technologies on the efficiency and inclusive growth of banks' services.

DOI: 10.4324/9781003095354-7

We use the method of narrative literature review and meta-synthesis from extant studies for inference and conclusions. Our results comprise the identification and typology of results from fintechs. Particularly, we conceptually reveal and describe preservation, modification, and creation effects triggering the efficiency of banks' services. These effects comprise different consequences for inclusive growth of banking services that would address disadvantaged market segments, including retail customer segments, micro-enterprises, and new ventures. Based on the literature review, we find a causal link between the advancement of technological change and broader possibilities for financial inclusion of underserved economic agents and social groups. The most comprehensive and radical transformation from fintechs are new financial ecosystems. Nevertheless, we also identify how the adoption of fintechs may limit the access to banking services, and we point to particular barriers to this access.

The remainder of the chapter is organized as follows. In the next section, we present the conceptual background for our method. Subsequently, we describe the method for literature review and report the results. Finally, we discuss the implications of the findings and their contributions to theory and practice.

Conceptual background

The essence of financial technologies, their mechanisms, and effects for the transformation of banking services

Digitization in the financial sector comprises two phenomena and related terms, namely: i) financial technology (fintech) meaning digital technology adopted in banking services, and ii) fintech businesses (Board-FSB, 2017, p. 7; EBA, 2017; Puschmann, 2017).

From the technological perspective, fintechs denote both intangible parameters of products and processes as well as their tangible manifestations, such as software, computer, and electronic devices (Frenken & Mendritzki, 2012; Sanchez & Mahoney, 2013). The major digital technologies in financial services are: artificial intelligence (AI) (bots, automation in finance, and algorithms), cloud computing, internet of things (IoT) and mobile technologies, distributed ledger technology (DLT) (blockchain, smart contracts), data applications (big data analysis, machine learning, predictive modelling), ecosystems (infrastructure, open-source, application programming interface – APIs), as well as portal and data aggregators (BIS, 2018, p. 9; Nicoletti, 2017). Fintech businesses are based on financial technologies and form a new industry, closely related with existing financial institutions both as contractors and competitors (Schueffel, 2016; Zavolokina et al., 2016).

The impact of fintechs on banking services can be seen from the perspective of transformation mechanisms and their effects as described by Malone et al. (1999). The concept of transformative mechanisms and effects has been recently adopted by Von Briel et al. (2018) to reveal the influence of ICT on business models and market opportunities. We apply this conceptual background in the specific case of fintechs as ICT technologies focused on banking services (Vives, 2019; Wewege & Thomsett, 2020). In this vein, fintechs are drivers of mechanisms that increase the efficiency and market reach of banking. Mechanisms describe causal relationships that lead to particular effects (Gross, 2009). The major effects of transformative mechanisms are preservation, modification, and creation (Malone et al., 1999; Von Briel et al., 2018).

With reference to the bank's activities, preservation means the retention or maintenance of extant activities, modification describes the change in the bunch of activities, and creation refers to the development of new activities. Von Briel et al. (2018) identify six enabling mechanisms that lead to these effects. Namely, compression (reduction of time required to perform an activity) and conservation (reduction of resources required for an activity) lead to the preservation of extant activities with the increased efficiency. Preservation happens through the compression mechanism when big data applications reduce the time for credit assessment. Expansion (increased availability and scope of an activity) and substitution (replacement of one activity with another) result in the modification of the scope of activities. Modification is accomplished through the substitution mechanism when personal customer support is replaced by robo advisors. Ultimately, combination (new combinations of extant resources and activities), and generation (entirely new resources and activities brought about) are mechanisms resulting in the creation of new activities. Creation is achieved through the generation mechanism when peer-to-peer lending platforms are established as completely new resources, or through the combination mechanism, when mobile wallet ecosystems are introduced as new configurations of extant services.

The above fintech-driven mechanisms affect the bank's core services, particularly, payments, lending, and wealth management. The preservation effect predominantly benefits the efficiency and performance of banks as well as provides value for extant customers. Modification and creation effects raise additional aspects of expanding both the service providers and potentially, the market segments as well. Faced with the referred mechanisms and potential effects, banks may choose between digitalization of their own activity, or establishing a model of cooperation with fintech businesses, or a combination of both. This means the options from modernizing own services, through fragmentation of the offered services and their deployment between incumbent banks and fintechs (on the basis of market cooperation or outsourcing), to the emergence of new, technology-driven banks (challenger banks or neo-banks) (BIS, 2018, pp. 14–21; Tanda & Schena, 2019, pp. 51–81). The expanded players in the banking services industry potentially increase the competition and offerings to customers, including underserved market segments (Vives, 2019).

The socioeconomic implications of financial technologies

The relationships between banking services, fintechs, and socioeconomic consequences should be placed in a wider context of the sharing economy. The efficient and client-centric digitalization requires fundamental changes in business models (Tanda & Schena, 2019). Instead of integrating technology into their structures, banks often determine to participate in the development of new financial ecosystems, contributing to the sharing economy. The idea of sharing economy (also known as collaborative economy) is reflected in such systems and platforms, which enable direct user-producer contracts. The finance sector is one of the key sectors of the sharing economy. The incumbent financial institutions focus on their core competencies in the value chain and provide other non-core activities in partnerships with fintechs (Nicoletti, 2017; Scardovi, 2017). It means the shift from owning technology and infrastructure to leveraging them. Another dimension of the sharing economy is peer-to-peer platforms that link contracting parties without the intermediation of banks (Iman, 2018; Jakšič & Marinč, 2019; Omarini, 2018).

As new players in financial services, fintechs are responsive to the needs of the real economy rather than to financial markets. An example of such solutions is mobile wallets created in South-East Asian countries by ride-hailing services. Companies, such as Grab or Gojek, provide solutions that enable cashless taxi services offered via smartphone applications. Moreover, they offer digital wallets topped up in cash with third parties (retail entities) and extend the range of services by small-business loans, microinsurance, and cross-border remittances (Economist, 2019; Loo, 2019). Consequently, banking services are developed in largely unbanked societies, where even 75–80% of population has no access to banks' offerings (Arner et al., 2020). Exclusion from the mainstream financial system applies not only to developing countries, but it is also the case in the United States or United Kingdom. This calls for broad and systemic approach to the growth of banking services, with the recognition of inclusion processes (Economist, 2018).

Financial technologies have demonstrated a high capacity to contribute to financial inclusion. The possibilities in this regard range from offering traditional banking services on-online to peer-to-peer lending platforms (Chatterjee, 2020; Mehrotra, 2019a; Sha'ban et al., 2019). Useful examples are mobile phone-based money transfer services, as well as payments and micro-financing services offered by such companies like M-Pesa (Hill, 2018; Tyce, 2020). The latter fintech business offers mobile banking services in such African countries like Kenya, Tanzania, South Africa, Ghana, Mozambique, or Egypt (Arslanian & Fisher, 2019, pp. 81–86; Noonan, 2019). The Chinese company Ant Financial has launched adjacent services in Asian countries (e.g. China, Bangladesh, India, Malaysia, the Philippines, and Thailand) (Economist, 2019). The main role of such companies as M-Pesa or Ant is not to challenge traditional banks or to displace them, but rather to help them to serve customers they would otherwise not be able to reach (Chen, 2016). Fintechs businesses are equipped with data and technical possibilities to reach nearly a quarter of the world's unbanked population (Economist, 2018). They do so by combining different services (e.g. loans and payment services linked with insurance or investment), and by offering these services in novel ways. Fintechs businesses not only reduce the costs of banking services as suppliers, but they directly offer these services in a better and cheaper way than traditional financial institutions. The quoted examples imply fintechs' and fintech-based companies' role in efficiency gains and inclusion in banking services. However, this socioeconomic impact from fintechs has been less explored and requires systematic and in-depth investigation based on extant empirical evidence (Effah, 2016; Nicoletti, 2017, p. 74). Moreover, there is an identified research gap regarding a comprehensive and theory-driven framework that would explain how different fintech-driven mechanisms and related effects jointly bring about efficiencies and socioeconomic inclusion in banking services (Ozili, 2018; Shofawati, 2019).

Material and method

In order to address the above research gaps, we adopted the method of narrative literature review and meta-synthesis from extant studies. Narrative reviews demonstrate qualitative, comprehensive, and up-to-date approach to a specified issue (Collins & Fauser, 2005). Although they are less objective than systematic reviews, the selection criteria for literature analysis need to be specified (Green et al., 2006). Narrative reviews are valued for the synthesis of the advancement of an individual topic, predominantly in its emerging or growing phase. They point to the latest achievements in the field, intending to launch new views (Green et al., 2006). Since our research aims to systemize a broad and growing topic of fintechs' impact channels on bank services, the narrative review and meta-synthesis are appropriate methods (Hoon, 2013).

The selection of literature for review embraced two phases. In the first phase, the general search was done in WoS and Scopus. The search used keywords: "bank" and "fintech", "fintech" and "inclusion", and it produced 502 items. Our review was not designed as systematic due to the explorative and novel conceptual background presented in section 2 that could not be investigated with more specified keywords. Nevertheless, the use of databases is intended to recognize the extant stock of knowledge. We found the majority of resources published in 2016–2020 and we focused on this period. The literature search embraced research papers, monographs, and research reports of both theoretical and empirical nature. By screening the abstracts and article bodies, we purposefully selected these contributions that addressed the impact channels of fintechs on banking and socioeconomic inclusion.

In the second phase, when reviewing articles bodies, we found some widely cited contributions are lacking, so we added these recognized items. Ultimately, we selected the literature relevant to perform the classifications and evaluations according to the constructs of our conceptual background. The final sample amounted to 40 items indicated in the list of references as the core items of our analysis.

The literature review was guided by the research framework based on the economics of banks and technology economics (Frenken & Mendritzki, 2012; Kotarba, 2016; Sanchez & Mahoney, 2013; Vives, 2019; Wewege & Thomsett, 2020). We adopted the categorization of fintech-driven mechanisms and effects by Malone et al. (1999) and Von Briel et al. (2018) to describe and explain the fintech transformation of banks' services. Further, we systemized these mechanisms and effects as to efficiencies and inclusive growth of banking services, pointing to advantages and limitations.

Results

Increased efficiency of banking services – A preservation effect from fintechs

The preservation effect is accomplished through fintech-driven mechanisms of compression and conservation (Table 7.1.). The compression mechanism ensures reduction of time required to perform such activities as credit rating assessment or payments. Credit rating assessment is accelerated due to the application of big data, which also improves quality of decision-making. When linked with machine learning, big data upgrades the pace and quality of the bank's broader internal processes. Automated payment systems and digital exchange platforms, in turn, speed up the execution of transactions and facilitate control over these operations.

Time compression can be also observed in improvement of the quality and increase of intensity of the bank's internal communication. Moreover, internal finance operations accelerate, since artificial intelligence collects data from all relevant sources (Bilan et al., 2019; Boot, 2017; Jakšič & Marinč, 2019). By combining machine learning with data capture technology, banks are able to supply intelligent document checking engines with transaction-level data streams on a continuous basis, even in real-time (Tanda & Schena, 2019).

The conservation mechanisms ensure reduction of tangible resources required to perform operations, such as the number of banks' branches, which can be centralized in one geographic location. Positive implications of these divestments for the overall performance are widely reported (Coetzee, 2018; Medina-Molina et al., 2019; Nam et al., 2016). Another driver of resource conservation is automation of internal processes that takes over some tasks earlier executed by human agents and performs them with the use of machines and software (Hernández-Nieves et al., 2020; Son et al., 2019).

Table 7.1 Preservation effects on the banking activity and socioeconomic inclusion

Mechanisms	Time compression	Resource conservation
Major fintechs to accomplish preservation effects	AI, automated payment system, big data, machine learning.	
Impact on efficiency	Increased efficiency through time compression, based on the application of big data to the credit rating assessment and automated payment systems to the payment services. Combining data from all required sources with machine learning leads to the improvement of the speed of the bank's internal processes.	Increased efficiency based on resource conservation – reduced number of bank branches, automation of selected internal banking operations, centralization of activities; engagement of customers into the transaction processing through depositor devices, video banking, self-service kiosks, etc.
Impact on socioeconomic inclusion	Time compression makes the banking services more comfortable, time-saving, and increasing productivity. AI and big data reduce information asymmetries and transaction costs, as well as allow for absorption of new technological standards.	Savings on resources that would otherwise be spent on direct physical interactions with bank service providers. Reduced human participation impedes interactions between the bank and its customers, still, it might lower the quality of advisory, or even exclude some social groups with limited ICT skills and access to the internet.

Source: own elaboration based on Arslanian & Fisher, 2019; Bilan et al., 2019; Boot, 2017; Chatterjee, 2020; Chen, 2016; Coetzee, 2018; Frost, 2020; Hernández-Nieves et al., 2020; Holotiuk et al., 2018; Jakšič & Marinč, 2019; MacDonald et al., 2016; Medina-Molina et al., 2019; Mehrotra, 2019a; Mehrotra, 2019b; Nam et al., 2016; Ozili, 2018; Ramesh, 2019; Sibanda et al., 2020; Son et al., 2019; Tanda & Schena, 2019; Von Briel et al., 2018; Wewege & Thomsett, 2020.

The preservation effect from fintechs leads to the increased efficiency of banking services enabled by cost reduction and economies of scale (Boot, 2017; Holotiuk et al., 2018; MacDonald et al., 2016; Nam et al., 2016). Moreover, digital solutions improve quality of operations through smooth communication and support for decision-making. Fintechs' role is largely supportive to decision-making and does not fundamentally change the core processes of service delivery (Bilan et al., 2019; Coetzee, 2018).

The preservation effect and mechanisms leading to it can also be evaluated from the perspective of customers and wider socioeconomic impact. Customers do not need to spend a long time to get a loan, and they have easy access to other banking services through mobile applications on smartphones and personal computers (Hill, 2018; Kotarba, 2016; Ramesh, 2019). Moreover, reshaping the infrastructure towards higher agility ICT in the area of sales management, marketing, and customer intelligence, reduces "time to market" and allows for faster absorption of new technology standards. Time and resource efficiency of banking services improves customer comfort and saves his or her time. Overall, it reduces transaction costs related to information acquisition, processing of services, and monitoring the execution of services, ultimately increasing productivity. The application of solutions like AI and big data may alleviate information asymmetries between banks and customers (Bilan et al., 2019; Coetzee, 2018; Jakšič & Marinč, 2019). Time compression is valuable for virtually all groups of customers, from retail customers, who process their ongoing affairs, up to big investors who make significant investments in capital markets. Moreover, customers benefit from the conservation of resources that would otherwise be spent on direct physical interactions with bank service providers. The preservation effects primarily increase the utility of extant customers and stimulate the increased volume of transactions with these customers. Still, the consequences for broadening the market reach to new or underserved groups are limited.

Besides valuable benefits, there are some downside impacts and shortcomings from time compression and resource conservation by fintechs. Reduction of the direct human participation in some activities leads the changes in the nature of services (Frost, 2020; Kotarba, 2016). The quality of interactions without human factors might be inferior than the quality of services supported by human advice and assistance in some areas, e.g. in lending or wealth management (Jakšič & Marinč, 2019). Moreover, technologies flatten structures providing for direct relationships between clients and banks' back and front-offices, without necessity to use branch intermediaries. Still, the customers who lack adequate ICT-related skills or efficient access to internet connections might experience difficulties or even exclusion from digitized services.

Expanded market – A modification effect from fintechs

The modification effect stems from fintech-driven expansion and substitution mechanisms (Table 7.2.).

The expansion mechanism increases efficiency through scale economies and cost reductions. This is accomplished by broadening the scope of the services with mobile payments and lending operations (non-cash payment methods) executed via electronic platforms (Boot, 2017). The bank's front office is changed and forces the implementation of digital space for new customers inside incumbent banks (Bilan et al., 2019; Effah, 2016; Holotiuk et al., 2018; Japparova & Rupeika-Apoga, 2017; Nam et al., 2016). Wealth management services are transforming by application of many digital solutions,

Table 7.2 Modification effects on the banking activity and socioeconomic inclusion

Mechanisms	Expansion of bank services	Substitution of bank services
Major fintechs	AI and online solutions, cloud computing, data applications (big data, machine learning), DLT (blockchain), application program interfaces (APIs), IoT, and real-time processing.	
Impact on efficiency and the extent of the market	Increased efficiency (economies of scale and cost reduction) by expansion of the payment and lending activities via electronic platforms, digital payments, APIs, and online solutions. Wealth management services enhanced through AI and robo advisors.	Increased efficiency by substitution of lending activities delivered by humans with automated lending processes. Traditional direct contacts with customers substituted with non-bank networks, sensors, trackers, and transmitters. The efficiencies from the substitution of the bank's internal processes, e.g. accounting and data collection or analytics, with cloud accounting and cloud computing, using DLT technology, data applications, IoT, and real-time processing. Overall better control and monitoring over transactions.
Impact on socioeconomic inclusion	Banking services more accessible to customers with ICT skills who prefer digital tools over traditional banking. Mobile and online services broaden accessibility of banking, increase the number of users, and commoditizes some services, like savings and investments. Market expanded due to the inclusion of new, younger generation of customers (millennials, technology-oriented customers). AI and data applications enable better credit scoring and risk reduction in the services offered for these earlier underserved groups.	Traditional lending and payment substituted by digitized solutions and supported with customized advisory and cash management. Geographic proximity replaced by social proximity of social networks. Enlargement of market scope and size by new customers, predominantly younger generation preferring alternative financial products. The threat of exclusion for the customers unskilled in ICT tools and with limited broadband access.

Source: own elaboration based on Arner et al., 2020; Arslanian & Fisher, 2019; Bertsch et al., 2020; Bilan et al., 2019; Bömer & Maxin, 2018; Chatterjee, 2020; Chen, 2016; Coetzee, 2018; Effah, 2016; Frost, 2020; Gupta & Xia, 2018; Hedman & Henningsson, 2015; Hill, 2018; Holotiuk et al., 2018; Japparova & Rupeika-Apoga, 2017; MacDonald et al., 2016; Mehrotra, 2019a; Mehrotra, 2019b; Ozili, 2018; Schmidt et al., 2018; Sibanda et al., 2020; Vives, 2019; Von Briel et al., 2018; Wewege & Thomsett, 2020; Wonglimpiyarat, 2019; Zhao et al., 2019.

like trading applications, digital asset managers, digital, and robo advisers. Investments can be based on individual needs and personal investment portfolio, aggregated view and analysis of multiple accounts, as well as platforms for sophisticated investors (Gupta & Xia, 2018, p. 221). Besides efficiencies, these technologies lower the risks related to transactions they support.

Moreover, the expansion mechanism broadens the market scope. The massive use of DLT, together with APIs, and sometimes IoT leads to the increase of the number of communication channels and platforms available to customers (Bilan et al., 2019; Zhao et al., 2019, p. 4). As a result, the wider use of such channels of communication and automation enables the process of inclusion. The banking services market is broadened by the new groups of customers, particularly a younger generation of millennials and technology-oriented customers (Chatterjee, 2020; Coetzee, 2018; Frost, 2020; Vives, 2019).

The substitution mechanisms deepen the transformation of banking, enabling the replacement of tangible resources and direct services with intangible assets and fully online operations. Efficiency gains through substitution became crucial due to the growing pressure to operate with lower margins and to identify profitable and diverse services and new banking products (Bertsch et al., 2020; Bömer & Maxin, 2018; Medina-Molina et al., 2019). Costly and staff-assisted bank branches are substituted by digital banking with self-assisted services and automated solutions (Nam et al., 2016). Another example of substitution is the change of the banking services distribution channel from multi- to omnichannel (Nicoletti, 2017). The efficiencies pertain both to customer services and bank internal operations (accounting and analytics) enhanced by technologies like APIs, cloud computing, data applications (big data and machine learning), and DLT.

Similarly, as the expansion mechanism, substitution results in the inclusion of new groups of customers, who prefer digital channels of communication. Nevertheless, here we deal with the replacement and largely termination of traditional banking channels with the new, fintech-based operations (Effah, 2016; Hau et al., 2017; Hill, 2018; Wonglimpiyarat, 2019). Consequently, this mechanism brings the threat of exclusion to customers unskilled in ICT tools and with limited broadband access. The latter consequence appears even stronger than in the case we observed for the conservation mechanism within the preservation effect.

New financial ecosystem and inclusive growth – A creation effect from fintechs

The creation effect consists in the development of new environment for banking services on the basis of extant resources (combination), or in the replacement of traditional services by their alternative forms (generation) (Table 7.3.). In the combination mechanism, fintechs integrate their resources and activities into intertwined ecosystems.

Table 7.3 Creation effects on the banking activity and socioeconomic inclusion

Mechanisms	Combination banks' and fintechs' activities in bank's structure	Generation new activities offered by fintechs, outside the banking sector
Major fintechs	AI, data applications, open-source APIs, DLT, and other fintechs.	AI, APIs, data applications (big data, machine learning), DLT (blockchain technology).
Impact on efficiency	Efficiency increased based on new architecture of ecosystems. Banking activities combined into the SOA. Multifaceted interdependencies among functions and services in the financial ecosystem enhanced by APIs, AI, big data, and DTL.	Efficiency growth due to the generation of new, alternative fintech-based services that compete with extant bank services, e.g. crowdfunding platforms. The new services based on AI, data applications, and blockchain linked through APIs and executed more efficiently compared to traditional banking. In addition to new services, the efficiency is increased also by ecosystems, where fintechs play the role of integrators.
Impact on socioeconomic inclusion	Customer-centric and broadened banking with stronger participation of fintechs and fintech businesses. AI, APIs, data applications, and DTL link banking services (lending, payment), tailor them to society's lifestyle (e.g. shopping, travelling, or even investing), and better adjust the services to customer needs (e.g. disabled people).	Fintechs enrich the banking services environment, make the bank services more agile, and accelerate the process of financial inclusion. Alternative services like crowdfunding (peer-to-peer lending), cryptocurrency payments, or high-frequency trading. Addressed both refined customers with specialized needs, and disadvantaged and excluded clients without collateral – e.g. individuals, micro-firms, new, innovative ventures. Financially enhanced both commercial, and social-purpose projects (charitable, cultural, ecological, etc.). The referred benefits unavailable for groups disadvantaged in the area of ICT and broadband access.

Source: own elaboration based on Arner et al., 2020; Arslanian & Fisher, 2019; Barberis & Arner, 2016; Börner & Maxin, 2018; Chatterjee, 2020; Chen, 2016; Effah, 2016; Frost, 2020; Gozman et al., 2018; Gupta & Xia, 2018; Hedman & Henningsson, 2015; Jagtiani & Lemieux, 2018; Lee & Shin, 2018; Loo, 2019; Nicoletti, 2017; Omarini, 2018; Ozili, 2018; Puschmann, 2017; Scardovi, 2017; Schmidt et al., 2018; Suryatmojo et al., 2018; Tyce, 2020; Von Briel et al., 2018; Zhao et al., 2019.

The combination of bank's activities and assets into more complex systems launches a new dimension of contemporary banking services. Traditional bank activities become parts of a broader financial ecosystem, namely Services Oriented Architecture (SOA), created due to the application of APIs. The deployment of AI, data applications, and DTL enable creation of new solutions and functionalities, e.g. bank's mobile wallets and payment ecosystems are integrated with payment providers like VISA or Mastercard (Effah, 2016; Hedman & Henningsson, 2015; Omarini, 2018, p. 114; Tyce, 2020). SOA is beneficial not only for banks' customers but also provides the improvement of the bank efficiency. It enables to consolidate several bank accounts and services, unify all bank balances, control spending, pay bills, among others (Lee & Shin, 2018; Suryatmojo et al., 2018). The example includes cloud accounting, which provides a fundamental transformation of the bank's internal activities like largely automated bookkeeping. Banks take advantage of newly created solutions, like platforms Xero, SageOne, or Clear Books, which link transaction accounts and create "financial web", enabling higher efficiency and better performance of the internal processes. The efficiency gains in the internal processes benefit indirectly customers as well. The customers, e.g. small and medium enterprises, can use online platforms for automatic reconciliation of their business banking transactions (Barberis & Arner, 2016; Schmidt et al., 2018). Overall, based on the combination mechanism, services are better executed, banks offer broader range of products, and finally the range of bank's customers is being widened (Frost, 2020; Gupta & Xia, 2018; Sibanda et al., 2020; Tyce, 2020).

The generation mechanism happens when banking services are offered by non-bank entities through digital channels, platforms, and portable devices, such as laptops mobile phones (BIS, 2018; Guo et al., 2015; Puschmann, 2017; Scardovi, 2017). Alike the creation mechanism, generation is supported with technologies like AI, APIs, data applications, and DLT. These fintechs enable spinning out the bank's standardized activities to external entities, structures, and processes. These new solutions capture a large part of the banks' legacy. Traditional lending, payments, and wealth management activities are offered through single payment solutions (near-field communication/NCF/or quick reference/QR/codes in payments), crowdfunding, or peer-to-peer lending platforms. As a result, banks and newly generated entities (fintech businesses), structures (crowdfunding platforms), and processes (online-transaction processing and payments) integrate into a comprehensive financial ecosystem, capable to serve a variety of customers, with diversified needs and financial affordability (Bömer & Maxin, 2018; Frost, 2020; Gupta & Xia, 2018; Hedman & Henningsson, 2015; Omarini, 2018; Scardovi, 2017).

The creation effect is relevant for attracting customers, who potentially have access to banking services, but demonstrate individual preferences in this regard. An example is young customers to whom simplicity matters. They easily accept solutions like the contactless services and biometric ways of identification that are consistent with their lifestyles (e.g. way of shopping, traveling, or even investing) (Boot, 2017; Economist, 2019). The combination of banking services with different fintechs enables to offer banking services also to people, who were excluded from such services due to their disability.

Another dimension of the creation relates to banking activities offered by nonbank companies to unbanked customers (Frost, 2020). Fintech businesses offer loans to lower-income consumers without collateral. Moreover, they serve micro-firms, new, innovative ventures, and real estate market (especially offered to those consumers who prefer faster, more accurate, safer, and more affordable services options than traditional mortgage lenders) with diversified and advanced methods of financing, including equity funding and securities (Chen, 2016; Gupta & Xia, 2018; Jagtiani & Lemieux, 2018, p. 3; Loo, 2019). Lending Club, Avant, and SoFi offer instruments based on peer-to-peer lending platforms, such as loans for variety of needs, including student loans, mortgages, personal loans, payday loans, and high interest credit cards (Jakšič & Marinč, 2019). Sometimes the web of participants of digitalization banking services is broader. Not only fintechs but also social media facilitate the development of communities through crowdfunding and peer-to-peer lending. Acting together with fintechs, they change the societies and markets, enabling people and businesses to raise funds for charity or venture capital (Gozman et al., 2018; Iman, 2018; Lee & Shin, 2018). The referred benefits for underserved markets are still unavailable for groups disadvantaged in the area of ICT and broadband access.

There is a great socioeconomic impact of the ecosystems created as the result of cooperation between banks and fintechs businesses. The multi-sided banks and external system integrators (dedicated platforms that govern the architecture of financial ecosystems) enable inclusion of wide social groups, formerly excluded due to poverty, lack of skills, geographical distance, or unaddressed particular needs. Banks are aware of some of these constraints, but they are not able to provide adequate solutions, as fintechs can do. For example, soft and non-standard information is important for evaluating lower-quality borrowers (Gozman et al., 2018; Jakšič & Marinč, 2019).

Fintech businesses continuously increase their importance in banking services, and in shaping the models of contemporary banking. Collaboration of fintechs and banks is a critical success factor in creating these new models and the pathway to the new sharing economy. (Schmidt et al., 2018; Zhao et al., 2019). Two main models of bank-fintech ecosystems have been emerging. In the first solution, the bank is in the center of the ecosystem and pursues technological and business development after the acquisition of fintech businesses. In the second one, fintech businesses are hubs of the ecosystem and provide multi-collaborative platforms that deliver value to involved banks. The latter solution is, however, less favorable for banks. Fintechs would capture rich and commercially sensitive information from different banks, and exploit this information, disadvantaging banks (Sibanda et al.,

2020). This is, however, beneficial for socioeconomic inclusion, as fintechs can offer broad range of financial (not only banking) services for formerly excluded clients.

Discussion and conclusions

Following the aim of this study, we have conceptually categorized and systemized the impact of fintechs on banking services, pointing to three major effects and mechanisms that underlie these potentially emerging effects. The systemization of the effects and related mechanisms was based on the review of empirical and theoretical studies. Our review points to the causal links between types of effects and consequences for efficiency and inclusive growth of banking services. Preservation effects maintain traditional ways of performing services, which are complemented by fintechs to increase efficiency and volume of operations within extant customer base (Nam et al., 2016; Ramesh, 2019). However, these effects raise limited consequences for market expansion and particularly, for reaching out underserved customers. Modification effect combines efficiency gains with considerable market expansion towards the groups with developed ICT skills and demands. Technology lowers risks in addressing some underserved customer groups by more comprehensive and reliable credit scoring as well as control and monitoring over transactions. It also enables substitution of some of the channels of banking services distribution with non-bank solutions (Gozman et al., 2018; Japparova & Rupeika-Apoga, 2017; Zhao et al., 2019). Creation effects bring about new instruments that are alternative to traditional financial operations and institutions offering them (Omarini, 2018). The consequences are the most comprehensive in this case, embracing increased efficiencies, expanded market, and ultimately, the most significant socioeconomic impact, comprising the inclusion of disadvantaged individuals and organizations. The referred relationships between fintech-based mechanisms and socioeconomic consequences point to the increased efficiencies and inclusive growth when more advanced and transformative fintechs are applied.

Nevertheless, we also find reverse effects and the threats from exclusion of social groups with lower ICT skills and limited access to technical infrastructure, such as broadband access, and with lower income that prevents ongoing investment in personal hardware and software. Our recommendations to alleviate these barriers target both decision-makers in banks, alternative financial institutions, and policy-makers. Financial institutions, both traditional and fintech businesses, need to consider education and training tools for customers, as well as adopting solutions that acknowledge open standards and compatibility to enable the ease of upgrading rather than completely new investment in hardware and software to use financial services (Jakšič & Marinč, 2019; Kotarba, 2016). Policy recommendations comprise educational, infrastructure, public procurement, and intellectual property arrangements. Educational policy needs to address the development of education programs and training for wide society that would integrate financial knowledge and ICT skills. Infrastructure policy should actively diminish ICT exclusion, both in the area of broadband access and access to basic equipment and devices that might be freely available to lower-income groups. Public procurement needs to raise demand for innovations that are directed at financial affordability of fintech-based banking services. Finally, intellectual property policy might actively promote open standards and compatibility through public purchases strengthening these solutions.

The results of our study complement and advance the earlier research on bank services affected by fintechs (Bömer & Maxin, 2018; Hedman & Henningsson, 2015; Holotiuk et al., 2018; Jakšič & Marinč, 2019; Omarini, 2018). The extant studies are largely focused on some selected aspects of fintechs in banking, such as new business models or relationships between banks and fintech businesses. We add to this research by theory-driven and thus comprehensive view of banking services affected by fintechs and evaluated according to efficiency and inclusive growth. Nam et al. (2016), Ramesh (2019), and Schmidt et al. (2018) highlight the relationships among banks and fintech businesses as well as related effects on value creation in business models. We complement these studies by explaining not only effects, but also the mechanisms leading to these outcomes. Moreover, Gozman et al. (2018) identify the process of disintermediation of some banking activities by third parties. We considered this process within the creation effects from fintechs, and we highlighted broader consequences for the social and economic inclusion or exclusion from banking services.

This research intends to provide the contributions to theory and practice. First, it advances the theory by a comprehensive view of the bank services affected by fintechs, as well as by the systemization of efficiencies and inclusive growth prospects from fintechs (Bilan et al., 2019; Bömer & Maxin, 2018; Loo, 2019). Second, the theoretical perspective on the ICT impact on banking services has been enhanced by the categorization of fintech mechanisms and effects (Gozman et al., 2018; Chen, 2016; Schmidt et al., 2018). Third, the categorization of mechanism and effects of financial technologies on banks' services forms a conceptual background for further empirical studies (Bilan et al., 2019; Coetzee, 2018). Fourth, this study proposes practical implications for decision-makers in banks and fintech businesses, such as utility of particular technologies for efficiency and socioeconomic impact, as well as related consequences and challenges (Arner et al., 2020; Frost, 2020).

References

*Sources selected from the Scopus and Web of Science databases as the core 40 items for the analysis.

*Arner, D. W., Buckley, R. P., Zetzsche, D. A., & Veidt, R. (2020). Sustainability, FinTech and financial inclusion. *European Business Organization Law Review, 21*, 7–35.

Arslanian, H., & Fisher, F. (2019). *The future of finance: The impact of FinTech, AI, and crypto on financial services*. Palgrave Macmillan.

*Barberis, J., & Arner, D. W. (2016). FinTech in China: From shadow Banking to P2P lending. In P. Tasca, T. Aste, L. Pelizzon, & N. Perony (Eds.), *Banking beyond banks and money. New economic windows* (pp. 69–96). Springer.

*Bertsch, C., Hull, I., Qi, Y., & Zhang, X. (2020). Bank misconduct and online lending. *Journal of Banking & Finance*, *116*, 105822.

*Bilan, A., Degryse, H., O'Flynn, K., & Ongena, S. (2019). *How banks and financial technology are reshaping financial markets*. Palgrave Macmillan.

BIS. (2018). *Sound practices. Implications of fintech developments for banks and bank supervisors*. https://www.bis.org/bcbs/publ/d431.pdf.

Board-FSB. (2017). *Financial stability implications from fintech: Supervisory and regulatory issues that merit authorities' attention*. https://www.fsb.org/wp-content/uploads/R270617.pdf.

Boot, A. W. A. (2017). The future of Banking: From scale & scope economies to fintech 2020. *European Economy. Banks, Regulation, and the Real Sector*, *2*, 77–95.

*Bömer, M., & Maxin, H. (2018). Why fintechs cooperate with banks – Evidence from Germany. *Zeitschrift Für Die Gesamte Versicherungswissenschaft*, *107*(4), 359–386.

*Von Briel, F., Davidsson, P., & Recker, J. (2018). Digital technologies as external enablers of new venture creation in the IT hardware sector. *Entrepreneurship Theory and Practice*, *42*(1), 47–69.

*Chatterjee, A. (2020). Financial inclusion, information and communication technology diffusion, and economic growth: A panel data analysis. *Information Technology for Development*, *26*(3), 607–635.

*Chen, L. (2016). From fintech to finlife: The case of fintech development in China. *China Economic Journal*, *9*(3), 225–239.

*Coetzee, J. (2018). Strategic implications of Fintech on South African retail banks. *South African Journal of Economic and Management Sciences*, *21*(1). doi : https://doi.org/10.4102/sajems.v21i1.2455.

Collins, J. A., & Fauser, B. C. (2005). Balancing the strengths of systematic and narrative reviews. *Human Reproduction Update*, *11*(2), 103–104. doi: https://doi.org/10.1093/humupd/dmh058.

EBA. (2017). *Discussion Paper on the EBA's approach to financial technology (FinTech)* (EBA/DP/2017/02).https://www.eba.europa.eu/sites/default/documents/files/documents/10180/1919160/7a1b9cda-10ad-4315-91ce-d798230ebd84/EBA%20Discussion%20Paper%20on%20Fintech%20%28EBA-DP-2017-02%29.pdf.

Economist (2018). *Exclusive access*. https://www.economist.com/special-report/2018/05/04/financial-inclusion-is-making-great-strides.

Economist(2019).*Thebankinyourpocket*.https://www.economist.com/special-report/2015/05/07/the-bank-in-your-pocket.

Effah, J. (2016). Institutional effects on e-payment entrepreneurship in a developing country: Enablers and constraints. *Information Technology for Development*, *22*(2), 205–219.

Frenken, K., & Mendritzki, S. (2012). Optimal modularity: A demonstration of the evolutionary advantage of modular architectures. *Journal of Evolutionary Economics*, *22*(5), 935–956.

*Frost, J. (2020). *The economic forces driving fintech adoption across countries* (BIS Working Paper No. 838). Bank for International Settlements. https://www.bis.org/publ/work838.htm.

*Gozman, D., Hedman, J., & Sylvest, K. (2018). *Open banking: Emergent roles, risks & opportunities* (Association for Information Systems Research Papers 183). https://aisel.aisnet.org/ecis2018_rp/183/.

Green, B. N., Johnson, C. D., & Adams, A. (2006). Writing narrative literature reviews for peer-reviewed journals: Secrets of the trade. *Journal of Chiropractic Medicine, 5*(3), 101–117.

Gross, N. (2009). A pragmatist theory of social mechanisms. *American Sociological Review, 74*(3), 358–379.

Guo, Z., Kauffman, R. J., Lin, M., & Ma, D. (2015). Mechanism design for near real-time retail payment and settlement systems. *2015 48th Hawaii International Conference on System Sciences*, 4824–4833.

*Gupta, A., & Xia, C. (2018). A paradigm shift in Banking: Unfolding Asia's FinTech adventures. In *Banking and finance issues in emerging markets* (pp. 215–254). Emerald Publishing Limited. doi: https://doi.org/10.1108/S1571-038620180000025010.

Hau, H., Huang, Y., Shan, H., & Sheng, Z. (2017). *TechFin in China: Credit market completion and its growth effect.* Proceedings of the BFER 6th Annual Conference. http://52.76.234.106/media/abfer-events-2018/annual-conference/international-macroeconomics/AC18P1014_Ant_Financial_and_Growth_Effect_Paper_first_draft.pdf.

Hayen, R. (2016). *FinTech: The Impact and Influence of Financial Technology on Banking and the Finance Industry.* CreateSpace Independent Publishing Platform.

Hedman, J., & Henningsson, S. (2015). The new normal: Market cooperation in the mobile payments ecosystem. *Electronic Commerce Research and Applications, 14*(5), 305–318.

*Hernández-Nieves, E., Hernández, G., Gil-González, A. B., Rodríguez-González, S., & Corchado, J. M. (2020). Fog computing architecture for personalized recommendation of banking products. *Expert Systems with Applications, 140*, 112900.

*Hill, J. (2018). *Fintech and the remaking of financial Institutions.* Elsevier.

*Holotiuk, F., Klus, M. F., Lohwasser, T. S., & Moormann, J. (2018). *Motives to form alliances for digital innovation: The case of banks and fintechs.* BLED 2018 Proceedings. 22. https://aisel.aisnet.org/bled2018/22.

Hoon, C. (2013). Meta-synthesis of qualitative case studies: An approach to theory building. *Organizational Research Methods, 16*(4), 522–546.

Iman, N. (2018). Assessing the dynamics of fintech in Indonesia. *Investment Management and Financial Innovations, 15*(4), 296–303.

*Jagtiani, J., & Lemieux, C. (2018). Do fintech lenders penetrate areas that are underserved by traditional banks? *Journal of Economics and Business, 100*, 43–54.

*Jakšič, M., & Marinč, M. (2019). Relationship banking and information technology: The role of artificial intelligence and FinTech. *Risk Management, 21*(1), 1–18.

*Japparova, I., & Rupeika-Apoga, R. (2017). Banking business models and the digital future: The case of Latvia. *European Research Studies Journal, XX*(3A), 846–860.

Kaur, H., Lechman, E., & Marszk, A. (2017). *Catalyzing development through ICT adoption: The developing world experience.* Springer International Publishing AG.

*Kotarba, M. (2016). New factors inducing changes in the retail banking customer relationship management (CRM) and their exploration by the fintech industry. *Foundations of Management, 8*(1), 69–78.

Lechman, E. (2015). *ICT diffusion in developing countries. Towards a new concept of technological takeoff.* Springer International Publishing AG.

*Lee, I., & Shin, Y. J. (2018). Fintech: Ecosystem, business models, investment decisions, and challenges. *Business Horizons*, *61*, 35–46.
*Loo, M. K. L. (2019). Enhancing financial inclusion in ASEAN: Identifying the Best growth markets for fintech. *Journal of Risk and Financial Management*, *12*(4), 181.
Marszk, A., Lechman, E., & Kato, Y. (2019). *The emergence of ETFs in Asia-Pacific*. Springer International Publishing AG.
MacDonald, T. J., Allen, D., & Potts, J. (2016). Blockchains and the boundaries of self-organized economies: Predictions for the future of Banking. In P. Tasca, T. Aste, L. Pelizzon, & N. Perony (Eds.), *Banking beyond banks and money. New economic windows* (pp. 279–296). Springer.
Malone, T. W., Crowston, K., Lee, J., Pentland, B., Dellarocas, C., Wyner, G., Quimby, J., Osborn, C. S., Bernstein, A., Herman, G., Klein, M., & O'Donnell, E. (1999). Tools for inventing organizations: Toward a handbook of organizational processes. *Management Science*, *45*(3), 425–443.
*Medina-Molina, C., Rey-Moreno, M., Cazurro-Barahona, V., & Parrondo, S. (2019). The adoption of mobile banking applications from a dual perspective. *Sociology & Technoscience*, *9*(2), 1–22.
*Mehrotra, A. (2019a). Financial inclusion through FinTech –A case of lost focus. *Proceedings of the International Conference on Automation, Computational and Technology Management (ICACTM)*. doi: https://doi.org/10.1109/ICACTM.2019.8776857.
*Mehrotra, A. (2019b). Artificial Intelligence in financial services – Need to blend automation with human touch. *Proceedings of the International Conference on Automation, Computational and Technology Management (ICACTM)*. doi: https://doi.org/10.1109/ICACTM.2019.8776741.
*Nam, K., Lee, Z., & Lee, B. G. (2016). How internet has reshaped the user experience of Banking service? *KSII Transactions on Internet and Information Systems*, *10*(2), 684–702.
Nicoletti, B. (2017). *The future of fintech. Integrating finance and technology in financial services*. Palgrave Macmillan.
Noonan, L. (2019). Banks use fintechs to make up for lost time on financial inclusion. *The Financial Times*. Retrieved from https://www.ft.com.
*Omarini, A. E. (2018). Fintech and the future of the payment landscape: The mobile wallet ecosystem – a challenge for retail banks? *International Journal of Financial Research*, *9*(4), 97–116.
*Ozili, P. K. (2018). Impact of digital finance on financial inclusion and stability. *Borsa Istanbul Review*, *18*(4), 329–340.
*Puschmann, T. (2017). Fintech. *Business & Information Systems Engineering*, *59*(1), 69–76.
*Ramesh, L. (2019). FinTech: A new avenue of banks to enhance customer digital experience (DX). *International Journal of Innovative Technology and Exploring Engineering (IJITEE)*, *8*(8), 644–648.
Sanchez, R., & Mahoney, J. T. (2013). Modularity and economic organisation: Concepts, theory, observations, and predictions. In A. Grandori (Ed.), *Handbook of economic organisation: Integrating economic and organization theory* (pp. 383–399). Elgar.
*Scardovi, C. (2017). *Digital transformation in financial services*. Springer International Publishing AG.
*Schmidt, J., Drews, P., & Schirmer, I. (2018). *Charting the emerging business ecosystem of Fintechs and banks: Seven types of collaborative business models*

(Association for Information Systems Research Paper No. 104). https://aisel.aisnet.org/ecis2018_rp/104.
Schueffel, P. (2016). Taming the beast: A scientific definition of fintech. *Journal of Innovation Management*, 4(4), 32–54.
Sha'ban, M., Girardone, C., & Sarkisyan, A. (2019). Financial inclusion: Trends and determinants. In *Frontier topics in Banking* (pp. 119–136). Palgrave Macmillan.
Shofawati, A. (2019). *The Role of Digital Finance to Strengthen Financial Inclusion and the Growth of SME in Indonesia.* Proceedings of the International Conference on Islamic Economics, Business, and Philantropy (ICIEBP). doi: https://doi.org/10.18502/kss.v3i13.4218.
*Sibanda, W., Ndiweni, E., Boulkeroua, M., Echchabi, A., & Ndlovu, T. (2020). Digital technology disruption on bank business models. *International Journal of Business Performance Management*, 21(1–2), 184–208.
*Son, Y., Kwon, H. E., Tayi, G. K., & Oh, W. (2019). Impact of customers' digital banking adoption on hidden defection: A combined analytical–empirical approach. *Journal of Operations Management*, 66(4), 418–440. doi: https://doi.org/10.1002/joom.1066.
*Suryatmojo, A., Kaburuan, E. R., Fajar, A. N., Sutarty, S., & Girsang, A. S. (2018). Financial technology integration based on service oriented architecture. *Proceedings of the International Conference on Orange Technologies (ICOT)*.doi: 10.1109/ICOT.2018.8705824.
*Tanda, A., & Schena, C. M. (2019). *FinTech, BigTech and banks. digitalisation and its impact on banking business models.* Palgrave Macmillan.
*Tyce, M. (2020). Beyond the neoliberal-statist divide on the drivers of innovation: A political settlements reading of Kenya's m-PESA success story. *World Development*, 125, 104621.
*Wewege, L., & Thomsett, M. C. (2020). *The digital banking revolution. How fintech companies are transforming the retail banking industry through disruptive financial innovation* (3rd ed.). De Gruyter.
*Wonglimpiyarat, J. (2019). FinTech banking industry: A systemic approach. *Foresight*, 19(6), 590–603.
*Vives, X. (2019). Competition and stability in modern banking: A post-crisis perspective. *International Journal of Industrial Organization*, 64, 55–69.
Zavolokina, L., Dolata, M., & Schwabe, G. (2016) Fintech – What's in a name? *Proceedings of the International Conference on Information Systems.* doi: https://doi.org/10.5167/uzh-126806.
*Zhao, Q., Tsai, P. H., & Wang, J. L. (2019). Improving financial service innovation strategies for enhancing China's Banking industry competitive advantage during the fintech revolution: A hybrid MCDM model. *Sustainability*, 11(5). doi: https://doi.org/10.3390/su11051419.

Part 3:
Digitalization of financial institutions

8 The prospect of cryptocurrencies becoming money

Andrzej Sławiński

Introduction

Cryptocurrencies, as part of the Fintech revolution, have the potential to improve the existing monetary system. However, the early hopes that they would replace the bank-based one proved to be unrealistic. They did not take sufficiently into consideration the institutional setting, which is indispensable for any monetary system to operate properly (Danielsson, 2019; Eichengreen, 2019). Money is a social construct based on peoples' trust in public institutions which makes it stable and legally protected (Mersch, 2019; Simmel, 1907). None of this can be replaced by the trust in blockchain technology.

Admittedly, the existing monetary system has been far from perfect. Central banks' dependence on governments after World War II led to accelerated inflation in the late 1960s and the stagflation of the 1970s.[1] Periods of unwarranted liberalization of banking regulations tended to be followed by unsustainable lending booms and the resulting financial crises (Reinhart & Rogoff, 2009; Saka et al., 2019). Nonetheless, the above-mentioned events led to today's independence of central banks' and the emergence of macroprudential policy as an important countercyclical tool, which made the monetary system more resilient to potential disturbances.

The undoubtedly positive contribution of the FinTech revolution to the functioning of the monetary system is the emergence of non-bank payment service providers (PSPs), which made money transfers more efficient and enabled financial inclusion of millions of unbanked households in the developing economies. However, attempts to pass cryptocurrencies off as new international monies are problematic. Although the high volatility of Bitcoin and other initially issued cryptocurrencies led to the emergence of stablecoins, the latter does not constitute a genuine breakthrough since they only borrow their stability from the main international currencies through the currency board mechanism. In the long run, the ascent of stablecoins may have a positive impact on the evolution of the monetary system, but launching them hastily on a massive scale, as was planned for Facebooks' Libra, would pose excessive risks to monetary and financial stability. The

DOI: 10.4324/9781003095354-8

rising awareness of these risks brought a proposed alternative solution in the form of Central Bank Digital Currencies (CBDCs).

This chapter argues that despite its weaknesses, the existing monetary system has certain features that call for improvement (using also FinTech innovations) rather than wholesale replacement with cryptocurrencies. The main advantage of the current bank-based system is its ability to provide simultaneously price stability and flexibility of credit and money adjustments to the needs of the economy. The source of this advantage is the two-tier institutional structure of the modern monetary system, which is the outcome of its long evolution.

The remainder of this chapter is structured as follows. Second section highlights the main features of the two-tier monetary system and the role of non-bank payment service providers (PSPs) as its new advantageous component. Third section discusses why Bitcoin could not become a digital successor of the gold standard system and why the launch of Facebook's Libra faced strong opposition from regulators, supervisors, and central banks. Fourth section analyzes the *pros* and *cons* of issuing the CBDCs. Final section contains conclusions.

The bank-based monetary system and the PSPs as its new advantageous component

The two-tier structure of the modern monetary system, based on the separation of commercial and central banking, resulted from past experiences. One of them was that the success story of the Bank of Amsterdam, one of the 17th century's proto-central banks, ended abruptly when it incurred large losses on its commercial loans portfolio (Knot, 2019; Schnabel & Shin, 2018). Another example is the Bank of England, which ceased to extend commercial loans to eliminate the conflict of interest related to its role as lender of last resort for its commercial competitors (Bordo, 2014).

Each of the two tiers of the modern monetary system serves a different role. Technically speaking, central banks are clearinghouses responsible for managing the payment system (Goodhart, 1988). From the macroeconomic perspective, their task is to stabilize the value of money and play the role of lenders of last resort. The key second-tier institutions of the monetary system are commercial banks, whose lending adjusts the supply of credit and money to the needs of the economy.

In the two-tier monetary system, the two kinds of means of payment are used. The central bank issues legal tenders – paper money and bank liquid reserves, which are obligatory in interbank settlements. Commercial banks issue deposit money thus providing the bulk of money supply.

Liquid reserves are issued when central banks buy assets (mainly foreign exchange and treasuries) from commercial banks or extend liquidity loans to them[2]. The issuance of deposit money results from commercial banks' lending (Goodhart, 2009; Tobin, 1963). Money supply increases when bank

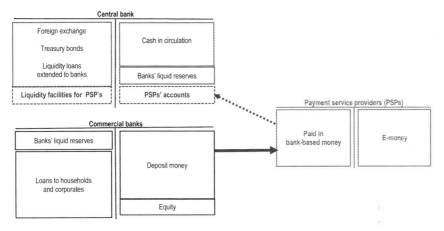

Figure 8.1 The bank-based monetary system with PSPs as its new component.

Source: own elaboration.

net lending grows and shrinks when bank net lending falls (McLeay et al., 2014). The reason why privately issued deposit money is widely accepted as a means of payment is its convertibility into paper money – the legal tender.

Central banks control credit and money creation mainly by changing the interest rate level. After the painful 2007–2009 crisis, macroprudential policy emerged as a new counter-cyclical policy tool (Blanchard, 2012).

A new component of the bank-based monetary system is electronic money (e-money) issued by non-bank payment service providers (PSPs). As it is illustrated in Figure 8.1., e-money is not a new *kind* of money; it is only a new *form* of money. In fact, e-money represents cash or deposit money paid into electronic wallets of PSPs' clients, which enables them to make payments using their cell phones or other mobile devices.

The emergence of the PSPs introduced more competition into the payments systems, which incentivized commercial banks to offer their customers faster and cheaper ways of money transfer (Segendorf et al., 2019). PSPs still settle their transactions via commercial banks in which they hold their settlement accounts. Nonetheless, as illustrated by the dotted arrow in Figure 8.1, regulators tend to allow PSPs to hold their settlement accounts directly at central banks to promote competition among bank and non-bank payment services providers (BIS, 2020). The Bank of England was the first to consider such a possibility (Carney, 2016), which materialized in 2019 (Bank of England, 2020).

PSPs' considerable positive contribution is that they offer indirect access to basic bank services to millions of unbanked households and small firms in developing economies. The most widely known examples are M-Pesa in Kenya and PayTM in India (Joshi et al., 2019; Ntara, 2019).

The positive consequences of the emergence of the PSPs are analogous to that of the emergence of the Eurodollar market. Both developments helped to alleviate the important challenges associated with the functioning of the monetary system. The Eurodollar market contributed to overcoming the global shortage of dollars that were needed to finance international trade after World War II (McCauley et al., 2015)[3], whereas PSPs successfully addressed the problem of low financial inclusion in many developing economies. Both developments brought about significant positive outcomes without causing undue financial frictions.

Cryptocurrencies

E-money provides an example of how the Fintech revolution has successfully contributed to the modernization of the existing monetary system. In contrast, the balance of costs and benefits associated with the emergence of cryptocurrencies is markedly different. Even though the potential benefits that accrue from their issuance are similar to those of e-money, they pose several substantial risks to monetary and financial stability.

Cryptocurrencies did not meet the expectations which accompanied their emergence. The main reason was the oversimplified assumptions on the functioning of the monetary system, which led to the belief that cryptocurrencies might easily become global currencies.

Behind Bitcoin's failure to become a 'digital gold' were the misguided assumptions on how the gold standard system actually worked. The main reason why plans to issue Libra – the Facebook-backed stablecoin – encountered strong negative reactions from central banks, regulators, supervisors, and governments in many countries was that its proponents failed to take into consideration the fact that using the currency board mechanism to stabilize Libra is far from sufficient to make it as safe as the existing international currencies as the dollar or the euro.

The arguments of the cryptocurrencies promoters

Even though the consequences of the global financial crisis of 2007–2009 were greatly reduced by central banks and governments, it was still the worst financial crisis since the Great Depression of the early 1930s. Among others, it led to an erosion of trust in the bank-based monetary system, which facilitated the emergence of cryptocurrencies. In the midst of the 2007–2009 crisis, Satoshi Nakamoto declared that the bank-based monetary system should be superseded by cryptocurrencies, and Bitcoin was touted as a new global currency (Nakamoto, 2008).

His proposal resulted from the belief that there were two systemic flaws in the design of the existing monetary system: that central banks tend to debase money,[4] whereas commercial banks pose a risk to financial stability due to the fractional reserve system (Nakamoto, 2009). Actually, historical experience demonstrates precisely the opposite. Central banks do not exhibit inflation bias as long as they remain independent. The fractional reserve system is not the cause of the unsustainable lending booms. They resulted mainly from inadequate supervision over commercial banks, which is expected to change thanks to the emergence of macroprudential policy.

The argument advanced by Bitcoin's promoters that due to the fractional reserve system bank deposits are at risk is especially misleading since depositors are protected by both the deposit insurance system and the central bank role as lender of last resort for commercial banks. If it was not true, we would have witnessed massive retail depositors' runs on banks during the 2007–2009 global banking crisis. In fact, it is cryptocurrencies that are exposed to confidence crises due to the lack of such an institutional safety net.

The demands to replace the existing monetary system with cryptocurrencies were also driven by concerns that central banks' quantitative easing (QE) programmes might lead to massive money printing which might instigate inflation. In reality, QE programmes are not about massive money printing. They considerably increase the volumes of commercial banks' liquid reserves, but not the supply of money.[5] The latter would grow rapidly only if these programs were able to instigate highly optimistic expectations among economic agents, which, in turn, would stimulate a sharp rise in bank lending and deposit money creation. This did not materialize as the QE programmes were pursued during periods of recession or economic stagnation when they could not instigate sharp recoveries characterized by a rapid acceleration of bank lending. Thus, QE programmes did not produce inflation. Their goal was mainly to shield individual economies from deflation.[6] For example, the Bank of Japan has been conducting its QE programs for the last two decades, but it has barely been able to overcome deflation, let alone achieve its 2% inflation target (Shirai, 2018).

Could bitcoin become a digital gold standard system?

The promoters of cryptocurrencies expected Bitcoin to be stable due to the cap imposed on its issuance, and as a result, to become the successor of the gold standard system (Weber, 2016). However, this assumption was based on a misconception of how the latter actually operated. The way to stabilize the value of money is not to limit its supply, but to keep it adjusted to the demand for money consistent with an equilibrium rate of gross domestic product (GDP) growth (Friedman, 1959). By a lucky coincidence, when the gold standard was in force, the supply of gold (from new discoveries) had been growing at a similar rate as the rate of global GDP growth, which stabilized prices in all the countries participating in the system (Cassel, 1931). Moreover, the distribution of gold was proportional to the GDP volumes of individual countries since – due to the absence of exchange rate risk – the gold standard facilitated constant capital flows from surplus to deficit countries, which, in turn, ensured a steady growth of gold reserves in all central banks (Jonung, 1979).

Behind the idea of making Bitcoin a global currency lay the belief that simple solutions, like imposing a cap on its issuance, can suffice to ensure price stability. However, the gold standard was not as simple a system as Bitcoin's promoters would have it. It was the product of a kind of financial revolution resulting from the needs of the first industrial revolution, which required a monetary system that ensured both price stability and money supply swiftly adjusting to the historically unprecedented acceleration in economic growth. The outcome was the development of the banking system, which was fairly sophisticated even by today's standards (e.g. in the 19th century the City of London was comprised of the central bank, merchant banks, bills brokers, discount houses, commercial banks, and other highly specialized financial institutions; (Bordo, 2014)).

In general, the history of the gold standard confirms that trust in money is secondary to trust in institutions. The success of the gold standard was based on its developed institutional structure with *de facto* independent central banks (Capie, 1995). The equally important factor was the rule of law in international trade and capital flows, which facilitated the smooth functioning of the gold standard as an international monetary system (Selgin, 2015).

Without a proper institutional setting, Bitcoin did not really stand a chance of becoming global money; instead, it was destined to become a speculative crypto-asset rather than a stable currency widely used in international trade and finance.[7] The volatility of Bitcoin and other cryptocurrencies turned out to be far greater than that of stock indices or foreign exchange rates (Danielsson, 2019). Moreover, Bitcoin and several other cryptocurrencies quickly gained popularity in illicit transactions (Houben et al., 2018).

Currency board as a way of issuing stablecoins

As Bitcoin and other cryptocurrencies were too volatile to become money, the next logical stage in the development of cryptocurrencies was the emergence of stablecoins, which are stabilized owing to their convertibility at a fixed rate into international currencies, mainly into the US dollar, as it is the case with Tether, the first widely used stablecoin.[8]

Stablecoins are usually portrayed as new international currencies, but initially, the actual purpose of their issuance was to provide safe assets for investors who wanted to park their profits from trading in crypto-asset markets without leaving the blockchain environment (ECB, 2019). It was not necessary to issue massive amounts of stablecoins to this end. The real challenge to the existing monetary system came with the proposed introduction of Libra – a digital currency spearheaded by Facebook, an online social media and networking service with more than 2 billion users (Libra Association, 2019).

Its widespread acceptance could generate demand for Libra not only as a safe asset for short-term investors on cryptocurrencies' trading platforms but it might also generate a genuine demand for money, i.e. for Libra-denominated transactional balances, which people would hold to cover their current expenditures on goods and services. Even though there are not that many objective reasons why people should hold Libra rather than their domestic state-backed currencies, the convenience of using a digital currency in the social media ecosystem and lower costs of money transfers exercised on the same platform might incentivize Facebook users to hold a part of their transactional balances in Facebook-sponsored money.

As was the case with other stablecoins, Libra was supposed to borrow its stability from the existing international currencies via the currency board mechanism in order to peg Libra to the dollar, the euro, or a basket of currencies.[9] The name of the planned currency board was Libra Reserve, which was to be managed by the Libra Association, a consortium based in Geneva. There would be also 'authorized resellers' (probably reputable banks) intervening in the market to stabilize the currency's exchange rate (Libra Association, 2019).

The Libra Association's *White Paper* (2019) implied that the Libra Reserve would function much like the Hong Kong currency board, but this analogy is not fully accurate. The difference between the Libra Reserve and a typical currency board is that the latter is actually a central bank, which issues a currency at a permanently fixed exchange rate. In Hong Kong, Bulgaria, and other economies having currency boards, the deposit money is created by commercial banks. Currency boards issue only liquid reserves and paper money.

Initially, Libra was to be issued only by being purchased for the main international currencies. But this was expected to change over time as Calibra was an electronic wallet system resembling a commercial bank, which could start extending Libra-denominated loans and create Libra-denominated deposits this way (Schmeling, 2019). In such an event, the Libra Reserve would have to be backed by a much larger pool of international liquidity than that which would result from selling Libra for dollars, euros, and other currencies.

To draw a comparison with Hong Kong again, its Monetary Authority (currency board) holds foreign exchange reserves twice as large as its monetary base (M0) to shield the Hong Kong dollar against speculative attacks (IMF, 2019). If Libra started to be issued also by way of Calibra extending Libra-denominated loans, the Libra Reserve would be forced to substantially increase its foreign exchange reserves to cover the growing volume of Libra-denominated deposits or tokens.

The source fuelling the stock of Hong Kong foreign exchange reserves are trade surpluses and foreign capital inflows (Hong Kong Monetary Authority, 2013). However, Libra would be money without a state and an economy. Therefore, how exactly the Libra Reserve planned to increase its foreign exchange holdings to adjust them to the growing supply of Libras resulting from CaLibra's lending remains an open question. Without solving this problem, a potential confidence crisis might trigger a run on the Libra Reserve similar to the Argentinian currency board crisis of 2001–2002 (De la Torre et al., 2003).

In contrast to the collapse of Argentina's currency board, a debacle of the Libra Reserve could have serious international repercussions. This is why the announcement of Libra's early and large-scale launch (Libra Association, 2019) almost immediately faced strong negative reactions on the part of policymakers, regulators, and supervisors in many countries. In the United States, the Federal Reserve called for the Libra project to be postponed (Reuters, 2019).

The reasons behind the postponement of Libra's launch

Policymakers in different countries emphasized that widespread use of Libra might erode the monetary sovereignty of their economies (Federal Ministry of Finance, 2019). What they meant was that a massive acceptance of Libra would reduce their monetary policy effectiveness and autonomy (Cecchetti & Schoenholtz, 2019).

The reason is that at the heart of monetary policymaking is adjusting money supply to the demand for money which is consistent with an economy's potential rate of growth (Friedman, 1959). If Facebook users in a given country started to increase their Libra holdings at the expense of their domestic currency, it would amount to the 'libraization' (analogous to dollarization) of its monetary system. The ensuing fall in the demand for the domestic currency would reduce the effectiveness of the local central bank's monetary policy, especially in the case of developing economies (Segendorf et al., 2019).

In the past, dollarization usually resulted from the eroding trust in the capacity of the domestic monetary authorities to stabilize inflation. This is why the prospect of 'libraization' was often interpreted as a potential advantage for poorly managed developing economies. Nonetheless, it could also create problems in middle-income economies with stable inflation. Recent examples include Eastern and Central European countries, where before the 2007–2009 crisis, central banks were unable to contain foreign exchange lending booms by way of raising domestic interest rates (EIB, 2019; Slawinski, 2020).

The source of concerns related to Libra's launch is not only that it might prove to be a destabilizing factor, but also that Libra itself may be unstable. The Financial Stability Board expressed concern that due to the Libra Reserve's operational setting, it may have problems with fending off a speculative attack against its currency even before it started to be loanable and still had a 100% foreign exchange backing (BIS, 2020). Hence, from the very beginning, the Libra Reserve would need an international liquidity backstop provided by main global central banks (Adrian & Mancini-Griffoli, 2019).

Yet the prospect that central banks would provide the Libra Reserve with access to their liquidity facilities seems remote (Reuters, 2019), since the elementary precondition is that Libra must first comply with all the necessary regulatory standards in force (EBA, 2019; ESMA, 2019; FSB, 2019). This should not be perceived as an attempt to impede technological progress, but as the necessary condition for building up trust in Libra. Let us remember that what led to the 2007–2009 global financial crisis was the belief that the new methods of measuring and managing risk were so effective that only light banking regulation and supervision were needed (Bayoumi, 2017). The subsequent crisis proved that this view was much too optimistic, which brought today's worldwide tightening of banking regulations (Basel Committee on Banking Supervision, 2017).

Especially after the painful 2007–2009 crisis, central banks, which are also responsible for financial stability, would not offer the Libra Reserve access to their liquidity loans until it complied with strict regulatory standards. This will postpone for long the moment when Facebook's sponsored money could count on central bank liquidity backing during a potential confidence crisis.

It is symptomatic that while the PSPs were increasingly granted access to central banks' liquidity facilities, the Libra Reserve was unlikely to achieve it quickly. The reason is that PSPs are institutions whose operations improve the effectiveness of the current monetary system and make it accessible to still unbanked households, while a premature launch of Libra would lead to the emergence of an alternative monetary system with a host of risks that would be very difficult to supervise and control.

Another thorny issue is why central banks should provide their liquidity backstop to stablecoins if only the issuers of the latter were to benefit from seigniorage. In the bank-based monetary system seigniorage is transferred to the state budget (Danielsson, 2019).

It is also difficult to assume that regulators and supervisors at both domestic and international levels would swiftly learn to identify and contain the risks incurred by a large-scale issuance of Facebook's digital money. If the Libra Reserve started to operate too early, the likely scenario may be similar to that involving Argentina's currency board, where after a period of complacency the accumulating risks produced a run on the peso.

Central Bank Digital Currency: Risks and benefits

The risk that the growing circulation of stablecoins may destabilize demand for domestic currencies and thus reduce the effectiveness of monetary policy in individual countries led to the idea of issuing the CBDC, which, in practical terms, would amount to allowing households and firms to hold their money deposits not only at commercial banks but also at the central bank.

The expected benefits of introducing CBDCs would involve giving households and firms direct access to central banks' instant and cheap payment systems. Moreover, it would pave the way for the elimination of cash, which would enable central banks to set deeply negative interest rates during recessions, since households would be unable to escape into paper money (Bordo & Levin, 2017; Meaning et al., 2018). Even though negative interest rates may indeed help to alleviate economic downturns, they are unlikely to be sufficiently effective in economies that suffer from a negative feedback loop between protracted stagnation and persistently pessimistic expectations, which produces stubbornly low expected rates of return on investments (Palley et al., 2019).

Central bankers' main concern is that CBDC might pose a risk to financial stability in periods of high uncertainty when households would *en masse* transfer their deposits from commercial banks to the central bank (Jordan, 2019). The source of this risk is that, for obvious reasons, central banks should not be involved in extending commercial loans. This implies that the emergence of CBDCs should not lead to the creation of retail deposits by central banks, which should restrict themselves only to accepting household and firm deposits.

While the implementation of the CBDC proposal would not lead to the emergence of a different monetary system, but only to a modification of the existing one, it would create the risk of deposit flights from commercial to central banks.

Actually, the CBDC proposal is very much in vein with the *narrow banking* concept formulated back in the 1930s. It envisaged that people should keep their transactional balances at narrow banks, which would hold their assets exclusively in the form of central bank liquid reserves and short-term treasury bills (Simons, 1936). Consequently, household deposits held in narrow banks would have been safe thanks to the 100% backing in assets instantly convertible into cash (Pennacchi, 2012).

The narrow banking solution was proposed in the wake of the disastrous banking crisis in the United States in the early 1930s when the Federal Reserve failed to provide commercial banks with sufficient liquidity, which they would have converted into paper money to meet their customers' cash withdrawals. That, in turn, could have stopped runs on banks and their resultant massive suspensions.

The narrow banking proposal was put forward as a way of guaranteeing cash withdrawals. Nevertheless, the US authorities chose a simpler way to achieve this objective. The Federal Deposit Insurance Corporation was established in 1933. The main reason why the narrow banking proposal was not implemented was precisely the mentioned above the risk of deposit flights from commercial to narrow banks.

The same risk may result from launching CBDCs; the only difference being that in times of heightened uncertainty, households would move their deposits not to narrow banks, but directly to the central bank (Grym et al., 2017). Hence the introduction of CBDCs would expose commercial banks to the risk of periodic loss of a large proportion of their liabilities. Although central banks could replenish commercial banks' liabilities by extending liquidity loans to them, the question remains if the benefits from launching CBDCs are indeed worth exposing commercial banks to the risk of losing a substantial part of their retail deposits, which usually constitute a stable part of their sources of funding.

In order to reduce the risk to financial stability posed by CBDCs, it was proposed to limit the scale of potential household deposit flows back and forth between commercial and central banks by way of imposing caps on their volumes which would effectively reduce the CBDCs role to a digital substitute of cash (Bank of England, 2020; Bindseil, 2020).

Discussions on the introduction of CBDCs reveal that, paradoxically, it is difficult not only to replace the existing monetary system with an alternative one, based on cryptocurrencies but even to modify its two-tier structure. Actually, it is only to be expected, since such an arrangement gives the monetary system its ability to simultaneously stabilize money and adjust its supply to the needs of the economy.

Concluding remarks

The 2007–2009 global banking crisis exposed the fragility of the existing bank-based monetary system, which led to demands to replace it with cryptocurrencies. These calls proved to be unsubstantiated since trust in the blockchain technology cannot substitute for trust in reputable public institutions that protect the stability of money and shield the monetary system against illicit activities.

For the same reason, the hopes that stablecoins would quickly become important international currencies were largely misplaced. Today, the international role of the dollar, the euro, the yen, and the pound sterling results not only from the fact that they are widely used in international trade and finance. An equally important factor is that investors all over the world trust the competencies and independence of public institutions that manage the financial systems in the United States, the Eurozone, Japan, and the United Kingdom (Eichengreen & Kawai, 014). At the moment, the prospect of stablecoins having such institutional backing seems remote.

The institutions that manage, regulate, and supervise the monetary system cannot be replaced by algorithms, as some proponents of stablecoins are disposed to believe (Al-Naji et al., 2017). The world we live in is non-ergodic, which entails policymaking based on a substantial dose of informed discretion, even if it is increasingly supported by artificial intelligence (Danielsson, 2020).

On the whole, FinTech innovations may improve the existing monetary system e.g. by reducing the costs of financial intermediation (Philippon, 2016), including those associated with cross-border payments (CPMI, 2020). A prominent positive example of FinTech innovation is the emergence of PSPs' e-money, which made the monetary system accessible for millions of unbanked households and small firms in developing economies and promotes more inclusive global growth (Pazarbasiouglu et al., 2020).

Finally, the case for stablecoins soon becoming an important element of the international monetary system is not very compelling. While in December 2020, after complying with some relevant regulations, Facebook confirmed its intention to issue a global stablecoin rebranded as Diem (Diem Association, 2020), the risks related to the issuance of a stateless cryptocurrency, which is intended to be international, remain substantial and untested. Under the circumstances, the Facebook-sponsored stablecoin cannot count on backing from central banks or other public institutions. This reduces the chances that Facebook's Diem will become as safe as bank money in the foreseeable future.

Notes

1. The only countries that did not experience high inflation in the 1970s were Germany and Switzerland, since their central banks were already independent from government (Bernanke et al., 1999, p. 41–87).
2. Cash in circulation remains on central banks' balance sheets, but they do not decide how much of it is issued at a given time. It depends on how much of their liquid reserves commercial banks convert into banknotes in order to meet their customers' demand for cash.
3. On the Eurodollar market, foreign banks domiciled outside the United States (initially in London), extend dollar-denominated loans and hold US dollar deposits. They settle their customers' transactions through the Fedwire via their correspondent American banks. The emergence of the Eurodollar market contributed to avoid the Triffin dilemma, i.e. the risk that the United States would have had to run very large trade deficits in order to meet global demand for its currency (Bordo & McCauley, 2018).
4. The notion that hyperinflations are caused by central banks is misplaced. They usually result from the collapse of the public finance system during war or political turmoil, when tax revenues rapidly shrink and governments resort to printing money in order to maintain the basic functions of the state (Lopez & Mitchener, 2018)
5. This has changed to an extent during the Covid-19 pandemic, when central banks 'printed' money e.g. through buying corporate bonds, but it was necessary to reduce the scale of bankruptcies and layoffs.
6. As far as asset prices are concerned, the QE programmes contributed to the rise in stock indices as commercial banks invested part of their excess liquid reserves on e.g. repo market, which is the main source of funding for institutions, such as hedge funds, known as active stock-market investors.
7. One of the reasons why Bitcoin and other crypto-assets are highly volatile is that their issuance is impossible to coordinate (Aizenman, 2019)
8. The belief that algorithms could stabilize cryptocurrencies through adjusting supply and demand on their markets (Al-Naji et al., 2017) does not take into account the fact that confidence crises cause a massive flight from a given asset (Eichengreen, 2019).
9. In 2020, the Libra Association decided that in order to make things easier Libra would be stabilized mainly against individual currencies (Libra Association, 2020).

References

Adrian, T., & Mancini-Griffoli, T. (2019). The rise of digital money. *Fintech Note, International Monetary Fund*, Note 19/01, 1–20.

Aizenman, J. (2019). On the Built-in Instability of Cryptocurrencies. *VOX CEPR Policy Portal, February 12*.

Al-Naji, N., Chen, J., & Diao, L. (2017). *Basis: A price-stable cryptocurrency with an algorithmic central bank.* https://www.basis.io/basis_whitepaper_en.pdf.

Bank for International Settlements (2020). Central Banks and payments in the digital era. *BIS Annual Economic Report*, Chapter III, 67–95. https://www.bis.org/publ/arpdf/ar2020e.htm

Bank for International Settlements (2020). *Investigating the impact of stablecoins*. G7 Working Group on Stablecoins, Basel.

Bank of England (2020). Central bank digital currency: Opportunities, challenges and design. *Discussion Paper*, 1–12. https://www.bankofengland.co.uk/paper/2020/central-bank-digital-currency-opportunities-challenges-and-design-discussion-paper

Basel Committee on Banking Supervision (2017). *Basel III: Finalising post-crisis reforms*. Basel Committee on Banking Supervision, Basel.

Bayoumi, T. (2017). *Unfinished business: The unexplored causes of the financial crisis and the lessons yet to be learned*. Yale University Press.

Bernanke, B., Laubach, T., Mishkin, F., & Posen, A. (1999). *Inflation targeting. Lessons from international experience*. Princeton: Princeton University Press.

Bindseil, U. (2020). Tiered CBDC and the financial system. *European Central Bank Working Paper Series, 2351*, 1–40.

Blanchard, O. (2012). Monetary policy in the wake of the crisis. In O. Blanchard, D. Romer, M. Spence, & J. Stiglitz (Eds.), *In the wake of the crisis. Leading economists reassess economic policy* (pp. 7–14). The MIT Press

Bordo, M. (2014). Rules for a lender of last resort: A historical perspective. *The Journal of Economic Dynamics and Control, 49*, 126–134.

Bordo, M., & Levin, A. (2017). Central bank digital currency and the future of monetary policy. *NBER Working Paper, 23711*, 1–32.

Bordo, M., & McCauley, R. (2018). Triffin Dilemma or Myth. *NBER Working Paper. 24195*, 1–40.

Capie, F. (1995). The evolution of central banking. *Policy Research Working Paper, The World Bank, 1534*, 1–25.

Carney, M. (2016). *Enabling the FinTech transformation – Revolution, restoration, or reformation*. Speech at the Lord Mayor's Banquet for Merchants of the City of London, Bank of England.

Carstens, A. (2019). *The future of money and the payment system: What role for central banks?*. Speech at the Central Bank of Ireland, Basel.

Cassel, G. (1931). The monetary character of the present crisis. *Journal of the Institute of Bankers, 52*, 323–342.

Cecchetti, S., & Schoenholtz, K. (2019). Libra's dramatic call to regulatory action. *VOX CEPR Policy Portal*, August 28.

Committee on Payments and Market Infrastructure (2020). *Enhancing cross-border payments: building blocks of a global roadmap: Stage 2 report to the G20 – Technical background report*. Bank for International Settlements, Basel.

Danielsson, J. (2019). Cryptocurrencies: Policy, economics and fairness. *Systemic Risk Center Discussion Paper, London School of Economics, 86*, 1–33.

Danielsson, J. (2020). Artificial intelligence as a central banker. Cryptocurrencies: Policy, economics and fairness. *VOX CEPR Policy Portal*, March 6.

De la Torre, A., Levy Levy-Yeyati, E., & Schmuckler, S. L. (2003). Living and dying with Hard pegs: The rise and fall of Argentina's currency board. *Economia Journal, The Latin American and Caribbean Economic Association, Spring, 20*, 43–108.

Diem Association (2020). *White Paper*. https://www.diem.com/en-us/white-paper/.

European Central Bank (2019). Stablecoins - no coins, but are they stable? *In Focus, 3*, 1–10. https://www.ecb.europa.eu/paym/intro/publications/pdf/ecb.mipinfocus 191128.en.pdf?adf9157e3e022dceaadac7b24b54ed0b

European Investment Bank (2019). *Ten years of the Vienna Initiative*: 2009-2019, Luxemburg, 396 https://www.eib.org/attachments/efs/10years_vienna_initiative_en.pdf

Eichengreen, B. (2019). From commodity to fiat and now to crypto: What does history tell us? *NBER Working Paper, 25426*, 1–18.

Eichengreen, B., & Kawai, M. (2014). Issues in renminbi internationalization: An overview. *Asian Development Bank Institute Working Paper, 454*, 1–10.

European Banking Authority (2019). *Report with advice for European Commission on crypto-assets*, Paris. 1-30, https://www.eba.europa.eu/sites/default/documents/ files/documents/10180/2545547/67493daa-85a8-4429-aa91-e9a5ed880684/EBA% 20Report%20on%20crypto%20assets.pdf

European Securities and Market Authority (2019). *Initial Coin Offerings and Crypto-Assets*. ESMA 50-157-1391, Paris. https://www.esma.europa.eu/sites/default/files/ library/esma50-157-1391_crypto_advice.pdf

Federal Ministry of Finance & Ministere de Economie et des Finances (2019). *Joint statement on Libra*. Helsinki, September 13. https://www.bundesfinanzministe rium.de/Content/EN/Standardartikel/Topics/Financial_markets/Articles/2019- 09-17-Libra-download.pdf?__blob=publicationFile&v=3

Financial Stability Board (2019). *Regulatory issues in stablecoins*. Bank for International Settlements, Basel. https://www.fsb.org/wp-content/uploads/P181019.pdf

Friedman, M. (1959). The demand for money: Some theoretical and empirical results. *Journal of Political Economy, 67*(4), 327–351.

Goodhart, C. (1988). *The evolution of Central banks*. Cambridge, London: The MIT Press.

Goodhart, C. (2009). A steadfast refusal to face facts. *Economica, 76*, 821–830.

Grym, A., Heikkinen, P., Kauko, K., & Takala, K. (2017). Central Bank digital currency. *Bank of Finland Economic Review, 5*, 1–11.

Hong Kong Monetary Authority (2013). Monetary operations under Currency Board System: The Experience of Hong Kong. BIS Papers chapters. In Bank for International Settlements (ed.) *Sovereign risk: A world without risk free assets?, 73*, 145-154. Bank for International Settlements.

Houben, R., & Snyers, A. (2018). *Cryptocurrencies and blockchain. Legal context and implications for legal crime, money laundering and tax evasion*. Brussels: European Parliament.

International Monetary Fund (2019). *People's Republic of China – Hong Kong special administrative region*. Washington D.C.

Jonung, L. (1979). Knut Wicksell and Gustav Cassel on secular movements in prices. *Journal of Money, Credit and Banking, 2*, 165–181.

Jordan, T. (2019). *Currencies, money and digital tokens*. Speech at University of Basel, Swiss National Bank.

Joshi, T., Sharmista Swasti Gupta, S. S., & Rangaswamy, N. (2019). Digital wallets 'turning corner' for financial inclusion: A study of everyday PayTM practices in India. In Nielsen P., Honest Ch. K. (Eds.), *Advances in information and communication technology*, 552, 280–293, Springer.

Knot, K. (2019). Risks and benefits of modern financial technology; Lessons from a 17th century stablecoin. Speech at the RiskMinds International seminar, De Nederlandsche Bank, December 2.

Libra Association (2019). *Libra White Paper*. https://libra.org/en-US/white-paper/.

Libra Association (2020). *Libra White Paper v2.0. Cover Letter from Libra Association Members.* https://libra.org/en-US/white-paper/.

Lopez, J. A., & Mitchiner, K. J. (2018). Uncertainty and hyperinflation: European inflation dynamics after World War I. *Federal Reserve of San Francisco Working Paper, 2018–06*, 1–51.

McCauley, R., McGuire, P., & Sushko, V. (2015). Global dollar credit: Links to US monetary policy and leverage. *Economic Policy, 30*(82), 187–229.

Mersch, Y. (2019). *Money and private currencies: Reflections on Libra*. Speech at the ECB Legal Conference, European Central Bank, September 2.

McLeay, M., Radia, A., & Ryland, T. (2014). Money creation in the modern economy. *Bank of England Quarterly Bulletin, Q1*, 14–27.

Meaning, J., Dyson, B., Barker, J., & Clayton, E. (2018). Broadening narrow money: Monetary policy with a central bank digital currency. *Staff Working Paper, 724*, 1–36.

Nakamoto, S. (2008). *Bitcoin: A peer-to-peer electronic cash system*. https://bitcoin.org/bitcoin.pdf.

Nakamoto, S. (2009). *Bitcoin open source implementation of P2P currency*. https://satoshi.nakamotoinstitute.org/posts/p2pfoundation/threads/1/.

Ntara, C. (2019). An analysis of m-pesa use in international transactions. *European Journal of Business and Management, 7*(17), 73–79.

Palley, T., Rochan, L.-P., & Vallet, G. (2019). The economics of negative interest rates. *Review of Keynesian Economics, 7*(20), 135–136.

Pazarbasiouglu, C., Mora, A. G., Uttamchandani, M., Natarajan, G., Feyen, E., & Saal, M. (2020). *Digital financial services*. Washington D.C: World Bank.

Pennacchi, G. (2012). Narrow Banking. *Annual Review of Financial Economics, 4*, 141–159.

Philippon, T. (2016). The Fintech opportunity. *NBER Working Paper, 22476*, 1–25.

Reinhart, C., & Rogoff, K. (2009). *This time is different. Eight centuries of financial folly*. Oxford: Princeton University Press.

Reuters (2019). *Fed chief call for Facebook to halt Libra project until concern addressed*. https://www.reuters.com/article/ctech-us-usa-fed-powell-libra-idCAKCN1U5IVE-OCATC

Saka, O., Campos, N., De Grauwe, P., Ji, Y., & Martelli, A. (2019). Financial crises and liberalization: Progress or reversals? *IZA Discussion Paper Series, 12393*, 1–48.

Schmeling, M. (2019). What is Libra?. Understanding Facebook's. *Currency. SAFE Policy Letter, 76*, 1–13.

Schnabel, I., & Shin, H. S. (2018). Money and trust: Lessons from the 1920s for money in the digital age. *BIS Working Papers, 698*, 1–36.

Segendorf, B., Ekloof, A., Gustafsson, P., Landelius, A., & Cicovic, S. (2019). What is Libra? *Sveriges Riksbank Economic Commentaries*, *9*, 1–13.

Selgin, G. (2015). Law, legislation and the gold standard. *Cato Journal*, *35*(2), 251–272.

Shirai, S. (2018). *Mission impossible. Reflating Japan's economy.* Tokyo: Asian Development Institute.

Simmel, G. (1907). *Philosophy of money.* Routledge: London.

Simons, H. C. (1936). Rules vs. authorities in monetary policy. *Journal of Political Economy*, *XLIV*, 171–179.

Slawinski, A. (2020). Central, eastern and southeastern Europe's reunion with Europe. In R. Holzmann, D. Ritzberger-Grunwald, & H. Schuberth (Eds.), *30 years of transition in Central, Eastern and southeastern Europe* (pp. 94–104). Edward Elgar.

Tobin, J. (1963). Commercial banks as creators of money. *Cowles Foundation Discussion Papers*, *159*, 1–18.

Weber, W. (2016). A bitcoin standard: Lessons from the gold standard. *Bank of Canada Staff Working Paper*, *2016–14*, 1–37.

9 Employing artificial intelligence in investment management

Tomasz Miziołek

Introduction

Asset management (AM) industry is becoming increasingly competitive, as more and more entities enter the financial market, aiming to capitalize on growing importance of effective money management in various areas of human activity. Among the essential qualities necessary to succeed in this sector one can find the following: an ability to differentiate oneself from the competition, an ability to provide low-cost funds, offering repeatable investment strategies that yield strong performance overall, and a willingness to prudently adapt to the changing competitive landscape (Morningstar, 2019). Concurrently, asset managers have to face many challenges resulting from trends occurring in financial markets, such as regulatory changes, digital and data revolution, more demanding investors with a growing preference for non-traditional assets, new competitors providing non-traditional assets, and globalization. It is digital technologies and data innovation that are particularly transforming operational aspects of asset management, thus becoming one of the most significant sources of competitive advantage (Shub et al., 2014).

This applies to both US-based asset managers, who have a dominant position in the market globally, and entities from other parts of the world, including European ones who have to cope with the challenges resulting from fragmented financial market. Regardless of the specifics of different regions of the world, the main trends in this industry have been unchanged in recent years – it is the ongoing shift from active to passive investment products, and focus on relative as well as absolute fund investment performance and fees. In these circumstances, artificial intelligence (AI) – defined as a suite of technologies, enabled by adaptive predictive power and exhibiting some degree of autonomous learning that dramatically advance people's ability to recognize patterns, anticipate future events, create good rules, and make good decisions – has a prominent role to play (Halpin & Dannemiller, 2019). This is confirmed, inter alia, by a survey conducted in 2020 by Calastone among European asset managers, according to which AI and distributed ledger technology (DLT) will have a major impact on the future of the asset management industry (Calastone, 2020)[1].

DOI: 10.4324/9781003095354-9

The main aim of the chapter is to provide an in-depth insight into theoretical and practical AI applications in the AM industry, especially in portfolio management. In the first part of the chapter the main application areas of AI in asset management are discussed, particularly those that offer new development opportunities to this financial sector, and at the same time meet investors' expectations. In particular, attention is paid to the portfolio management, including basic types of artificial intelligence techniques utilized in this area, obtained benefits, as well as main groups of AI adopters among investment managers. Second section outlines some risks and challenges connected with adopting and deploying AI in portfolio management. The final part presents the most interesting practical applications of AI in investment management on the example of exchange-traded funds (ETFs) – listed on stock exchanges both in the United States and in Europe. The chapter ends with conclusions.

Artificial intelligence in investment management

Artificial intelligence is reshaping all sectors of financial services, including deposits and lending, payments, insurance, capital markets, market infrastructure, and asset management. With regard to the latter, AI can be employed in various, often completely different activities, both directly related to the main activity, as well as those of a supplementary nature. For example, in the area of securities trading, it is applied in trade execution, as part of post-trade operations in transaction reporting, reconciliations or tax operations, while in the field of risk management and control, it can facilitate enterprise risk management. Additionally, AI offers unique opportunities to client servicing, especially in client relationship management (CRM) – e.g. for client authentication or to support relationship managers in client interactions. It is widely employed in information technology (IT), mostly in cybersecurity where AI algorithms are used to analyze, identify, and prevent potential cybersecurity threats by identifying unusual activity patterns. The main areas of compliance wherein AI is used, cover regulatory horizon scanning and compliance, anti-money laundering and surveillance, employee surveillance, market abuse and conduct. Finally, AI and machine learning (ML) combined with data analytics may facilitate the operation of legal activities (e.g. to read, interpret, and summarize key information from contractual documents, perform contract analysis, and visualize contract risk), and human resources management (AI can be a key tool for identifying candidates in the recruitment process) (EY, 2016).

One of the areas in asset management where AI is increasingly used is robo-advising. Robo-advisors are computer programs that provide financial investment advice based on mathematical rules or algorithms customized to investors' needs and preferences. Robo-advisors can not only enhance investment performance but also rebalance portfolios, automatically managing the portfolio's risks and minimizing transaction costs.

Simultaneously, they are also less prone to behavioral biases, mistakes, and illegal practices. AI is often the key element of typical robo-advising algorithms known as recommender systems that produce optimal, diversified portfolios tailored to investors' risk appetites (Bartram et al., 2020). These portfolios are mainly (often exclusively) based on ETFs, that are effective, easily accessible, and cost-competitive financial instruments for achieving the diverse investment strategies and providing exposure to different asset classes.

However, among the many diverse AI applications in asset management, one of the most sophisticated areas seems to be its employment in the investment (portfolio) management process. Portfolio management entails making asset allocation decisions to construct a portfolio with specific risk and return characteristics. AI techniques can contribute to this process in-different ways. They can mitigate the shortcomings of classical portfolio construction techniques, facilitate fundamental analysis through quantitative or textual data analysis, or generate novel investment strategies (Bartram et al., 2020). Generally, traditional asset managers, i.e. mutual funds, pension funds, and insurance funds, use AI and ML[2] to enhance financial products' performance by supporting multiple aspects of the investment process, including the data and research processes that drive the creation of alpha signals and models, pre-trade analysis, and understanding investment risks in an investment portfolio (Novick et al., 2019).

Disruptive technology solutions help improve efficiency of portfolio management, including stock selection and portfolio allocation. This applies both to actively managed portfolios and index (passive) investment products, i.e. index mutual funds and ETFs. Asset managers in actively managed funds study and interpret various datasets of varying levels of complexity to identify patterns and insights as inputs to the investment decision-making process. This includes – in the case of equity investing – mostly analyzing and compiling commonly available, "traditional" datasets such as obligatory company filings, macroeconomic data, as well as brokers' or analysts' reports and recommendations. Notwithstanding, more and more frequently, AI and ML are also used to analyze new, "alternative" types of datasets, usually available online, mainly through social networks (they encompass e.g. internet searches, tweets, posts), as well as GPS data or satellite imagery. These sources enable asset managers to identify the latest socioeconomic trends and, based on that, to find the patterns that are potentially useful for better portfolio construction.

Technological innovations are perhaps even more readily used in passive management, wherein the main challenge is not to select the best securities for the portfolio from perspective of the assumed investment goal but to be precise in the benchmark tracking. Artificial intelligence may facilitate efficient and accurate index replication and manage the mechanical trading processes. As regards asset managers offering smart (strategic) beta funds, i.e. funds or portfolios that combine selected features of an active (in the field of index portfolio construction) and passive investment approach (in terms of index replication quality), AI can support their decisions concerning both spheres of activity.

The most avid adopters of AI and ML are also managers who deal with systematic (quantitative) funds, mainly hedge funds. They use sophisticated technological solutions to devise non-standard, often tailor-made investment strategies. The main aim is to identify signals on price movements out of a vast amount of available data. These signals facilitate making predictions about price levels or volatility over different time periods and among various asset classes, and thus to generate alpha (Financial Stability Board, 2017).

One can recognize three types of AI and big data applications in investment management. First, natural language processing (NLP), computer vision, voice recognition, and optical character recognition applications are employed to efficiently process a text, image, and audio data from a variety of public sources and internal/vendor databases. In most cases, such programs automate what is traditionally a manual and repetitive task performed by analysts. The programs also increase human capacity by saving the time otherwise spent on manual work. According to the survey conducted by Chartered Financial Analyst (CFA) Institute among investment professionals[3], one of the most popular AI/ML techniques is sentiment determination via NLP of news, Twitter, transcripts, etc. (e.g. by counting positive or negative words) (Cao, 2019).

Second, more sophisticated AI techniques – ML and deep learning (DL)[4] – are used to improve the effectiveness of algorithms used to generate signals in the investment decision-making process. DL algorithms are often applied to improve the results of NLP, computer vision, and voice recognition programs. They can also help extract useful information from large piles of data. Additionally, newly developed ML algorithms – such as gradient boosted regression trees, artificial neural networks, random forests, and support vector machines – may be more effective than linear regression models. Although the latter is commonly used in traditional statistics and econometrics, ML programs are often more effective, especially in the case of multicollinearity (where explanatory variables are correlated). They can also uncover complex patterns and hidden relationships, including nonlinear and contextual relationships that are often difficult to identify with linear algorithms (Rasekhschaffe & Jones, 2019).

Third, AI techniques enable processing big data, including alternative and unstructured data[5]. Extracting signals from this kind of data – e.g. satellite images, earnings, conference call recordings and transcripts, social media postings, consumer credit and debit card data, and e-commerce transactions – may be a new method of generating alpha. It is true especially for analysts and investment managers preferring a fundamental approach and managing discretionary portfolios, who use these data as single input in the investment decision-making process (Cao, 2019).

Risks and challenges in AI adoption

Artificial intelligence techniques may offer a variety of advantages to asset managers, including portfolio managers, but this does not mean that their practical adoption and implementation is simple, costless, and risk-free.

CFA Institute identified main obstacles in applying AI in investment management, among which there are three worth taking a closer look: cost, talent, and technology (Cao, 2019). Firstly, implementing AI/ML techniques – due to their complex nature – usually involves significant upfront cost as well as ongoing maintenance costs. This applies especially to the so-called "early adopters" who incur huge expenditures on new, often sophisticated and not fully proven technologies, and who, at the same time, must take into account that their application will not always bring the expected outcomes (e.g. in the form of better investment results), at least in the short term. This may prove to be a particular challenge for small, niche companies that frequently do not have sufficient resources to purchase appropriate licenses or technologies.

A very serious obstacle in the use of AI may also be the difficulty in obtaining appropriately qualified, skilled, and experienced employees, particularly scientists dealing with AI or related technologies. Although the number of AI specialists is steadily increasing, the demand for their services from many different industries is growing at an even faster pace. Skill shortages and limited availability of experienced and trained staff necessary to effectively deploy and operate AI solutions often become a very serious hurdle. In this situation, asset managers have to face enormous competition, not only from technology companies, which is usually associated with very high employee costs.

Another significant challenge is an extremely rapid development of technology. Asset management companies already using AI must constantly keep up with innovation in this area, otherwise they will be overtaken by late adopters. They must stay up to date with the latest technological developments, which can be a significant obstacle for the entities with limited financial, organizational, and human resources. Additionally, like any other software, it requires regular upgrading so as to adapt it to the changing environment and, in the case of breakdown, it poses the risk of losing important data. Meanwhile, the system restoration is often time-consuming and costly. In terms of technology, integration of new systems with existing ones can also be challenging, just like making them interoperable with other platforms.

When the above difficulties are overcome, unavailability or poor quality of data may be a serious barrier to AI implementation. Data are often inconsistent, which presents a challenge to companies expecting to create value from AI at scale. Even if adequate quality data can be accessed, their sorting, linking, and properly using may become difficult as the amount of unstructured data ingested from sources such as the web, social media, mobile devices, sensors, and the Internet of Things is constantly increasing (Cheatham et al., 2019). Thus, the transformation of new types of data to make them fit investment process often becomes the greatest challenge for asset managers.

Referring to the data, it should also be noted that ML techniques usually perform better in a test environment (i.e. based on the training data set), and do not always respond adequately to new situations and circumstances. The main challenge in this case is overfitting[6]. Although ML algorithms can uncover contextual and nonlinear relationships, overfitting poses a major challenge when one is trying to extract signals from noisy historical data. Algorithms often work well in a sample when the conditions under which they operate are relatively permanent. However, when tested out of the sample, in the real, constantly changing world, their effectiveness leaves much to be desired (Cao, 2019).

AI/ML algorithmics do not adapt well to rare situations such as political coups, pandemics or natural disasters. Nor can ML predict future events if they are not closely related to past trends, such as the 2008 financial crisis. Algorithms themselves can also exhibit significant biases derived from the data sources used in a training process, or from their own shortcomings. Additionally, many of the patterns ML identifies in large data sets are often only correlations that do not have to reflect the underlying drivers. Even if such patterns are considered sensible, consistent and predictive, they are not always easily convertible into profitable investment decisions (Pozen & Ruane, 2019).

The use of AI may also prove problematic for asset managers, given the fact that these techniques are characterized by a very high level of complexity and ambiguity, and therefore they are often opaque. The low level of transparency may be negatively perceived by some investors interested in financial products involving this type of technological solution. The consequence of this may be lack of confidence in these techniques, which in turn may lead to the abandonment of financial instruments applying them. This particularly refers to the periods of growing uncertainty on financial markets, when a significant number of investors almost automatically stop using more complex financial products in favor of relatively simple instruments that are believed to be more secure.

Looking at the problem comprehensively, it is worth emphasizing that AI should be human-centric, ethical, sustainable, and respects fundamental rights and values. However, like other advanced systems, it may create significant ethical, moral, and social challenges.

According to European Parliament (2020), main ethical implications and moral issues that arise from the development and implementation of artificial intelligence technologies are visible in six areas: on society, on human psychology, on the financial system, on the legal system, on the environment and the planet, and on trust. The most important concerns are related to human rights and well-being, emotional harm, accountability and responsibility, security, privacy, accessibility and transparency, safety and trust, social harm and social justice, lawfulness and justice, control and the ethical use (or misuse) of AI, environmental harm and sustainability, informed use, and existential risk.

To seize fully the opportunities that AI offers, while at the same time meeting the aforementioned challenges associated with its application, all activities in this area should be properly designed, carried out and primarily be oriented towards the interests of people and their environment. This is achieved by various strategies and regulations implemented at various levels, both national[7] as well as international[8]. Although they differ in terms of their goals, the extent, and their commitment, they all are aimed at promoting a sustainable and orderly AI development, as well as mitigating adverse effects of its implementation.

Ethical initiatives in the field of AI fundamentally aim to identify and set up clear ethical frameworks and guidelines that put human beneficence at the highest levels, and prioritize benefit to both human society and the environment. They also endeavor to mitigate the risks and negative impacts associated with AI focusing on ensuring that AI is accountable and transparent (European Parliament, 2020)[9].

AI practical applications – Examples from the ETF industry

Although still relatively few investment professionals use AI/big data techniques in their investment processes[10], more and more often examples of specific applications of these techniques in the investment sector can be found. It appears that passively managed funds (especially ETFs) and index providers are currently pioneers and main adopters in this respect. This is due to the fact that they apply a disciplined approach to investing, as most of them aim to track rules-based indices, i.e. benchmarks created upon a set of strict rules. In this case, the use of AI and ML techniques in particular may turn out to be notably beneficial since they are better suited to such systematic strategies. Selected examples of ETFs listed on the exchanges all over the world and using various AI techniques in investment management are characterized below[11].

One of the pioneering funds applying AI in the investment process was AI-Powered Equity ETF. It is an actively managed ETF, launched by ETFMG and EquBot in 2017 and listed on New York Stock Exchange (NYSE) Arca, which aims to utilize AI as a method for stock selection. The fund applies analytical algorithms to AI technology, which can process over one million pieces of information per day in order to build predictive financial models on 6,000 US companies. The fund harnesses the power of IBM Watson. It is a computing platform capable of answering natural language questions by connecting large amounts of data, both structured (e.g. spreadsheets) and unstructured (e.g. news articles), and learning from each analysis it conducts (e.g. by recognizing patterns) to produce a more accurate answer with each subsequent question. AI-Powered International Equity ETF launched in 2018, which offers exposure to developed markets (ex-US), has a similar investment profile (ETFMG, 2020).

The world's largest ETF provider and investment manager – BlackRock – introduced in March 2018 a suite of seven active ETFs employing an evolved approach to sectors that seeks to provide a more representative view of sectors within the US economy: iShares Evolved US Consumer Staples ETF, iShares Evolved US Discretionary Spending ETF, iShares Evolved US Financials ETF, iShares Evolved US Healthcare Staples ETF, iShares Evolved US Innovative Healthcare ETF, iShares Evolved US Media and Entertainment ETF and iShares Evolved US Technology ETF. This innovative approach uses text analysis, guided by ML statistical techniques, to identify words and phrases companies use to describe themselves in publicly available materials (e.g. regulatory filings, earnings reports). Companies are grouped into sectors based on similarities in the language each uses when describing their businesses (BlackRock, 2018).

Global X (currently owned by Mirae Asset Global Investments) – a specialist in providing thematic ETFs to the US market – manages several funds that track indices utilizing NLP in the stock selection. For example, the Global X Autonomous & Electric Vehicles ETF (launched in April 2018 and listed on National Association of Securities Dealers Automated Quotations – NASDAQ), the Global X E-commerce ETF (launched in November 2018 and listed on NASDAQ), and the Global X Video Games & Esports ETF (launched in October 2019 and listed on NASDAQ) seek to track Solactive indices in which selection of their constituents is based on the screening of publicly available information, such as financial websites, search engines or company publications, with the use of an NLP algorithm. Using keywords that describe a given index theme, the algorithm identifies companies that either have, or are expected to have a significant exposure to the field of autonomous and electric vehicles, e-commerce, as well as video games and esports, respectively (Global X, 2020).

NLP is also the chief technology applied by Direxion Connected Consumer ETF, launched by Direxion in August 2020 and listed on NYSE Arca. The fund offers exposure to companies across four technological pillars: home entertainment, online education, remote health and well-being, as well as virtual and digital social interaction (the so-called "connected industries"). It aims to replicate the performance of Solactive Connected Consumer Index whose constituents are selected for inclusion using index provider's NLP algorithm. It identifies the thematic exposure of a broad set of companies by analyzing more than 500,000 publicly available text documents related to them (e.g. annual reports, business descriptions, and financial news), and determines their degree of thematic relevance based on theme-related keywords given to the algorithm as an input (Direxion, 2020).

The offer of ETFs utilizing various cutting-edge AI technologies in the investment process is not just limited to the US asset managers. One of the world's first indices that applied AI-related algorithms to select companies exposed to artificial intelligence was the STOXX AI Global Artificial Intelligence Index, launched by STOXX in January 2018. It selects companies from a wide range of industries that invest heavily in increased development and adoption of AI-related technologies, via an innovative selection process relying itself on an AI system. When creating the index, STOXX collaborated with the AI company Yewno whose AI algorithms, involving knowledge graph techniques[12] were used to identify index constituents from the universe of the STOXX Developed and Emerging Markets Total Market Index. The key criterion used in stock selection is patent filings related to AI intellectual property, thereby identifying AI innovators as well as AI adopters (STOXX, 2018). The aforementioned index is tracked by Amundi Stoxx Global Artificial Intelligence – UCITS ETF, launched by Amundi in September 2018 and now listed on five European exchanges.

The ETF of a similar nature is Xtrackers Artificial Intelligence & Big Data UCITS ETF, launched by Deutsche Bank in January 2019, listed on Deutsche Boerse Xetra and SIX Swiss Exchange. Its aim is to replicate the NASDAQ Yewno Global Artificial Intelligence and Big Data Index. This benchmark is designed to track performance of companies from developed and emerging markets that show material exposure to the themes related to AI, data processing and data security, including DL, NLP, image recognition, speech recognition & chatbots, cloud computing, cybersecurity, and big data. Additionally, the index providers – NASDAQ and Yewno, applying screening and analytical processes to determine index constituents, employ a filtering methodology established with the use of AI processing. This process includes, among others, analyzing patent data, market size, trading volume, market listing, and foreign ownership restrictions (Xtrackers, 2020).

NLP is applied by a range of thematic ETFs launched by Lyxor International AM (Société Générale Group) in the first quarter of 2020 and listed on multiple European exchanges: Lyxor MSCI Millennials ESG Filtered (DR) UCITS ETF, Lyxor MSCI Smart Cities ESG Filtered (DR) UCITS ETF, Lyxor MSCI Digital Economy ESG Filtered (DR) UCITS ETF, Lyxor MSCI Disruptive Technology ESG Filtered (DR) UCITS ETF and Lyxor MSCI Future Mobility ESG Filtered (DR) UCITS ETF. Methodology of indices replicated by these ETFs employs a set of keywords for theme-related products, services, and concepts developed with the help of NLP and data analysis techniques. These words and phrases permit identification of relevant companies that could benefit from increased adoption and utilization of products and services linked to the respective theme (Lyxor, 2020).

Ossiam World ESG Machine Learning UCITS ETF utilizes ML to detect financial opportunities in environmental, social and governance (ESG) data. This is an actively managed fund launched by Ossiam in November 2018 and listed on Deutsche Boerse Xetra and Borsa Italiana. It uses a quantitative model that implements a rule-based approach aiming to assess large and mid-cap equities from developed markets, based on financial data and

ESG ratings. This model applies ML techniques to integrate and process a very large set of ESG and financial data and to select the patterns that show a significant link between ESG characteristics and financial performance for the securities in the investment universe. Securities classified as "investment opportunity" are categorized as "machine learning universe" and considered for further selection. The final portfolio is made up of opportunity stocks weighted (using optimization procedures) to minimize volatility and to achieve the fund's ESG objectives (Ossiam, 2018).

AI-driven ETFs are also developed by Asian companies. An example may be Qraft Technologies – a South Korea-based provider of AI investment systems. It launched, together with Exchange Traded Concepts (ETF advisor), three actively managed ETFs that are listed on NYSE Arca – two in May 2019 (AI-Enhanced US Large-Cap ETF, and AI-Enhanced US Large Cap Momentum ETF) and one in February 2020 (AI-Enhanced US High Dividends ETF). The funds are designed to enhance quantitative investment strategies with the help of AI technologies and extract out of the data these investment opportunities that portfolio managers may not seize. In order to create optimal factor weights (quality, size, valuation, momentum, and low risk), the first fund employs AI technologies to continuously learn the correlation of factor returns with various macroeconomic and valuation conditions. The investment system delivers stock weights that are in line with the factor weights targeted for the portfolio. The second fund applies AI to determine how a company's momentum would change and/or affect the company's performance over time and thus recommends weighting of such a company based on its potential for maximum return as compared to other companies. The third fund utilizes AI to identify attractive high dividend and quality stocks. Then it aims to learn which factors are most predictive of three-month forward performance and selects only the stocks offering the potential for best performance (Qraft, 2020).

Conclusions

Although the concept of artificial intelligence has been known for over 60 years, it is a relatively recent increase in vast computing power at lower prices, advanced statistical modelling advancements, as well as capability to analyze big data that made it possible to use AI more and more commonly in financial services, including asset management industry. The versatility of AI applications in this field is noteworthy – it is applied in, inter alia, client service applications, trading, post-trade operations, regulatory and compliance software, computer security, and fraud detection. However, one of the most fascinating and demanding areas of AI implementation seems to be investment management.

Asset managers apply a variety of forms of AI, among which ML and DL are one of the most widely used. They enable powerful algorithms to analyze large data sets in order to make predictions against defined goals. Thanks to this, it is possible, for example, to identify potentially outperforming equities by finding new patterns in existing datasets or reduce the negative impact of human biases on investment decisions. Other AI techniques also prove to be extremely useful, especially in analyzing alternative and/or unstructured datasets, including NLP, computer vision, voice recognition, and optical character recognition.

Even though AI has considerable limitations, and its adoption by portfolio managers often poses serious challenges, especially cost, technological, and time-related, its role is systematically growing. Various AI techniques are deployed both by active investment managers (particularly of quant funds and hedge funds) as a method to generate alpha, and by passive managers aiming to develop more attractive investment strategies, reducing transaction costs, improving index quality replication, and minimizing market impact. There is a noticeable increase in interest in the use of AI among the latter, which is confirmed by a growing number of new ETFs launched in recent years that use ML, DL, NLP, and other sophisticated technological solutions in the portfolio management process. They are implemented mainly by US and European asset managers, and – interestingly – both by market giants (e.g. BlackRock, Amundi, Deutsche Bank, Lyxor), medium-sized companies (e.g. Global X, Direxion), as well as small, niche ETF providers (e.g. Ossiam). Their products are developed usually in cooperation with index providers (e.g. Stoxx (Qontigo), Solactive) and technological firms specializing in AI (e.g. EquBot, Yewno, Qraft).

Despite the above-mentioned examples, AI is relatively rarely used in the portfolio management across the global asset management market. Still, few investment professionals are currently utilizing computer programs typically associated with AI. However, there are many symptoms that its role is going to increase systematically. Along with rapid development of technology, AI techniques are becoming more and more available, not only to the largest asset managers. There is also growing awareness that advanced technological solutions – not only in the area of product distribution or contacts with clients but also in new products development and in the investment process – can be a key factor in gaining and/or maintaining an advantage in the increasingly competitive asset management market[13]. This is evidenced by the results of the 2020 survey by Calastone, in which respondents indicated – for the first time ever – AI as the factor (selected out of emerging technologies) with the greatest impact on the asset management industry. It is good to know that asset managers are aware of the role AI will play in their business in the future. However, this should be followed by concrete, decisive actions, thanks to which asset management companies will be able to meet the requirements of present times and offer financial products and services that will satisfy customers' expectations.

Notes

1. Interestingly, the percentage of respondents that identified AI as having most potential impact on the funds industry has risen from 22% in 2018, to 26% in 2019, and to 30% in 2020. In 2020, AI was the dominant response in this survey for the first time.
2. The terms "AI" and "ML" are often used interchangeably, however AI is a broader term. ML is a subset of AI that reflects evolution of AI. ML programs learn to perform tasks by finding patterns in large datasets and making inferences instead of following explicit task-specific instructions that have already been programmed.
3. The survey was conducted in 2019 among 513 equity and credit analysts, portfolio managers, chief investment officers (CIOs), and private wealth managers from all over the world.
4. Deep learning is a type of ML that is based on artificial neural networks (a type of learning modeled on the human brain).
5. Alternative and unstructured data, in contrast to structured data that are digitized and stored in relational databases, refer to the data that are often found in text, image, or voice formats and are not readily processable. These two notions are related, but not identical. Alternative data are often unstructured when first discovered, while unstructured data are usually not used by mainstream investors, making them alternative.
6. Overfitting is a modeling error that can happen when a function is too closely fitted to a limited set of data points. It occurs when a model describes noise rather than signal and, as a result, it finds patterns that are actually not there.
7. The first national strategy on AI was launched by Canada (Pan-Canadian Artificial Intelligence Strategy) and Japan (Artificial Intelligence Technology Strategy) in March 2017, followed in the same year by e.g. China (Next Generation Artificial Intelligence Development Plan), Singapore (AI Singapore), and Finland (Artificial Intelligence Programme).
8. First initiatives on the international level were taken by European Union in 2018 when two documents (Artificial Intelligence for Europe and Coordinated Plan on Artificial Intelligence) were published. The next undertaking in this area implemented by the EU included publishing consultation document (White Paper on Artificial Intelligence – A European approach to excellence and trust) in February 2020. It presents policy options to enable a trustworthy and secure development of AI in Europe. Other international strategies were taken by, inter alia, G7 in 2018 (Common Vision for The Future of AI), and OECD in 2019 (OECD Principles for AI).
9. The most significant documents on ethical considerations concerning AI were published in 2019 by European Commission (Ethics Guidelines for Trustworthy AI), and Institute of Electrical and Electronics Engineers (IEEE)) (Ethically Aligned Design: A Vision for Prioritizing Human Well-being with Autonomous and Intelligent Systems).
10. According to the CFA Institute survey, only 10% of portfolio manager respondents have used AI/ML techniques in the past 12 months.
11. It should be emphasized that this overview does not include ETFs focused on artificial intelligence and/or automation and robotics as an investment theme, i.e. funds that *invest* in stocks of companies directly involved in developing new products, services or technological improvements related to AI, as well as companies whose business is positively impacted by an increasing development of AI. Examples of these funds on the European market are: Amundi Stoxx Global Artificial Intelligence – UCITS ETF, iShares Automation & Robotics UCITS ETF, L&G ROBO Global Robotics & Automation

UCITS ETF, Lyxor Robotics & AI UCITS ETF, and WisdomTree Artificial Intelligence UCITS ETF. A similar investment theme on the US market represents e.g. First Trust NASDAQ Artificial Intelligence and Robotics ETF, Global X Robotics & Artificial Intelligence Thematic ETF, iShares Robotics and Artificial Intelligence ETF, ROBO Global Artificial Intelligence ETF, and TrueShares Technology, AI & Deep Learning ETF.
12. Knowledge graph is a framework that turns unstructured data into quantifiable metrics. It scans documents and relates them to one another, similarly to what a search engine does with individual pages. However, it needs to extract a meaning from the text instead of simply identifying which pages are connected via hyperlinks. To do so, the algorithm scans all patents and extracts a set of potentially associated concepts for each of them (Andreetto, 2018).
13. The use of advanced technologies can be a marketing differentiator, and thus may allow to reach customers more effectively. This is especially true of millennials, as they are poised to become the increasingly important target market for asset managers in the nearest future. Such positioning in the financial market may be an important argument while competing with well-known technology companies (e.g. FAANG). According to the survey carried out by Calastone (2019), young investors would, if offered, purchase investment products through such companies, which indicates that loyalty to traditional, current financial services providers will decrease over time.

References

Andreetto, M. (2018). Big data and AI in investment innovation. *Canadian ETF Watch*, 9(1), 8–9. https://www.canadianetfwatch.com/reports/CanadianETFWatch-Volume9Issue1.pdf.

Bartram, S. M., Branke, J., & Motahari, M. (2020). *Artificial intelligence in asset management*. CFA Institute Research Foundation. https://www.cfainstitute.org/-/media/documents/book/rf-lit-review/2020/rflr-artificial-intelligence-in-asset-management.ashx.

BlackRock. (2018). *iShares launches seven sector ETFs powered by machine learning*. https://www.ishares.com/us/literature/press-release/ishares-evolved-release.pdf.

Calastone. (2019). *Millennials and investing: A detailed look at approaches and attitudes across the globe*. https://www2.calastone.com/millennialsresearch.

Calastone. (2020). *The changing face of funds distribution. Technology and innovation in the asset management industry 2020*. https://www2.calastone.com/changingfaceoffunddistribution.

Cao, L. (2019). *AI pioneers in investment management. An examination of the trends and use cases of AI and big data technologies in investments*. CFA Institute. https://www.cfainstitute.org/-/media/documents/survey/AI-Pioneers-in-Investment-Management.ashx.

Cheatham, B., Javanmardian, K., & Samandari, H. (2019). *Confronting the risks of artificial intelligence*. McKinsey Quarterly. https://www.mckinsey.com/business-functions/mckinsey-analytics/our-insights/confronting-the-risks-of-artificial-intelligence.

Direxion. (2020). *Direxion connected consumer ETF factsheet*. https://www.direxion.com/product/connected-consumer-etf/.

ETFMG. (2020). *AI powered equity ETF fact sheet*. https://etfmg.com/funds/aieq/.

EY. (2016). *Capital markets: Innovation and the FinTech landscape. How collaboration with FinTech can transform investment banking*. https://www.ey.com/Publication/

vwLUAssets/EY-capital-markets-innovation-and-the-finTech-landscape/$FILE/EY-capital-markets-innovation-and-the-fintech-landscape.pdf.

Financial Stability Board. (2017). *Artificial intelligence and machine learning in financial services. Market developments and financial stability implications.* https://www.fsb.org/wp-content/uploads/P011117.pdf.

Global, X. (2020). *Global X autonomous & electric vehicles ETF factsheet. Global X e-commerce ETF factsheet. Global X video games & esports ETF factsheet.* https://www.globalxetfs.com/.

Halpin, L., & Dannemiller, D. (2019). *Artificial intelligence. The next frontier for investment management firms.* Deloitte.https://www2.deloitte.com/content/dam/Deloitte/global/Documents/Financial-Services/fsi-artificial-intelligence-investment-mgmt.pdf.

Lyxor. (2020). *Lyxor index fund SICAV prospectus.* https://www.lyxoretf.co.uk/en/instit/products/equity-etf/lyxor-msci-millennials-esg-filtered-dr-ucits-etf-acc/lu2023678449/eur#.

Morningstar. (2019). Identifying winners and losers in a more competitive market during the next decade for our US-based asset manager coverage. *Asset Manager Observer.* March 2019.

Novick, B., Mayston, D., Marcus, S., Barry, R., Fox, G., Betts, B., Pasquali, S., & Eisenmann, K. (2019). *Artificial intelligence and machine learning in asset management.* BlackRock. https://www.blackrock.com/corporate/literature/whitepaper/viewpoint-artificial-intelligence-machine-learning-asset-management-october-2019.pdf.

Ossiam. (2018). *Ossiam IRL ICAV prospectus.* https://www.ossiam.co.uk/files/Shiller_ESG_Legal_doc/1526490242_Ossiam_IRL_ICAV_-_Prospectus_21_March_2018_UK.pdf.

Pozen, R. C., & Ruane, J. (2019). What machine learning will mean for asset managers, *Harvard Business Review.* https://hbr.org/2019/12/what-machine-learning-will-mean-for-asset-managers.

Qraft. (2020). *AI-enhanced US large cap ETF factsheet. AI-enhanced US large cap momentum ETF factsheet. AI-enhanced US high dividend ETF factsheet.* https://www.qraftaietf.com/.

Rasekhschaffe, K. C., & Jones, R. C. (2019). Machine learning for stock selection. *Financial Analysts Journal, 75*(3), 70–88. doi: https://doi.org/10.1080/0015198X.2019.1596678.

Shub, G., Bartletta, S., Beardsley, B., Hapelt, C., Donnadieu, H., Macé, B., Maguire, A., Tang, T., & Fages, R. (2014). *Steering the course to growth.* Boston Consulting Group. https://www.bcg.com/publications/2014/financial-institutions-global-asset-management-2014-steering-course-growth.

STOXX. (2018). *The economic impact of artificial intelligence.* https://www.stoxx.com/pulse-details?articleId=861904696.

Xtrackers. (2020). *Xtrackers artificial intelligence & big data UCITS ETF factsheet.* https://etf.dws.com/en-gb/IE00BGV5VN51-artificial-intelligence-big-data-ucits-etf-1c/.

10 Challenger bank as a new digital form of providing financial services to retail customers in the EU internal market

The case of Revolut

Michał Polasik, Paweł Widawski and Andrzej Lis

Introduction

Digital transformation has resulted in redefinition of business models and retail services in the financial sector. The emergence of challenger banks is found to be one of the manifestations of this transformation and an example of a financial innovation. 'Challenger banks' are banks or FinTech, non-banking start-ups, the operations of which are based on digital technologies and which challenge big, traditional banks. It is a new approach to provide financial services, where an agile organization and new technologies are the key success factors. Due to branchless and often mobile operations, challenger banks are focused on offering their customers better user experience and attractive pricing for selected financial services. Challenger banks are established in many European countries, e.g., Revolut and Monzo in the United Kingdom, N26 in Germany, Golden Sand Bank in Gibraltar, Aion in Belgium. Providing investment products to mass retail customers is a significant feature differentiating challenger banks from traditional banking institutions. An inclusive and simple formula of offering those products via mobile apps enables a numerous group of customers to invest in financial assets in a comfortable and comprehensible way. Nevertheless, provision of such an offer is a challenge requiring an innovative business model obeying strict legal regulations.

Due to their relative novelty, innovations in business models of challenger banks have not been studied thoroughly, yet. The topic has been discussed in only a handful of studies. Schepinin and Bataev (2019) and Bataev (2019) estimate efficiency of such organizations based on the number of their clients and operations performed by them. Cable (2014), in his analysis of the UK banking industry, notices growing intensity of competition due to the emergence of challenger banks. Bruggink and Coehlo (2020) observe the role of BNI Europa in servicing niche customers in some segments of the Portuguese market. Sibanda et al. (2020) employ a questionnaire survey in the context of the United Arab Emirates banking sector to analyze

DOI: 10.4324/9781003095354-10

the 'impact of digital technology, via Fin-Tech challenger banks on banks' business models'. Bataev et al. (2019) study development of a Russia-based Tinkoff Bank as well as they compare and contrast its profitability, return on assets and the long-term capital against traditional banking institutions.

An initial review of literature points out that research on challenger banks has been limited. Thus, taking into account the identified research gap, the aim of the study is to explore the operations of challenger banks and their new digital approaches to provide banking and investment services to retail customers in the EU Internal Market as an innovation in the financial market. Revolut, the most recognized challenger bank, which succeeded in attracting 12 million customers until 2020, is used as a unit of the single case study analysis.

The study combines a narrative literature review in its theoretical part with a single case study methodology in the empirical part. Due to a limited number of publications related to challenger banks, we decided to give up a systematic literature review (Tranfield et al., 2003) and employ a narrative review of refereed and non-refereed publications, in spite of limitations of this methodology. Nevertheless, as highlighted by Cook et al. (1997), narrative reviews are useful for describing development of an issue, especially if a research field is new and its scientific output is limited in number. Moreover, our literature review is embedded in a wider context of more advanced and abundant research on FinTech development (Gomber et al., 2018; Milian et al., 2019). The case study methodology (Myers, 2010; Patton & Appelbaum, 2003; Rowley, 2002) is used as a framework to analyze empirical data. The remainder of the chapter is structured as follows: firstly, digital innovations in the financial sector are discussed to provide the theoretical background for the study; secondly, the method of the study is explained; thirdly, Revolut's innovative services in the financial market and their legal formula are analyzed and finally, the findings from analysis are discussed.

Digital innovations in the financial sector

Digital technologies and new business models in the financial sector

Digitalization in the economy turned out to be a crucial breakthrough. These changes are referred to as the modern industrial revolution and are a part of the concept of Industry 4.0 which 'is based on the creation of value through the close interaction of all economic agents through digitalization' (Bilan et al., 2019, p. 70). Information and communication technologies (ICTs) completely change business models and the traditional way of providing financial services as well. This process is particularly visible in financial markets, which can be easily digitalized due to the intangible features of their products. Thus, the emergence of the 'FinTech' expression, which according to Philippon (2017) 'covers digital innovations and technology-enabled business model innovations in the financial sector'.

Traditional banking, associated with physical bank branches, is being increasingly replaced by e-banking (Nsouli & Schaechter, 2002). Within the e-finance business, which refers to forms of financial services performed with the use of electronic communication channels, many business models have emerged in the 1990s. They included the process of services automation and development of self-service interfaces, such as online banking, online brokerage services and even the first attempts of mobile banking and mobile payments (Gomber et al., 2018). The first important new business model – the Internet-only bank – was aimed to radically reduce fixed costs by resigning from owning the branches and taking advantage of the economies of scale (DeYoung et al., 2007). The low price strategy attracted mass customers, and the transaction volume generated the profit. In brokerage services, an online access enabled investors to quickly react to the changes in financial markets and to reduce commissions from transactions. This model was also gradually adapted to traditional banks and led to reducing the number of physical branches of banks and other traditional institutions, resulting in improvement of financial results (Akhisar et al., 2015; Hernando & Nieto, 2007).

New types of technologies contribute to the development of financial innovations. The crucial are blockchain- and distributed ledger technology (DLT)-based solutions, in particular cryptocurrencies (Polasik et al., 2016), but also new document storage and payment services, new solutions for creditworthiness research based on artificial intelligence, InsurTech and improvements in the regulatory requirements process – RegTech (Butor-Keler & Polasik, 2020). Through the years, mobile and other ICTs have been developed, which led to merging different services as well as creating new business models. The main direction in changing business models was the disintermediation and reintermediation of the financial services value chain (Schmidt et al., 1999; Sibanda et al., 2020). New FinTech business models vary and might include many different elements, such as crowdfunding, Person-2-Person (P2P) lending platforms, wealth management automation, robo-advisors mechanisms and mobile trading (brokerage) platforms (Lee & Shin, 2018). The latter solution is the most important for the study as it enables customers to make direct investments in financial assets, including alternative investments.

Socio-economic impact of digital finance innovations and financial inclusion

An important aspect of the development of new technologies and products is also strengthening the financial inclusion of society (Sahay et al., 2020). 'Mobile money' services offered in developing economies (Lashitew et al., 2019), where the mobile phone operators provide customers with basic banking services, e.g., M-PESA in Kenya, may be an example of inclusive innovations (Van Hove & Dubus, 2019). Another example of changes in the banking sector, resulting from financial innovations, is the emergence and development of challenger banks. As of 2020, as reported by International Money Fund (Sahay et al., 2020), digital finance has a significant impact on financial inclusion. It is also associated with a higher GDP growth in a country. It is worth noticing, that financial inclusion processes changed due to the global COVID-19 pandemic. The abovementioned report suggests that the digital financial inclusion might have an important role in recovering from both the economic as well as social crisis (Sahay et al., 2020). It might be due to the fact, that, as presented in a World Bank research from 2017 (Demirgüç-Kunt et al., 2018), 'mobile money services (...) can help improve people's income earning potential and thus reduce poverty'. The saving and investing inclusion remains an important issue also in the European Union (EU) countries (Korzeniowska & Huterska, 2020). The need for financial inclusion applies also to the current sanitary regimes as digital finance services enable dealing with financial matters without the need of a physical contact with a representative of a given financial institution. As noted by Financial Stability Board (2017), in the end, digital financial innovations might translate into a greater efficiency and transparency of services offered to customers. New entities on the market mean higher competition, which creates new ways for financial inclusion and economic growth, especially in developing economies.

Digital finance innovations have also an impact on the retail investors' accessibility to trading services, previously reserved (due to the high entry threshold) for a selected part of this group (Musabegović et al., 2019). Easier access for small investors to the investment offer may also affect the different investment patterns used by such persons compared to professional investors. The pioneer in this market segment was Robinhood Brokerage established in 2013, which introduced the 'investing for everyone' model (Robinhood, 2021). The FinTech entrants increase also the access to many types of alternative investments, such as gold certificates and cryptocurrencies. The development of mobile-based market offer directed to small investors is resulting in democratization of financial markets (Palladino, 2019).

Challenger banking

In our paper, we define challenger banks as banks or FinTech, non-banking start-ups, the operations of which are based on digital technologies and which challenge big, traditional banks. It is a new approach to provide financial services, where an agile organization and new technologies are the key success factors. These companies are focused on providing their customers with excellent user experience and they target their offerings at young people, mainly of those of the generation of millennials. In the literature, challenger banks are labelled also as 'mobile-only banks' or 'neobanks' (Gomber et al., 2018; Hopkinson et al., 2019), to highlight their radical approach to reject traditional distribution channels such as: branches, phone banking or even WWW transaction applications. Using their smartphones, customers are able not only to set up an account but also to make a wide array of other available financial operations (Capgemini & Efma, 2020).

Challenger banks are usually established as new entities without an extensive organizational structure. The basis for the functioning of challenger banks is constituted by the IT department, which 'occupies up to 80% of the entire institution, and therefore, introducing and developing this form of credit organization can be presented as an IT-project' (Schepinin & Bataev, 2019, p. 2). Challenger banks usually use a monthly subscription model that includes a selected service package.

Burdened neither with legacy systems nor inertia of employees accustomed to traditional banking, challenger banks are good at creating innovations and achieving cost-effectiveness. In consequence, they can provide customers with speed services at competitive prices, which are also available in cross-border options. Potential to increase competitiveness and challenging the traditional banking sector is an essential aspect of their operations. Thus, challenger banks are perceived as market disrupters (Lu, 2017).

Nowadays, bank customers are increasingly focused on the convenience and speed of transactions. Good customer experience is one of the characteristic elements of the functioning of challenger banks. As a result of the personalization of services and use of information technology, this type of bank has been consistently gaining popularity. According to the FT Partners Research report *The Rise of Challenger Banks. Are the Apps Taking Over?* (2020), first challenger banks began to emerge in Europe after the 2008 crisis (Lu, 2017), and this trend began to develop around the world. In the opinion of Schepinin and Bataev (2019), the development of challenger banks took place somewhat later, that is, in 2014 in the United Kingdom. What is important, the United Kingdom remains a leading European center in the development of financial innovations and FinTech (Polasik et al., 2020), including challenger banks.

Legal antecedents of new business models in the financial sector

The issue of a 'challenger bank' has not yet been thoroughly analyzed in the legal literature. However, we can find studies devoted to the broadly understood legal framework of financial innovation (FinTech), including those related to payment services. For instance, Gurrea-Martínez and Remolina (Gurrea-Martínez & Remolina, n.d.) explore the most common regulatory strategies used by financial regulators around the world to address the challenges generated by the rise of FinTech. According to Khiaonarong and Goh (2020), regulatory approaches and their legal foundations need to augment entity-based regulation with increasing focus on activities and risks as the market structure changes. On the other hand, there are studies dedicated to specific phenomena occurring in the activities of challenger banks. Romanova et al. (2018) study the impact of the Revised Payment

Services Directive (PSD2) on competitiveness of the financial sector. Remolina (2019) explains the open banking and BaaS foundations and what they exactly entail. The author also explores the benefits and risks of this interaction between financial institutions and third parties for the financial services industry and analyses from the comparative perspective different approaches that the financial, data privacy and competition regulators have implemented to boost the open banking phenomenon.

In regard to organizational efficiency, the phenomenon of regulatory arbitrage is used, which results in conducting cross-border activity within the EU on the basis of licenses issued in the Member States with favorable conditions for conducting operations and a friendly financial supervisory authority (Houston et al., 2012). In combination with a decentralized organizational structure, such a solution ensures a high level of cost competitiveness.

In regard to fractional shares trading, it should be mentioned as an example of legal innovation in investment services. In general, it is not a new legal institution/solution in securities law in a number of common law and civil law jurisdictions, therefore there is comprehensive legal literature in this field (Roberts, 1959). But fractional shares trading as a new phenomenon still demands in-depth analyses at the level of national legal systems.

In regard to cryptocurrency, Nabilou (2019) proposes a number of detailed policy recommendations for regulatory intervention in the cryptocurrency ecosystem. In the context of the EU regulatory framework, Nahorniak and Leonova (2016) investigate cryptocurrency, its legal basis in the EU, concluding that the lack of legal foundation of cryptocurrencies exists and proves the necessity of adopting the EU regulation. In September 2020, European Commission adopted legislative proposals on crypto-assets regulation (Proposal for a regulation of the European Parliament and of the Council on Markets in Crypto-assets, and amending Directive (EU) 2019/1937) (MICA). MICA proposes rules to regulate stablecoins (crypto-asset type) as well as sets out the provisions on authorization and operating conditions of crypto-asset service providers (CASPs).

Method of study

To explore financial innovations introduced by challenger banks, we employed the case study methodology, which is increasingly used in highly contextualized studies (Lis, 2018). The study process was structured in accordance with a five-step model including (Rowley, 2002; Yin, 2010): (*i*) definition of contextualized study questions, (*ii*) selection of the case and internal sampling, (*iii*) data collection, (*iv*) data analysis and discussion, (*v*) report production.

The study was focused on the following research questions: (*i*) What product innovations have been implemented by Revolut in regard to the customers' access to financial markets? (*ii*) How does Revolut compete with other challenger banks and traditional financial institutions? (*iii*) What are socio-economic consequences of innovations introduced by challenger banks? (*iv*) What is the legal formula of Revolut's operations?

Revolut was chosen as a unit of analysis for this descriptive and exploratory single case study analysis as it is the most recognized challenger bank, which succeeded in attracting more than 12 million customers at the end of 2020. The start-up was founded in 2015 in the United Kingdom by Nikolay Storonsky and Vlad Yatsenko. Revolut became famous for its quick and cheap currency exchange, thus meeting customer expectations. In 2018, Revolut became authorized Electronic Money Institution under number 08804411 (Financial Conduct Authority, 2021). In connection with Brexit, in 2020 Revolut obtained a banking license in Lithuania. At the end of 2018, Revolut operated in over 44 countries and enabled customers to make transfers in over 30 currencies, commodities, and cryptocurrencies. Single case study methodology provided an opportunity to explore thoroughly the case and its context as well as to identify the relationships used to formulate propositions for further studies.

In order to triangulate data collection methods, we used three following sources of data: (*i*) review of financial reports and other information publicly disclosed by Revolut; (*ii*) analysis of the Revolut's offering, compared with the offers of selected market competitors; (*iii*) expert interviews. Expert opinions for analysis were collected from qualitative structured interviews with a representative of the company under the study, its customers and FinTech experts. Due to the restrictions caused by the pandemic of COVID-19, the videoconference or telephone interview techniques were employed to collect the observations and insights of the respondents. Interviews were conducted in September of 2020. We employed the following techniques and mechanisms in order to ensure quality of the study and its appropriate validity: (*i*) construct validity: collecting data from diverse sources and revising the study report by key respondents; (*ii*) internal validity: pattern matching and explanation building; (*iii*) external validity: referring to theoretical assumptions; (*iv*) reliability: study protocol and database (cf. Rowley, 2002; Yin, 2010).

Revolut's innovations for financial markets

Product innovations and their mechanisms

Revolut is branchless and entirely digital and mobile, which enables it to provide services to a wide audience in many European countries. All the services are provided online via a mobile application. As a new and completely online business, the company is not burdened with old legacy systems and servicing unattractive products or channels. As indicated by the interviewed experts, comparing to traditional banks and other challenger banks, Revolut's strategy is characterized by a significant share of cross-border services in relation to its size and revenues.

Challenger banks in various areas of their activity apply technological, business and legal solutions that increase their product innovation or organizational effectiveness. Product innovations include, for instance, proactive implementation of open banking solutions based on the PSD2 directive. Payment services are the core of Revolute offer value proposition. It includes a source of earnings of Revolut – as a card issuer – i.e. interchange fees charged on merchants under international payment card schemes (Górka, 2018, pp. 14–19).

Moreover, other product innovations can be identified among investment products offered by Revolut, including:

- Investment brokerage solutions based on the concept of 'fractional share investing/trading'.
- Digital currencies trading platform.
- Commodity trading, including gold.

Fractional shares mechanisms offer an opportunity to invest in a part of a single stock, which allows customers to invest in stocks of high price and therefore allows even low-income customers to broaden their portfolio. The fractional shares scheme, provided by Revolut's subsidiary, i.e. Revolut Trading Ltd. Fractional Shares, is integrated with the online platform enabling even small investors to exercise their voting and dividend rights.

Crypto-currency trading platforms are integrated with the Revolut application and provide customer friendly mechanisms for crypto-assets investment. Their functionality is limited in comparison to trading platforms for crypto-assets that provide private wallets (cryptocurrency accounts) allowing to send or receive crypto-assets from external wallets. Revolut offers a service, in which customer's cryptocurrency is stored by Revolut as an agent in the virtual account that also holds cryptocurrencies for other Revolut's customers. In consequence, it can be considered that a customer holds not a cryptocurrency but a financial instrument that creates beneficial right to the cryptocurrency. This model creates higher compliance security for Revolut as the institution is less exposed to a number of risks, including money laundering, which is one of the main challenges for regular cryptocurrency exchange platforms.

Revolut offers services of exchanging e-money or cryptocurrencies into precious metals (e.g., gold and silver) for investment purposes. The precious metals held by Revolut's users are backed by real precious metals held in a secure third-party financial institution. This activity is not regulated. Most of the traditional banks do not offer this service.

Revolut focuses its operations on selected market niches, instead of providing a full scope of banking and investment services. Nevertheless, the delivered products are well designed. It seems that the high quality of user experience, often indicated as a benchmark for the industry thanks to its excellent ease of use and simplicity, constitutes another source of competitive advantage of Revolut (Deloitte, 2020). Although, some experts also noticed potential inconveniences for customers such as lack of possibility to have contracts in languages other than English or a lower level of legal security as Revolut's selected services are not always covered by national banks guarantee funds (e.g., in Poland).

Market strategy

The primary market target audiences of Revolut are young customers (millennials), who are active users of mobile technologies and frequent travelers or frequent online shoppers. For some young customers Revolut may be a bank of the first choice. Nevertheless, for the majority of customers, and especially those more demanding customers, it is usually a secondary bank that serves them with products not available in local traditional banks. Revolut started servicing small and medium-sized enterprises (SME) business customers, but this segment remains the secondary audience.

It is worth noticing that easiness of using Revolut's services with smartphones as well as affordable prices are essential enhancers of financial inclusiveness. Nevertheless, this effect is limited only to the digitally skilled customers, who still do not use the services of traditional banks. The inclusiveness effect is the most visible in the case of investment products, which enable customers to have an easier and cheaper access to financial markets.

The analysis of Revolut's offering and opinions of the interviewed experts indicate that the company employs the 'freemium' pricing model, i.e. it offers a free of charge basic package of services while going beyond basic limits is paid or it requires service upgrading. The experts highlight that additional charges for exceeding limits are relatively low and transparent for customers. Revolut offers three types of packages: Standard (free of charge), Premium (6.99 GBP per month) and Metal (12.99 GBP packages). The comparison of the investment offerings of Revolut, other challenger banks and traditional financial institutions is presented in Table 10.1.

The majority of challenger banks offer basic banking services such as: a current account, a foreign currency account, a debit card for the account. Some of them include in their offers savings products, e.g., safes or rounding the ends of amounts. Few challenger banks offer investment products such as: ETFs or buying shares (e.g., Aion, 2020; Vivid, 2020).

Compared to other institutions providing financial services, Revolut stands out of the crowd with its unique investment offer and user-friendly interface. These characteristics result in the number of more than 10 million downloaded applications and a very high assessment by users of the Google Play shop (4.7/5) (Google Play, 2021). Revolut's customers are offered unique services, mostly connected to investing in financial markets, e.g., stock trading in a fractional way, including the US stock exchanges (New York Stock Exchange (NYSE) and National Association Securities Dealers Automated Quotations (NASDAQ)) quoting global IT companies. Customer-friendly

Table 10.1 Comparison of the Revolut's offer to other challenger banks and traditional financial institutions

Revolut	Other challenger banks	Traditional institutions
Banking application Simple and intuitive (Arslanian & Fischer, 2019) No expert knowledge required for buying investment products	Simple and intuitive Opening a bank account in less than 5 minutes (Deloitte, 2020)	Technical and subject matter knowledge required The majority of traditional institutions do not offer a bank account and an investment account on one platform
Investment offer Broad investment offer in shares of more than 750 companies Possible investments from 1 USD	The offer of the majority of challenger banks limited to savings products Some challenger banks, e.g., Aion Bank, offer ETF funds Customers may invest from 100 euro (Aion, 2020)	Broad investment offer in brokerage houses Limitations in buying shares of foreign companies No possibilities of fractional shares investing in Poland
Buying and exchanging cryptocurrencies Possibility of buying and exchanging of many cryptocurrencies, e.g., Bitcoin, Ether, Litecoin etc. Customers can exchange between cryptocurrencies and several fiat currencies (Revolut, 2020)	Numerous challenger banks, e.g., Monzo, N26, Monese, have no option of buying and exchanging cryptocurrencies in their offers The British challenger Ziglu is the exception (Stevens, 2020)	Lack of possibility of buying and exchanging cryptocurrencies Moreover, as indicated by Marszałek (2019, p. 116): 'Lloyds Banking Group and Virgin Money apply a purchase ban of cryptocurrencies with the use of credit cards (like American JP Morgan Chase and Citigroup'
Costs of investment transactions Fees based on the subscription model Depending on the package, customers are allowed to from 3 free transactions to unlimited stock exchange transactions The cost of transactions beyond the limit is around 1 EUR (Poland – 4 PLN, the UK – 1 GBP, Eurozone countries – 1 EUR) and yearly fee 0.01% of the market value at the end of the purchase (Revolut, 2021b) Investing in Revolut's shares is free of charge and unlimited, regardless of a package (Revolut, 2021a)	Subscription model, depending on the package and individual offer of challenger banks For example, Aion Bank charges no investment fees and commissions (Aion, 2020)	Multi-component fees and commissions, e.g., for account management, making transactions, safekeeping of securities Investments in foreign markets may be charged with commission for orders settled in a foreign currency

Source: own study.

and interesting alternative investment offers should be mentioned, covering cryptocurrencies (e.g., Bitcoin) and commodities, e.g., gold. In the long term, it might be an option for Revolut to widen the scope of provided services. In the case of a typical retail customer, Revolut provides an inclusive offer for the above investment products.

Legal formula of Revolut's operations

Revolut operates across the EU on the basis of the EU passporting system enabling the provision of financial services throughout the EU on the basis of authorization granted in any EU or European Econocmic Area (EEA) state. The single passport regime is an emanation of the freedom to provide services and a key legal foundation that allows Revolut for cross-border activity and substantial reduction of regulatory and compliance costs.

Currently, customers from various Member States are served by various companies of the Revolut Group (Revolut Payments UAB, Revolut Bank UAB, Revolut Ltd., Revolut Trading Ltd.). From the legal point of view, the key service provided by the company is a payment account that holds electronic money. This legal concept is also applied in the case of the company operating under a banking license (Revolut Bank UAB). The customers of Revolut Bank have at least two parallel accounts (bank account and e-money account). The first one, a bank account, is for deposit-taking purposes. The second one is an e-money account which is used for payments as transfers to and from Revolut accounts are being made in electronic money.

Particularly noteworthy is the license of a specialized bank held by Revolut Bank UAB. The license of a specialized bank was introduced into the Lithuanian law in 2017. It is a unique concept in the EU jurisdictions. Originally designed to implement the credit union reform, currently this type of license serves as a basis for creating a more favorable regulatory environment, in which minimum capital requirements are much lower than in a traditional bank (EUR 1 million compared to EUR 5 million) and what is crucial a specialized bank license is considered as a credit institution and can benefit from the EU passporting regime[1]. Therefore, it enables Revolut to have an access to markets across the EU Member States and to significantly reduce operational costs. This approach is also optimal in the context of Brexit, which is currently the biggest regulatory challenge for Revolut. The issue is transfer of the customers from the UK jurisdiction to the Lithuanian one, which was confirmed by one of the experts in interview.

Regarding investment services, customers have contractual relations with Revolut Trading Ltd., which does not hold an investment license. Revolut Trading Ltd. has the status of an Appointed Representative and a Tied Agent from the investment firm Sapia Partners LLP, which is authorized for advising, arranging and managing investments. It remains fully and unconditionally responsible for any action or omission on the part of the tied agent when acting on behalf of the investment firm. Orders are transmitted from Revolut Trading via Sepia Partners LLP to the Third Party Broker

(DriveWealth LCC registered in USA) responsible for execution. In investment services, Revolut adopted fractional shares, which allows its customers to buy less than one share for the minimum value of 1 EUR.

The company's regulatory strategy of carrying out different activities by different entities (authorized in different jurisdictions) and serving clients in different countries by different companies seems to be effective. However, from the customer's point of view, this approach may be less beneficial. A client enters a legal relationship with a foreign entity, the operations of which are based on the foreign law (British or Lithuanian). Moreover, the text of the contract is written in a foreign language (i.e. English). The place of out-of-court dispute resolution is also a foreign entity (Bank of Lithuania). One of the experts noted that customers in most cases are not aware, which entity they enter a relationship with, whether it is a bank or an electronic money institution and what is a jurisdiction of this entity. In addition, customers funds are protected by the Lithuanian bank guarantee fund, which in case of insolvency of the company of this scale might not be efficient due to its size connected with the size of the banking sector. This is confirmed by interviews with experts. One of the experts indicated that provision of crypto services (services that allow customers to buy, sell, receive or spend cryptocurrency) by Revolut creates substantial risks, due to the regulatory uncertainty and differences in approaches in specific Member States as legal frameworks of provision of those services are not harmonized in the EU. The same applies to trading of commodities.

Discussion

Digitalization and technological innovations in the financial services market made it possible not only to save resources, accelerate processes, reduce costs and reduce process irregularities but above all to build competitive advantages (Bataev et al., 2019; Gomber et al., 2018). New types of financial institutions continue to emerge and banking itself is undergoing a transformation (Galazova & Magomaeva, 2019). At the same time, new technologies and process automation open up opportunities for the development of products. Financial services become tailor-made for clients. New, mobile distribution channels not only supplement but start marginalizing traditional channels (Aldiabat et al., 2019). Mobile technologies enhance financial inclusion (Sahay et al., 2020). The following factors contribute to the changes in the way financial services: digitalization, constant access to information, increased knowledge, globalization, convenience, speed of transactions, saving of funds and the use of new information and communication technologies by customers (Schepinin & Bataev, 2019). The COVID-19 pandemic, resulting in the need for social distancing, is a new factor stimulating digital transformation of financial services, both at the side of customers and financial institutions (Sahay et al., 2020).

Traditional financial institutions watch carefully the new entrants to the market. Nevertheless, their infrastructure and the management structure impede the implementation of innovations (Kasiewicz, 2018). This observation is confirmed by Lu (2017), who claims that new challenger banks benefit from lack of historical legacy. Challenger banks do not need branches to provide their services. The business models of challenger banks are simple, based on up-to-date solutions and IT infrastructure (Lu, 2017).

Revolut knowingly selected market niches, where customers' needs were not properly satisfied. Initially, it was currency exchange for travelers, which enabled the company to become one of the leaders of the pan-European market of financial services. Then, Revolut introduced significant innovations to both traditional and alternative investment products, offered with the use of a mobile application. Revolut was one of the first challenger banks to provide investment services consisting of stock and commodity trading. Thanks to this solution of fractional shares, investment services become more accessible to citizens with low levels of savings. What makes Revolut standing out of the crowd is the offer enabling small and non-technologically advanced investors to purchase gold and cryptocurrencies, which are inaccessible in traditional financial institutions.

The operations of challenger banks, and Revolut in particular, contribute to removing the barrier of inaccessibility to numerous financial services. So far, retail customers disposing only small amount of savings, usually young, less educated and low-income customers, had limited possibilities to diversify their investments (Goetzmann & Kumar, 2008). Their choices were confined mainly to the offer of mutual funds, which, however, were not giving the possibility to control investments, make free decisions and exercise investor rights. Fees and a long time of realization of transactions were additional barriers. The barrier of entrance to the investment market has never been so low as it is now, when customers may start buying shares from 1 USD. Thus, the offer of Revolut and other challenger banks is a significant factor in democratization of access to the investment market.

The sources of Revolut's success should be sought not only in its technological or product innovations but also in innovative legal solutions based on the EU legislation (Polasik et al., 2020). Revolut operates with the use of several companies registered in different Member States and having different licenses (electronic money institution license, banking license, investment firm license) for specific types of financial activities, such as payment services, investment activities and others. At the same time, the entity's operating activities are carried out from yet another country. The decentralized business model in legal terms is an expression of the use of the phenomenon of regulatory arbitrage (Houston et al., 2012) as an instrument to increase the efficiency of business operations and, as a result, to reduce fees for clients.

Conclusions

Revolut has been used as the case to analyze the challenger banking as a new digital form of providing financial services to retail customers in the EU Internal Market. The study has explored product innovations introduced by the company to make the capital market and alternative investments available for small investors. The analysis has included: the mechanisms of new services, the market strategy and the Revolut's offer compared to traditional financial institutions and other challenger banks. Moreover, it has explained the legal formula enabling the operations of Revolut.

Over the past years, challenger banks around the world have introduced significant financial innovations. Their innovative approach refers not only to the business offer or a technological side of products but also to the legal layer of operations. Thus, the Revolut's investment offer is an innovation, which increases financial inclusion and brings socio-economic benefits. What is more, it becomes a real challenge for traditional players in financial markets, both banks and mutual funds. Extreme decrease in the amount of money needed to start investments and providing the investors with the rights to online voting contribute to democratization of the financial market and sets new standards, the traditional players will be forced to respond to. The fact that other challenger banks and FinTech companies follow this innovation and introduce similar investment products indicates that the financial market is under permanent transformation triggered by the innovations presented in the study. Moreover, the study shows that the EU passporting system, in connection with the optimization of jurisdiction for authorization and friendly supervision authority combined with the right choice of authorization regime (electronic money institution, specialized bank), have a significant impact on the dynamic development of the company.

Discussing the findings of the study, the limitations of the research process should be explained. First of all, the study does not analyze the changes and risks for Revolut associated with Brexit, as it takes into account the legal status as of December 31, 2020. Secondly, we are aware of inherent weaknesses of the case study methodology, which is often criticized for insufficient scientific rigor. Therefore, although we have made all the efforts to ensure quality of the study and its validity, we refrain from attempts to make generalizations based on this single case and we rather use its exploratory potential to formulate propositions to be tested in further studies (cf. Flyvbjerg, 2006). Thus, replicating this study as well as conducting a multiple case study analysis and/or a survey among the other challenger banks seems to be a natural line of future research. Thirdly, limitations in data collection processes should be mentioned. In spite of efforts to have a balanced view of the Revolut's operations by combining the perspective of external stakeholders (FinTech experts and users of Revolut's services) and the company itself, only one representative of the company participated in the interview survey.

This exploratory study contributes both to the development of management studies and business practice. From the perspective of management theory, it identifies the mechanisms of developing and implementing financial innovations considering the opportunities resulting from advancement of ICTs, and changes in law. Regarding business practice, studying the case of Revolut may bring some observations, insights, lessons and best practices to be useful for other challenger banks. Whereas the issue of the impact of the challenger bank business model on financial inclusiveness will require further, thorough studies.

Acknowledgements

This work was supported by the National Science Centre, Poland under Grant No. 2017/26/E/HS4/00858.

The views expressed in the article are the personal views of the authors and do not express the official positions of the institutions, which they are employed by.

Note

1. In line with art. 33 of Directive 2013/36/EU of the European Parliament and of the Council of 26 June 2013 on access to the activity of credit institutions and the prudential supervision of credit institutions and investment firms, amending Directive 2002/87/EC and repealing Directives 2006/48/EC and 2006/49/EC (CRDIV).

References

Aion. (2020). *Asset management*. https://www.aion.be/en/asset-management.

Akhisar, İ, Tunay, K. B., & Tunay, N. (2015). The effects of innovations on bank performance: The case of electronic banking services. *Procedia – Social and Behavioral Sciences, 195*, 369–375. doi: https://doi.org/10.1016/j.sbspro.2015.06.336.

Aldiabat, K., Al-Gasaymeh, A., & Rashid, A. S. K. (2019). The effect of mobile banking application on customer interaction in the Jordanian banking industry. *International Journal of Interactive Mobile Technologies, 13*(2), 37–48. doi: https://doi.org/10.3991/ijim.v13i02.9262.

Arslanian, H., & Fischer, F. (2019). *The future of finance: The impact of FinTech, AI, and crypto on financial services*. Springer.

Bataev, A. (2019). Financial technology: Efficiency evaluation of challenger banks. In S. Shaposhnikov (Ed.), *2019 IEEE conference of Russian young researchers in electrical and electronic engineering (EIConRus)* (pp. 1371–1375). IEEE. doi: https://doi.org/10.1109/EIConRus.2019.8657260.

Bataev, A., Koroleva, L., & Gorovoy, A. (2019). Innovative approaches in the financial sphere: Assessment of digital banks' performance. *The Proceedings of the 14th European Conference on Innovation and Entrepreneurship (ECIE 2019)*, 141–149. doi: https://doi.org/10.34190/ECIE.19.038.

Bilan, Y., Rubanov, P., Vasylieva, T., & Lyeonov, S. (2019). The influence of industry 4.0 on financial services: Determinants of alternative finance development. *Polish Journal of Management Studies, 19*(1), 70–93. doi: https://doi.org/10.17512/pjms.2019.19.1.06.

Bruggink, D., & Coehlo, P. (2020). The payments landscape in Portugal: An interview with Pedro Coelho. *Journal of Payments Strategy and Systems, 14*(1), 6–9.

Butor-Keler, A., & Polasik, M. (2020). The role of regulatory sandboxes in the development of innovations on the financial services market: The case of the United Kingdom. *Ekonomia i Prawo. Economics and Law, 19*(4), 621–638. doi: https://doi.org/10.12775/EiP.2020.041.

Cable, V. (2014). Observations on the UK banking industry. *International Review of Financial Analysis, 36*, 84–86. doi: https://doi.org/10.1016/j.irfa.2014.11.011.

Capgemini, & Efma. (2020). *World Fintech Report 2020*. https://fintechworldreport.com/resources/world-fintech-report-2020/.

Cook, D. J., Mulrow, C. D., & Haynes, R. B. (1997). Systematic reviews: Synthesis of best evidence for clinical decisions. *Annals of Internal Medicine, 126*(5), 376–380.

Deloitte. (2020). *The DNA of digital challenger banks*. https://www2.deloitte.com/us/en/pages/financial-services/articles/digital-challenger-bank.html.

Demirgüç-Kunt, A., Klapper, L., Singer, D., Ansar, S., & Hess, J. (2018). *The Global Findex database 2017: Measuring financial inclusion and the FinTech revolution*. World Bank. doi: https://doi.org/10.1596/978-1-4648-1259-0.

DeYoung, R., Lang, W. W., & Nolle, D. L. (2007). How the internet affects output and performance at community banks. *Journal of Banking and Finance, 31*(4), 1033–1060. doi: https://doi.org/10.1016/j.jbankfin.2006.10.003.

Financial Conduct Authority. (2021). *Revolut Ltd*. https://register.fca.org.uk/s/firm?id=001b000002zyAwNAAU.

Financial Stability Board. (2017). *Financial stability implications from Fintech: Supervisory and regulatory issues that merit authorities' attention*. https://www.fsb.org/wp-content/uploads/R270617.pdf.

Flyvbjerg, B. (2006). Five misunderstandings about case-study research. *Qualitative Inquiry, 12*(2), 219–245. doi: https://doi.org/10.1177/1077800405284363.

FT Partners Research. (2020). *The rise of challenger banks. Are the apps taking over?* https://ftpartners.docsend.com/view/28mpmwt.

Galazova, S. S., & Magomaeva, L. R. (2019). The transformation of traditional banking activity in digital. *International Journal of Economics and Business Administration, 7*(2), 41–51. doi: https://doi.org/10.35808/ijeba/369.

Goetzmann, W. N., & Kumar, A. (2008). Equity portfolio diversification. *Review of Finance, 12*(3), 433–463. doi: https://doi.org/10.1093/rof/rfn005.

Gomber, P., Kauffman, R. J., Parker, C., & Weber, B. W. (2018). On the FinTech revolution: Interpreting the forces of innovation, disruption, and transformation in financial services. *Journal of Management Information Systems, 35*(1), 220–265. doi: https://doi.org/10.1080/07421222.2018.1440766.

Google Play (2021). *Revolut - Get more from your money*. https://play.google.com/store/apps/details?id=com.revolut.revolut&hl=en_US&gl=US.

Górka, J. (2018). *Interchange fee economics: To regulate or not to regulate?* Palgrave Macmillan. doi: https://doi.org/10.1007/978-3-030-03041-4.

Gurrea-Martínez, A., & Remolina, N. (n.d.). *Global Challenges and Regulatory Strategies to Fintech* (2020/01; SMU Centre for AI & Data Governance Research Paper). doi: https://doi.org/10.2139/ssrn.3576506.

Hernando, I., & Nieto, M. J. (2007). Is the internet delivery channel changing banks' performance? The case of Spanish banks. *Journal of Banking and Finance, 31*(4), 1083–1099. doi: https://doi.org/10.1016/j.jbankfin.2006.10.011.

Hopkinson, G., Klarova, D., Turcan, R. V., & Gulieva, V. (2019). *How neobanks' business models challenge traditional banks* (Aalborg University Young Graduate News). http://www.e-pages.dk/aalborguniversitet/769/html5/.

Houston, J. F., Lin, C., & Ma, Y. (2012). Regulatory arbitrage and international bank flows. *Journal of Finance*, *67*(5), 1845–1895. doi: https://doi.org/10.1111/j.1540-6261.2012.01774.x.

Kasiewicz, S. (2018). *PSD2. Krytyczny przystanek na drodze do nowej ery bankowości*. Oficyna Wydawnicza SGH.

Khiaonarong, T., & Goh, T. (2020). *Fintech and payments regulation: Analytical framework* (WP/20/75; IMF Working Paper). doi: https://doi.org/10.5089/9781513531496.001.

Korzeniowska, A. M., & Huterska, A. (2020). Saving inclusion in the European union countries – Trends and differences. In K. S. Soliman (Ed.), *Education excellence and innovation management: A 2025 vision to sustain economic development during global challenges* (pp. 9844–9854). International Business Information Management Association, IBIMA.

Lashitew, A. A., Van Tulder, R., & Liasse, Y. (2019). Mobile phones for financial inclusion: What explains the diffusion of mobile money innovations? *Research Policy*, *48*(5), 1201–1215. doi: https://doi.org/10.1016/j.respol.2018.12.010.

Lee, I., & Shin, Y. J. (2018). FinTech: Ecosystem, business models, investment decisions, and challenges. *Business Horizons*, *61*(1), 35–46. doi: https://doi.org/10.1016/j.bushor.2017.09.003.

Lis, A. (2018). Profiling and mapping the contexts of the case study research in business, management and accounting. *International Journal of Contemporary Management*, *17*(1), 179–196. doi: https://doi.org/10.4467/24498939ijcm.18.010.8389.

Lu, L. (2017). Financial technology and challenger banks in the UK: Gap fillers or real challengers? *Journal of International Banking Law and Regulation 2017*, *32*(7), 273–282.

Marszałek, P. (2019). Kryptowaluty – Pojęcie, cechy, kontrowersje. *Studia BAS*, *1*(57), 105–125. doi: https://doi.org/10.31268/StudiaBAS.2019.06.

Milian, E. Z., Spinola, M. M., & Carvalho, M. M. (2019). FinTechs: A literature review and research agenda. *Electronic Commerce Research and Applications*, *34*, 100833. doi: https://doi.org/10.1016/j.elerap.2019.100833.

Musabegović, I., Özer, M., Đuković, S., & Jovanović, S. (2019). Influence of financial technology (FinTech) on financial industry. *Ekonomika Poljoprivrede*, *66*(4), 1003–1021. doi: https://doi.org/10.5937/ekoPolj1904003M.

Myers, M. D. (2010). Case study research. In M. Frenz, K. Nielsen, & G. Walters (Eds.), *Research methods in management* (pp. 227–248). Sage.

Nabilou, H. (2019). How to regulate bitcoin? Decentralized regulation for a decentralized cryptocurrency. *International Journal of Law and Information Technology*, *27*(3), 266–291. doi: https://doi.org/10.1093/ijlit/eaz008.

Nahorniak, I., Leonova, K., & Skorokhod, V. (2016). Cryptocurrency in the context of development of digital single market in European Union. *InterEULawEast*, *3*(1), 107–124.

Nsouli, S. M., & Schaechter, A. (2002). Challenges of the "e-banking revolution." *Finance & Development*, *39*(3). https://www.imf.org/external/pubs/ft/fandd/2002/09/nsouli.htm.

Palladino, L. (2019). Democratizing investment. *Politics and Society*, *47*(4), 573–591. doi: https://doi.org/10.1177/0032329219878989.

Patton, E., & Appelbaum, S. H. (2003). The case for case studies in management research. *Management Research News*, *26*(5), 60–71. doi: https://doi.org/10.1108/01409170310783484.

Philippon, T. (2017). The FinTech opportunity. *BIS Working Papers, 655*, 1–29.

Polasik, M., Huterska, A., Iftikhar, R., & Mikula, Š. (2020). The impact of payment services directive 2 on the PayTech sector development in Europe. *Journal of Economic Behavior and Organization, 178*, 385–401. doi: https://doi.org/10.1016/j.jebo.2020.07.010.

Polasik, M., Piotrowska, A., Wisniewski, T. P., Kotkowski, R., & Lightfoot, G. (2016). Price fluctuations and the use of bitcoin: An empirical inquiry. *International Journal of Electronic Commerce, 20*(1), 9–49. doi: https://doi.org/10.1080/10864415.2016.1061413.

Remolina, N. (2019). *Open Banking: Regulatory Challenges for a New Form of Financial Intermediation in a Data-Driven World* (2019/05; SMU Centre for AI & Data Governance Research Paper).

Revolut. (2020). *Go from cash to crypto instantly.* https://www.revolut.com/en-AU/go-from-cash-to-crypto-instantly.

Revolut. (2021a). *Investing for growth with Revolut trading.* https://www.revolut.com/stock-trading

Revolut. (2021b). *What fees will I be charged for my trading?* https://www.revolut.com/en-PT/help/wealth/stocks/trading-stocks/what-fees-will-i-be-charged-for-my-trading/

Roberts, W. L. (1959). Fractional corporate shares. *Kentucky Law Journal, 47*(4), 507–514.

Robinhood. (2021). *Investing for everyone.* https://robinhood.com/us/en/.

Romanova, I., Grima, S., Spiteri, J., & Kudinska, M. (2018). The payment services directive II and competitiveness: The perspective of European FinTech companies. *European Research Studies Journal, 21*(2), 3–22. doi: https://doi.org/10.35808/ersj/981.

Rowley, J. (2002). Using case studies in research. *Management Research News, 25*(1), 16–27. doi: https://doi.org/10.1108/01409170210782990.

Sahay, R., Allmen, U., Lahreche, A., Khera, P., Ogawa, S., Bazarbash, M., & Beato, K. (2020). *The Promise of FinTech: Financial Inclusion in the Post COVID-19 Era* (20/09; IMF Departmental Paper Series). doi: https://doi.org/10.5089/9781513512242.087.

Schepinin, V., & Bataev, A. (2019). Digitalization of financial sphere: Challenger banks efficiency estimation. *IOP Conference Series: Materials Science and Engineering, 497*(1), 012051. doi: https://doi.org/10.1088/1757-899X/497/1/012051.

Schmidt, R. H., Hackethal, A., & Tyrell, M. (1999). Disintermediation and the role of banks in Europe: An international comparison. *Journal of Financial Intermediation, 8*(1–2), 36–67. doi: https://doi.org/10.1006/jfin.1998.0256.

Sibanda, W., Ndiweni, E., Boulkeroua, M., Echchabi, A., & Ndlovu, T. (2020). Digital technology disruption on bank business models. *International Journal of Business Performance Management, 21*(1/2), 184. doi: https://doi.org/10.1504/IJBPM.2020.106121.

Stevens, R. (2020). *A UK challenger bank goes peer-to-peer with crypto, with a catch.* https://decrypt.co/41023/ziglu-goes-peer-to-peer.

Tranfield, D., Denyer, D., & Smart, P. (2003). Towards a methodology for developing evidence-informed management knowledge by means of systematic review. *British Journal of Management, 14*(3), 207–222. doi: https://doi.org/10.1111/1467-8551.00375.

Van Hove, L., & Dubus, A. (2019). M-PESA and financial inclusion in Kenya: Of paying comes saving? *Sustainability*, *11*(3), 1–26. doi: https://doi.org/10.3390/su11030568.

Vivid. (2020). *Commission-free investing with no limits*. https://vivid.money/en-eu/investments/.

Yin, R. K. (2010). Designing case studies. In M. Frenz, K. Nielsen, & G. Walters (Eds.), *Research methods in management* (pp. 185–226). Sage.

Index

Note: *Italicized* page numbers refer to figures, **bold** page numbers refer to tables

Acorns 94
Adamska, A. 3–15
Africa 106
Aion 175
AI-Powered Equity ETF 167–168
Aitken, M. 19
Aktar, M. 40
Alam, N. 106
Alibaba 85, 92, 94, 95, 108
AliPay 94
Alphabet 91
alternative trading systems (ATSs) 7–8, 14
Amazon 85, 91
American depositary receipts (ADRs) 12
Ant Financial 126
Apple 85, 91
application programming interfaces (APIs) 84, 101, 132
Arellano, M. 24
Argentina 152
Armenia 109
artificial intelligence (AI) 84, 87, 101, 124, 130, 134, 161–171; adopters of 164; defined 161; in investment management 162–164; overview 161–162; practical application of 167–170; risks and challenges 165–167; types of 164; *see also* machine learning (ML)
asset management and mutual funds industry 92–96
assets under management (AUM) 94–95
Australia 109
Australian Stock Exchange 91
Austria 109
Aviso, K.B. 42

Baidu 85
Balp, G. 90
Bangladesh 109, 126; capital market of 44–47, **45**
Bangladesh Securities and Exchange Commission (BSEC) 39, 45
Bank of Amsterdam 146
Bank of England 146, 147
Bank of Lithuania 186
Bartlett's test of sphericity 114, **114**
Bataev, A. 175, 176, 179
BATS Global Markets 8
Belgium 109
Betterment 94
Big Bang 3
big data 124, 132, 164
BigTechs 84–88; anti-competitive practices 88; Chinese 94–95; defined 85; opportunities and threats 86
Bitcoin 145, 148, 150; as digital gold standard system 149–150; *see also* cryptocurrencies
Blackman, A., Jr. 62
BlackRock 94, 168
blockchain 90–91, 101, 102, 124, 177; *see also* FinTechs
Bloomberg 11
Blundell, R. 24
BNI Europa 175
Bond, S. 24
Boot, A. 83
Borsa Italiana 169
bots 124
Bouwman, H. 41
Bover, O. 24
Brazil 42, 108, 109
Bruggink, D. 175

Brundtland Commission 106
Buchuk, D. 26
Bullen, C.V. 103

Cable, V. 175
Caifuhao platform 95
Calibra 151
Canada 109
Cao, D.B. 103
CEE Stock Exchange Group (CEESEG) 10
Central Bank Digital Currencies (CBDCs) 146, 153–154
Central Depository Bangladesh Limited (CDBL) 39, 44
challenger banks 175–189; customer experience 179; definition of 178; digital technologies 176–177; legal antecedents 179–180; legal formula of operations 185–186; market strategy 183; mobile-only banks 178; neobanks 178; overview 175–176; product innovations 181–183; Revolut 180–188; services 182, **183**
Charles Schwab 7
Chartered Financial Analyst (CFA) Institute 164, 165
chatbots 101
Chen 109
China 109, 126
Chittagong Stock Exchange Broad Index (CSEX) 43, 45–47, *47*
Chittagong Stock Exchange (CSE). 39, 43, 45, 45–46, 47–54
Chittagong Stock Index 30 (CSE30) 43, 48
Chow, T. 103
Clear Books 134
client relationship management (CRM) 162
cloud computing 124, 132
Coehlo, P. 175
communications frictions 82, **83**
computer vision 164
connected industries 168
Conrad, J. 23
Contreras Pinochet, L.H. 109
Corda 91
Corinthian Colleges 12
COVID-19 pandemic 7, 38–40, 178
critical success factors (CSFs) 101–109; defined 103; for FinTechs 103–109, **110–111**; LASIC principles 108; types of 103

cross-selling 84
crowdfunding 83, 102, 103, 134
CrunchBase 105
cryptocurrencies 145–156, 182; and bank-based monetary system 146–148; Bitcoin 149–150; Central Bank Digital Currencies 153–154; currency board 150–152; overview 145–146; and payment service providers 146–148; regulation of 180; stablecoins 150–152
cryptocurrency 102
CSI 300 index 22

Dacca Stock Exchange 44
dark pools 8
data analytics 84
data applications 124, 132, 134, 164
Davis, F.D. 104
decimalization 4
deep learning 164
Demutualization Act (Bangladesh) 49
Denmark 109
Deutsche Bank 169
Deutsche Boerse Xetra 169
Dhaka Stock Exchange Broad Index (DSEX) 39, 43, 45–47, *47*, 49
Dhaka Stock Exchange (DSE) 39, 43, 44–54
Diemers 102
digital asset management platforms (DAMPs) 93–94
digital platforms 92–96
digitalization: defined 40; in developing countries 38–53; and exchange-traded funds 57; of market processes 3–5; in pandemic 38–53
direct electronic access (DEA) 22
Directorate of Defense Trade Controls (DTCC) 91
Direxion Connected Consumer ETF 168
distributed ledger technology (DLT) 84, 90–91, 124, 132, 134, 177; *see also* FinTechs
Dolley, J.C. 42
DriveWealth LCC 186
DSE Info app 43, 53
DSE-Mobile app 43, 53

East Pakistan Stock Exchange Association Limited 44
economics of imperfect competition 82
efficient market theory 42

196 *Index*

Egypt 126
Eickhoff, M. 105
electronic trading markets (ETMs) 5
Emerald Management 103
environmental, social and governance (ESG) 169
environmental CSFs 103
e-payments 103, 104
EquBot 167
equity index arbitrage complex 61
Essendorfer, S. 21–22
Estimize 92
ETFMG 167–168
Ethiopia 109
eToro 92
Etrade 7
Eurodollar 147–148
European Securities and Markets Authority (ESMA) 20, 26, 31
European Union 178, 180
Evans, P.C. 92
event study method 42
Everbright Securities Co. 7
exchange-traded funds (ETFs) 57–74; and adoption of ICT 59–61; advantages of 61; artificial intelligence in 167–170; diffusion of 65–74; digital platforms 93; elements of 61; empirical research 62–74; versus ICT 65; in Japan 64–74, *67*, **69**, *71*; and other index financial instruments 61–62; overview 57–58; in South Korea 64–74, *68*, **69**, *71*; versus stock index options *71*; substitution of 65–74, *72*
eXtensible Business Reporting Language (XBRL) 11

Facebook 85, 92, 145, 148, 150, 152
Fama, E.F. 26, 42
Federal Deposit Insurance Corporation 154
Federal Reserve 154
Felipe, I.J.S. 108
Ferreira, B.C.F. 108
financial web 134
FinTechs 81–96; in asset management and mutual funds industry 92–96; and banking services 123–137; and BigTechs 84–88; Chinese 106–107; cooperation 115; creation effects of 132–136, **133**; critical success factors 101–119, **110–111**; customer base 115; defined 85; distributed ledger technology 90–91; entry of 84–88; in Germany 103–104; and high-frequency trading 90; impact of 82–83, **83**, 118, 123–137; in Indonesia 104; and industrial organization theory 82, 84; Islamic 106; LASIC principles 108; management 115; modification effects 130–132, **131**; opportunities and threats 86, *86*; overview 81–82; Polish 107; products **112**, 115; services 102; socioeconomic implications of 126–127; and stock market 88–92; user demographics 111–112
Fisher, J.C. 62
Fisher-Pry transformation 63
flash trading 21
Fors, A.C. 40
France 109
French, K.R. 26
Futoready 104

Gancarczyk, M. 123–137
Garvey, R. 90
Gaver, J.J. 42
Gawer, A. 92
Gen Z 7
generalized method-of-moments (GMM) 24, 28
Germany 109
Ghana 126
global depositary receipt (GDRs) 12
global financial crisis of 2007-2009 148
Global X Autonomous & Electric Vehicles ETF 168
Global X Video Games & Esports ETF 168
Goh, T. 179
Gojek 126
Golden Sand Bank 175
Gong, Y. 22
Google 85
Google News 11
Google Play 183
Grab 126
Great Depression 148
Greece 109
gross domestic product (GDP) 9, 39, 104, 149–150, 178
Grygiel-Tomaszewska, A. 19–33
Gurrea-Martinez, A. 179

Haberly, D. 94
Hammerschlag, Z. 106
Hansen test 24
Harasim, J. 81–96, 84

Hau, H. 23, 32
He, D. 83
Hendershott, T. 90
high-frequency trading (HFT) 5–7, **89**; advantages of 21; colocation 22–23; flash trading 21; and geolocation of financial institutions 19–33; legal restrictions 22; overview 19–20; single participants 22; technical requirements 21; transactions in Europe 20; ultra 21
Hong, C.Y. 95
Hong Kong 109, 151
horizontal integration **83**, 84
Hungary 111

IBM Watson 167
index funds 93
India 111, 126, 147
industrial organization economics (IO) 82–84
industry CSFs 103
information and communication technologies (ICTs) 3–15; and changes in market structure and competition model 14; versus diffusion and substitution of financial innovations 57–74; and digitization of market processes 3–5; and emergence of new market players 7–9; and ETFs 59–61; and incumbent stock exchanges 9–10; and investor behaviors 5–7; overview 3; regulatory response 13; and situation of issuers 11–12
information asymmetry 82–83, **83**
initial public offering (IPO) 12
InsurTech 104, 177; see also FinTechs
International Money Fund 178
Internet of things (IoT) 101, 132, 166
Investment Corporation of Bangladesh (ICB) 39
investor behaviors 3–5
Ireland 111
iShares ETFs 168
ISI Web of Knowledge 103
Islamic FinTechs 106
Italy 111

Jain, P. 90
Japan 111; ETFs in 64–74, *67*, **69**, *71*

Kaiser-Meyer-Olkin Measure of Sampling Adequacy **114**, 114
Kenya 126, 147

Khiaonarong, T. 179
Knight Capital 7, 12
KUDO 104

Lasak, P. 123–137
LASIC principles 108
Latvia 111
Lechman, E. 57–74
Lee, D.K.C. 108
Leong, K. 106
Leonova, K. 180
Libra 145, 148, 150–153; *see also* cryptocurrencies
Libra Association 151
Libra Reserve 151, 152–153
libraization 152
LiCaitong platform 94
Lithuania 111
Liu, D.Y. 42
Lloyds Banking Group 7
London Stock Exchange (LSE) 3, 10
Losiewicz-Dniestrzanska, E. 19–33
LSE Group 8
Lyxor International AM (Société Générale Group) 169

machine learning (ML) 84, 87, 101, 124, 132, 162, 166; *see also* artificial intelligence (AI)
Malaysia 111, 126
Malone, T.W. 124, 128
Malta 111
management CSFd 103
Marchetti, C. 62
Markets in Financial Instruments Directive 8
Marszk, A. 57–74
Mastercard 134
mergers and acquisitions (M&As) 10
Meyer, P. 63
Microsoft 91
Microsoft Azure 118
MiFID II 22
millennials 7
Millennium Bank 118
Millennium Goodie 118
Mirae Asset Global Investment 168
Mishkin, F.S. 26
Mitrega-Niestroj, K. 84
Miziolek, T. 161–171
mobile payments 103, 104, 177
mobile-only banks 178
Moinul Islam, A.N.M. 38–53
money supply 146–147

198 *Index*

Mongolia 111
Monzo 175
Moulton, P.C. 90
Mozambique 126
M-Pesa 108, 126, 147, 177
multilateral trading facilities (MTFs) 8
Muslims 106

N26 175
Nahorniak, I. 180
Nakicenovic, N. 62
Narayan, P.K. 42
NASDAQ 3, 168
NASDAQ Yewno Global Artificial Intelligence and Big Data Index 169
National Market System (NMS) 14
natural language processing (NLP) 164, 168, 169
neobanks 178
Netherlands 111
New York Stock Exchange (NYSE) 3–4
next generation trading system (NGTS) 39
Numerai 92
NYSE Arca 167, 168, 170
NYSE Euronext 10

OMX 10
online brokers 7
optical character recognition (OCR) 164
Ossiam World ESG Machine Learning UCITS ETF 169

P2P lending 103, 104, 106, 109, 126, 177
Pakistan 111
Parviainen, P. 40
pattern matrix 114–115, **115**
payment service providers (PSPs) 145–148, *147*
PayTM 147
peer-to-peer (P2P) platforms 83
Personal Capital 94
Phan, D.H. 42
Philippines 111, 126
Philippon, T. 176
Poland 42, 107, 109
Portugal 111
predictive modeling 124
ProQuest 103
Pry, R.H. 62

Qraft Technologies 170
quantitative easing (QE) 149
Quantopian 92

R3 consortium 91
Rahat, M.R. 38–53
RegTech 177
regulations 13
Remolina, N. 179
return on assets (RoA) 23, 24, **25**, 28, **30**, 31
Revised Payment Services Directive (PSD2) 179–180
Revolut 175, 176, 180–188; history 181; legal formula of operations 185–186; market strategy 183; product innovations 181–183; services 182, **183**
Revolut Bank UAB 185
Revolut Trading Ltd. 185
Revolut Trading Ltd. Fractional Shares 182
ride-hailing services 126
Robinhood 7, 178
robo-advisors 162, 177
robotic process automation 101
Rockart, J.F. 103
Roeder, J. 105

SageOne 134
Schena, C.M. 126
Schepinin, V. 175, 179
Scholtens, B. 82
Scree plot *116*
Sepia Partners LLP 185
Serbia 111
services oriented architecture (SOA) 134
Shafer, S.M. 103
Shanghai Stock Exchange 7
Shanghai-Shenzhen Stock Exchange Consortium 49, 51
Sheng, C. 106–107
Sibanda, 175
Singapore 111
Singh, S. 104
single payment solutions 134
SIX Swiss Exchange 169
Slawinski, A. 145–156
smart contracts 124
social distancing 7
social media 83
Sohrab Uddin, S.M. 38–53
Solactive Connected Consumer Index 168
South Africa 111, 126
South Korea 111; ETFs in 64–74, *68*, **69**, *71*
Spain 111

stablecoin 148, 150–152; *see also* cryptocurrencies
Staszkiewicz, L. 23
Staszkiewicz, P. 19–33, 23
State Street 94
stock exchanges: digitization of market processes 3–5; and FinTech 88–92; response to ICTs 9–10
stock index futures 61–62
stock index options 61–62, *71*
stock split 42
Stockholm Stock Exchange 9
Stocktwits 92
Stolterman, E. 40
Storonsky, N. 181
STOXX AI Global Artificial Intelligence Index 169
STOXX Developed and Emerging Markets Total Market Index 169
Strampelli, G,. 90
strategy CSFs 103
Streak 92
Sweden 111
Switzerland 111

Taiwan 111
Tanda, A. 126
Tanzania 126
Taralite 104
TD Ameritrade 7
TechInsurance 102
technological substitution 62
technology acceptance model (TAM) 103
Teixeira, J.C.A. 26
Tel Aviv Stock Exchange 90–91
temporal CSFs 103
Tencent 85, 94
Teo, E.G.S. 108
Thailand 111
Thompson, A.J. 42
Thomsett, M.C. 125
Tinkoff Bank 176

TMX Group 10
Tokyo Stock Exchange 23
Toronto Stock Exchange 91
transaction costs **83**, 83

Ukraine 111
ultra high-frequency trading 21
United Airlines 11
United Kingdom 111, 179
United States 111

Van Wensveen, D. 82
Vanguard 94
venture capitalists 104
vertical integration **83**, 84
Vietnam 111
VISA 134
voice recognition 164
Von Briel, F. 125, 128

Wang, Y.H. 42
Wang, Z. 105
Wealthfront 94
Werth, O. 103–104
Wewege, L. 125
Wizzard Software Corporation 12
World Commission on Environment and Development 106
Wu, F. 90

Xero 134
Xtrackers Artificial Intelligence & Big Data UCITS ETF 169

Yatsenko, V. 181
Yeh 109
Yermack 106
Yewno 169
Yu, K. 42
Yu'e Bao platform 94
YuEbao 105

Zipline 92